Linguistically Motivated Principles of Knowledge Base Systems

Functional Grammar Series

This series comprises monographs and collections written in the framework of Functional Grammar.
The aim is to seek explanations for a wide variety of linguistic phenomena, both language-specific and cross-linguistic, in terms of the conditions under which and the purposes for which language is used.

General address:
Institute for General Linguistics
Functional Grammar
Spuistraat 210
NL-1012 VT Amsterdam
The Netherlands

Other books in this series:

1. A.M. Bolkestein, C. de Groot and J.L. Mackenzie (eds.)
   Syntax and Pragmatics in Functional Grammar
2. A. M. Bolkestein, C. de Groot and J.L. Mackenzie (eds.)
   Predicates and Terms in Funtional Grammar
3. Michael Hannay
   English Existentials in Functional Grammar
4. Josine A. Lalleman
   Dutch Language Proficiency of Turkish Children born in the Netherlands
5. Jan Nuyts and Georges de Schutter (eds.)
   Getting one's Words into Line
6. Johan van der Auwera and Louis Goossens (eds.)
   Ins and Outs of the Predication
7. Judith Junger
   Predicate Formation in the Verbal System of Modern Hebrew
8. Ahmed Moutaouakil
   Pragmatic Functions in a Functional Grammar of Arabic
9. Simon C. Dik
   The Theory of Functional Grammar
10. John H. Connolly and Simon C. Dik (eds.)
    Functional Grammar and the Computer
11. Casper de Groot
    Predicate Structure in a Functional Grammar of Hungarian

Other studies on Functional Grammar include S.C. Dik, *Functional Grammar* (1978), T. Hoekstra et al. (eds.), *Perspectives on Functional Grammar* (1981). All published by FORIS PUBLICATIONS.

Linguistically Motivated Principles of Knowledge Base Systems

1990
FORIS PUBLICATIONS
Dordrecht - Holland/Providence RI - U.S.A.

Published by:
Foris Publications Holland
P.O. Box 509
3300 AM Dordrecht, The Netherlands

Distributor for the U.S.A. and Canada:
Foris Publications USA, Inc.
P.O. Box 5904
Providence RI 02903
U.S.A.

Distributor for Japan:
Sanseido Book Store, Ltd.
1-1, Kanda-jimbocho-cho
Chiyoda-ku
Tokyo 101, Japan

CIP-DATA

Weigand, Hans

Linguistically motivated principles of knowledge base systems / Hans Weigand. - Dordrecht [etc.]: Foris. - Ill. - (Functional grammar series ; 12)
Also published as thesis Vrije Universiteit Amsterdam, 1989. - With ref. - With summary in Dutch.
ISBN 90-6765-491-4
SISO 521.2 UDC 681.3.02:801.5
Subject heading: databases

ISBN 90 6765 491 4

Printed in The Netherlands by ICG Printing, Dordrecht.

Contents

1. INTRODUCTION

1.1 From database to knowledge base *1*
- 1.1.1 Data independence *1*
- 1.1.2 Artificial Intelligence *3*
- 1.1.3 Aristotle on knowledge *4*
- 1.1.4 Knowledge base research *7*

1.2 From knowledge base to language base *8*
- 1.2.1 The transcendental character of language *8*
- 1.2.2 Linguistically motivated knowledge representation *11*
- 1.2.3 Antithesis *13*
- 1.2.4 Language versus linguistic theory *15*
- 1.2.5 The language base *17*

1.3 Summary and conclusion *18*

1.4 Outline of thesis *19*

2. OUTLINE OF FUNCTIONAL GRAMMAR

2.1 Introduction *20*

2.2 Lexicon *22*

2.3 Terms *25*

2.4 Predication *26*

2.5 Proposition *30*

2.6 Message *32*

2.7 Negation *33*

2.8 Formal representation *35*

2.9 Expression rules *38*

2.10 Conclusion *42*

3. SEMANTICS

3.1 Introduction *43*

3.2 Scott information system *45*
- 3.2.1 The elements of a system *46*
- 3.2.2 Consistency by entailment *49*
- 3.2.3 Functions *49*
- 3.2.4 Product systems *52*

3.2.5 Entailment bases *53*
3.2.6 Data algebra *56*
3.3 Application *57*
3.3.1 Type level *57*
3.3.2 Instance level *59*
3.3.3 Situations *63*
3.4 Truth *66*
3.5 Summary and conclusion *72*

4. THE STRUCTURE OF THE LEXICON

4.1 Introduction *75*
4.1.1 Objectives *77*
4.1.2 Organization *77*
4.1.3 Some problems *79*
4.2 Predicates and predicate frames *81*
4.2.1 Predicates *81*
4.2.2 Predicate frames *84*
4.2.3 Predicate formation *87*
4.2.4 Semantic functions *90*
4.2.5 Places and paths *96*
4.3 Lexical structures *98*
4.3.1 Taxonomy *98*
4.3.2 Semantic fields *102*
4.3.3 Information system *105*
4.4 Complex frames *105*
4.4.1 Frame subsumption *105*
4.4.2 Complex predicate frame *106*
4.4.3 Meaning conditions *109*
4.4.4 Secondary semantic functions *113*
4.5 Predicate schemata *114*
4.5.1 Meaning definitions *116*
4.5.2 Predicate schema formation *117*
4.5.3 Sublanguages *119*
4.6 Application *121*
4.7 Summary *123*

5. TERMS

5.1 Introduction: how to denote things with words *125*

5.2 Terms in database languages *127*

5.3 Definition *130*

- 5.3.1 T-frames *131*
- 5.3.2 Term instantiation *132*
- 5.3.3 Restrictors *133*
- 5.3.4 Number and cardinality *137*

5.4 Interpretation *139*

- 5.4.1 The information structure of entity referents *140*
- 5.4.2 Masses and measures *141*
- 5.4.3 Grouping *144*
- 5.4.4 Qualifiers *146*
- 5.4.5 Locations *148*
- 5.4.6 The predicative use of terms and restrictors *149*

5.5 Conclusion *150*

6. PROPOSITIONS

6.1 Introduction *152*

6.2 Integrity constraints in knowledge bases *154*

6.3 Definition *157*

- 6.3.1 Predication versus proposition *157*
- 6.3.2 From P-frame to proposition *158*

6.4 Interpretation *164*

- 6.4.1 Chronicles *164*
- 6.4.2 Time domain *167*
- 6.4.3 Temporal logic *168*
- 6.4.4 Aspectual logic *171*
- 6.4.5 Data logic *171*
- 6.4.6 Dynamic logic *175*
- 6.4.7 Deontic logic *177*
- 6.4.8 Example *178*
- 6.4.9 Counterhistoricals *179*

6.5 Conclusion *180*

7. MESSAGES

7.1 Introduction: how to do things with words *182*
7.1.1 Example *183*
7.1.2 Information system modeling *184*
7.1.3 Speech acts *184*
7.1.4 Discourse analysis *185*
7.1.5 Message systems *187*
7.1.6 Interface design *188*
7.1.7 Summary *191*
7.2 Definition *191*
7.2.1 Illocutionary frame *192*
7.2.2 Epistemological modality *193*
7.3 Communication model *195*
7.3.1 A simple model of dialogue *198*
7.3.2 Epistemological modality *199*
7.4 EoD specification *201*
7.5 Reasoning as a language-game *203*
7.6 Summary *206*

APPENDIX A: f-structures *207*
APPENDIX B: example *214*

References

Die Sprache ist überall Vermittlerin, erst zwischen der unendlichen und endlichen Natur, dann zwischen einem und dem andern Individuum: zugleich und durch denselben Act macht sie die Vereinigung möglich, und entsteht aus derselben; nie liegt ihr ganzes Wesen in einem Einzelnen, sondern muß immer zugleich und aus dem andern errathen, oder erahndet werden; sie läßt sich aber auch nicht aus beiden erklären, sondern ist (wie überall dasjenige, bei dem wahre Vermittlung stattfindet) etwas Eignes, Unbegreifliches, aber nur durch die Idee der Vereinigung des, für uns und unsre Vorstellungsart, durchaus Geschiedenen Gegebenes, und nur innerhalb dieser Idee Befangenes... Man muß sich nur durchaus von der Idee losmachen, daß sie sich so von demjenigen, was sie bezeichnet, absondern lasse, wei z.B. der Name eines Menschen von seiner Person, und daß sie, gleich einem verabredeten Chiffre, ein Erzeugniß der Reflexion und der Übereinkunft, oder überhaupt das Werk der Menschen (wie man den Begriff in der Erfahrung nimmt) oder gar des Einzelnen sei.

WILHELM VON HUMBOLDT

1

Introduction

1.1. FROM DATABASE TO KNOWLEDGE BASE

We define a database informally as a collection of stored operational data used by certain application systems of some particular enterprise. The collection of data stored is probably large and requires special software for efficient processing. Usually, the data consists of shared information and several users may be accessing the database at the same time. The system manipulating the data in the database is called the database management system (DBMS). The DBMS does not only ensure efficient query processing, but also consistency control, recovery control, concurrency control and security control.

1.1.1. Data independence

An important objective of modern DBMS's is the provision of *data independence*. This concept is best understood by considering first applications that are data-*dependent*. This means that the way in which the data is organized in secondary storage and the way it is accessed are both dictated by the requirements of the application, and moreover that knowledge of the data organization and access technique is built into the application logic. Therefore it is not possible to change the storage structure or access strategy without affecting the application. We can define data independence as the immunity of applications to such changes (Date, 1977). Data independence was one of the most significant contributions of the relational model (Codd, 1970). The relational model provides a mathematical structure for the organization of data and algebraic operations on this structure. For the application program, it is indifferent how these operations are implemented.

Data independence is achieved by isolating the domain-specific parts of the database system from the general (supporting) parts. This process is sometimes called *knowledge abstraction* (Abbott, 1987) and is not restricted to databases. For example, the use of abstract data types in programming languages gives the programmer the ability to specify certain operations on a data type without having to bother about the internal representation of the instances. In databases, the domain-knowledge is called the *conceptual model*, which is typically stored in a *data dictionary*. It follows that the more "knowledge" is put in the conceptual model, the less remains for the application programs. In the ideal case, the DBMS provides a general database facility that needs only be fed with a conceptual model in order to perform the functions required in the particular application. An important advantage of this is that the conceptual model can be changed or updated easily, since all the domain knowledge is held together and represented explicitly. This allows for efficient design and maintenance.

When the objective of data independence is realized in full, we speak about a knowledge base management system (KBMS). The term "knowledge" is justified by the presence of an explicit conceptual model. In the last decades or two, several aspects of data independence have been studied each one going beyond the relational model. We mention the following:

- data structure independence. We already mentioned the relational database that abstracts from the way the data is stored (physical access pointers and the like);
- data item versus entity. Traditional databases do not make a distinction between the representation of an entity and the entity itself. For example, they identify the entity with its name. This causes problems if the names are changed, or if names are not unique. In the *Binary Relation Model* (Abrial, Nijssen), a distinction is made between linguistic objects (LOT's - an example is the string "Rita") and non-linguistic objects (NOLOT's, an example is the girl Rita). In the Extended Relational model (Codd, 1978), *surrogates* are used to identify the entities independent of their attribute values or physical address in memory (cf. Khoshafian & Copeland,1986).
- attribute independence. In the relational model, attributes are defined in relations. If the information of a certain entity is split over several relations, and the user wants to know the value of a certain attribute for this entity, he must know the relation in which the attribute occurs. Under the *Universal Relation assumption* (Maier et al, 1984), this is not necessary. It is assumed that the attribute can be defined independently.
- storage independence. Some data in the database are basic, whereas others can be derived (inferred) from these. The latter type of data need not be stored. It has been especially the introduction of Prolog and its coupling with databases that have brought logic into databases. A logical database contains not only facts, but also deduction rules. For the user asking a query, it does not matter whether the data retrieved was already stored in the system, or was computed at the spot (except perhaps for response time).
- time independence. In conventional databases, old data is deleted end new data is inserted under updates. Thus only current information resides in the database. In many applications it is not appropriate to discard old information. This problem is usually solved outside the system by storing the printouts in an archive, but this is obviously a non-solution, decreasing the data accessibility drastically. So in general it is necessary to associate time values with data to indicate their periods of validity. The incorporation of time leads to a so-called *temporal database* (Anderson, 1981; Jones et al, 1979; Snodgrass, 1987; Clifford & Warren, 1981; Gadia, 1988). A temporal database abstracts from the snap-shot interpretation of data.
- integrity constraints. A lot of work traditionally performed by the application program involves checks to preserve data integrity. Examples are range checks on values, but also more complex user-defined constraints, such as that no manager earns less than his subordinates. These constraints can be abstracted from the application program and put in the data dictionary too.

One of the consequences of data independence for database research, is that a new topic is added to the traditional research topics such as access methods, transaction specification and distribution: the *knowledge representation language* (including a *conceptual model*) that is used for specifying the domain-model. Since implementation issues are less relevant, other criteria determine the adequacy of the knowledge representation. One general requirement is of course that everything that is relevant in the domain, must be expressible in the language. This is called the *100 Percent Principle* in (van Griethuysen 1982). Moreover, the conceptualization must be as close to the conceptual model of the users as possible. As Bjorne Langefors already remarked once, data provide information to people only if the data are conformal with the conceptions and perceived needs of the users.

1.1.2. Artificial Intelligence

Knowledge representation is not only a topic in database theory, but also a central theme in Artificial Intelligence (AI). Of course, there are differences in perspective. Whereas databases traditionally deal with vast amounts of homogeneous data, AI programs usually deal with a small microworld with heterogeneous data. Typical examples are microworlds that are built as the result of an interpretation process of some natural language document, such as a story (Wilensky, 1983). Expert systems, another well-known application of AI, contain rules and data, but the data portion is usually small.

AI differs from database theory also in research goals. The most widely understood goal of Artificial Intelligence is to model and emulate intelligence, whereas database theory has the more modest goal of supporting communication and information storage. In practice, this distinction may become diffuse. For example, a database interface must be cooperative and "intelligent" to a certain degree in order to function properly.

Notwithstanding the differences, data independence is a central concept in AI too. This can be illustrated by the following statement of Brian Smith (1982) which he dubbed the *Knowledge Representation Hypothesis*:

> Any mechanically embodied intelligent process will be comprised of structural ingredients that a) we as external observers naturally take to represent a propositional account of the knowledge that the overall process exhibits, and b) independent of such external semantical attribution, play a formal but causal and essential role in engendering the behaviour that manifests that knowledge.

Two things have to be noted in this formulation (cf. Brachman and Levesque, 1986:71). First, the data structures of the system must be interpretable as *propositions*. Whatever form these propositions may take (frames, networks, object classes, clauses, etc), they must be identifiable as statements about some world. Implicit in this constraint is that the structures have to be expressions in a language that has a *truth theory*. Whether the structures allow for efficient access and processing is of secondary importance.

The second requirement concerns the causal role of the knowledge units. It is not enough when the knowledge is contained in some data dictionary, independent from the actual behavior of the system. In traditional database systems, the data dictionary was used only for documentation. The term *data-dictionary driven* has been used sometimes to indicate systems in which the behaviour of the database is determined by the contents of the data dictionary.

Finally, it must be noted that the hypothesis does not require that the system has to be aware in any mysterious way of the interpretation of its structures and their connection to the world; but for us to call it a knowledge base, *we* have to be able to understand its behaviour as if it believed these propositions.

Brachman and Levesque (1986) make a distinction between the Knowledge Level and the Symbol Level (cf. also Brachman, 1983). The Symbol Level deals with the "how" of the representation. The Knowledge Level involves "looking at what an agent knows about the world, not in terms of the symbolic representation and inference techniques used, but in terms of the *world itself* - what it would have to be like if what the agent held as true were in fact true" (p.70). They conjecture that under the view of the Knowledge Level, there is no fundamental difference between databases and (AI) knowledge bases. Both manage facts about a world.

1.1.3. Aristotle on knowledge

We used the term "knowledge base" for a database that achieves full data independence. This use of this word "knowledge" needs some more justification. It occurs to me that such a justification can be given by going back to classical definitions of knowledge, in particular, the one of Aristotle.

In *Metaphysics A*, Aristotle opens with the observation that all men by nature desire to know. He then starts by distinguishing knowledge from experience. Experience is also found in animals:

> By nature animals are born with the faculty of sensation, and from sensation memory is produced in some of them, though not in others. And therefore the former are more intelligent and apt at learning than those which cannot remember; those which are incapable of hearing sounds are intelligent though they cannot be taught, e.g. the bee, and any other race of animals that may be like it; and those which besides memory have this sense of hearing can be taught.

Aristotle makes a distinction between the mere faculty of sensation and memory. Memory makes animals more intelligent. This has an analogue in computers. Electronic devices become interesting when they have a memory capacity.

Memory is also a necessary (though not sufficient) condition for teachability, which makes those animals even more intelligent. But memory and teachability are still not sufficient for having knowledge. Let us proceed.

> The animals other than man live by appearances and memories, and have but little of connected experience; but the human race lives also by art (techne) and reasonings (logismos). Now from memory experience is produced in men; for the several memories of the same thing produce finally the capacity for a single experience. ... Science (techne) arises when from many notions gained by experience one universal judgement about a class of objects is produced. For to have a judgement (hypolepsis) that when Callias was ill of this disease this did him good, and similarly in the case of Socrates and in many individual cases, is a matter of experience; but to judge that it has done good to all persons of a certain constitution, marked off in one class, when they

were ill of this disease, e.g. to phlegmatic or bilious people when burning with fever - this is a matter of science.

Memory enables living beings to gain experience. Multiple sensations result in connected experience, just as in modern neural networks (Rumelhart & McClelland, 1986). However, this does not yet produce science (techne): that requires a *judgement*. The judgement involves the recognition of a *universal* rather than a set of particulars. The Philosopher hastens to warn us that for the practical purposes, science is in no way superior to experience:

> With a view to action experience seems in no respect inferior to science, and men of experience succeed even better than those who have theory without experience. The reason is that experience is knowledge of individuals, science of universals, and actions and productions are all concerned with the individual; for the physician does not cure *man* (except in an incidental way), but Callias or Socrates or some other called by some such individual name who happens to be a man. If, then, a man has the theory without the experience, and recognizes the universal but does not know the individual included in this, he will often fail to cure; for it is the individual that is to be cured.

This warning must be taken to heart when we are applying knowledge bases or expert systems in specific contexts. An expert system may have more explicit knowledge than the experienced physician, but that does not make him more successful in curing a particular individual. What is then the advantage of knowledge?

> Scientists know the cause, but men of experience do not. For men of experience know that the thing is so, but do not know why, while the others know the "why" and the cause ... thus we view them as being wiser not in virtue of being able to act, but of having the theory for themselves and knowing the causes. And in general it is a sign of the man who knows and of the man who does not know, that the former can teach, and therefore we think science more truly knowledge then experience is; for scientists can teach, and men of mere experience cannot.

Here the Philosopher mentions two characteristics of knowledge: knowledge is knowledge of the causes, and knowledge can be communicated. All this is to show the distance that knowledge separates from experience. The Philosopher does not tell us how this process (judgement) is achieved, but evidently, *language* (some symbol system) is indispensable: the symbols provide tokens for the universals, and enable communication.

The fact that knowledge is communicable, by definition, means that it is explicit and comprehensive. In terms of databases, this means that the knowledge is represented explicitly (data-independence) and in such a way that human agents can make sense of it.

Another characteristic of knowledge involves knowledge of the causes. For Aristotle, the word "cause" has a specific meaning. He speaks about causes in four senses (A,3):

> In one of these, we mean the substance, i.e. the essence (for the "why" is reducible finally to the definition, and the ultimate "why" is a cause and principle); in another the matter or substratum, in a third the source of the change, and in a fourth the cause opposed to this, the purpose and

the good (for this is the end of all generation and change).

The four senses of "cause" are treated further in *Physics*, but the present summary is sufficient for our purposes. I will not go into the metaphysical claims and assumptions contained in Aristotle's conception of the causes, but reduce it to its methodological consequences. Scientific knowledge is knowing the causes, in the four senses spelled out. Going back to knowledge bases, we can say that a knowledge base is a database that can answer "why" questions. Traditional database languages, such as SQL, allow only "what" questions (SELECT). Following Aristotle, four kinds of why-questions can be distinguished:

(a) *formal cause*: the essence or substance. For example, a user may not only ask which suppliers live in Athens, but also what *is* a supplier. This definition is to be extracted from the conceptual model. A definition, according to the Philosopher, consists of a genus proximum (a nearest supertype in some taxonomic ordering) and differentiae that distinguish it from sister concepts.

(b) *material cause*: what the thing is made of. For example, a statue can be made of bronze or iron. It is not that material causes always refer to "materials", in the chemical sense. For Aristotle, "bronze" has a formal, effective and final cause too. It depends on the level of composition.
In an information system, a sales order consists of various parts, such as the part list, delivery conditions etc. A string is composed of characters.

(c) *effective cause*: the source of change. The facts stored in the database usually refer to (dynamic) events in reality. States ("X is responsible for project Y") of course also have a beginning. A user may not only want to ask who is responsible for a certain project, but also how this employee has become responsible. The effective cause includes then the *action* as well as the responsible actor (the manager in question who assigned the responsibility). In order to answer such questions, the knowledge base must have the notion of actions, an abstract specification of actions (for example, in the form of pre- and postconditions). This is in contrast to those traditional databases, in which only the current "snap-shot" is stored. Actions were executed *on* the database, but they were not objects *in* the database.
In medieval scholastics, a further distinction was made between *causa fiendi* and *causa cognosciendi*. The causa fiendi is the effective cause proper. The causa cognosciendi is the information source. For example, a user may ask why a certain employee is responsible for a project, and the knowledge base may answer by specifying the agent who told him so or by mentioning the reasons that led him to this conclusion by inference. These would be cases of causa cognosciendi. The fact that the board of directors had decided to assign the project to the EDP manager, may be the causa fiendi of the responsibility.

(d) *final cause*: for comprehending a set of data, or a story, it is crucial to know the purposes and goals of the agents. For example, a client orders certain parts because he wants to have these parts. Sometimes, the final cause is inherent in a certain action (such as ordering), sometimes the final cause differs from one case to another. In the first case, the final cause may be specified in the conceptual schema, otherwise it can be represented as a feature of the fact.

For Aristotle, the final cause is the *telos* of a thing, the state to which the thing is evolving. This involves more than "purposes" and "goals". Closer to Aristotle's conception is perhaps the following example. An organization such as an hospital has certain objectives, for instance, healing people. All the actions, rules and the material equipment in the hospital are directed at fulfilling this objective. A knowledge base for a certain organization should know this final cause and how the different activities are related to it.

In knowledge base research, a lot of work has been done on the formal causes, in the form of conceptual models (e.g., Brodie, Mylopoulos,Schmidt, 1984). The specification of actions has also been an important topic (Borgida et al, 1984; Lingat et al, 1987). Explanation facilities are an indispensable part of expert systems and much research in Artificial Intelligence and cognitive psychology has been devoted to it. Very little research has been done on representing final causes and reasoning with them. In AI, some work has been done on the analysis of goals and purposes in narratives as part of a discourse understanding program (Wilensky, 1983). In information system design, one of the initial phases includes the *functional* analysis, the analysis of the functions that the new system must fulfil. These functions are not isolated, but embedded in the management objectives of the organization.

We can summarize the Philosopher's contribution to the conception of knowledge as follows:

> Knowledge does not guarantee better performance; it differs from experience in that it is explicit and communicable. Having knowledge involves the ability to answer "why"-questions.

This definition of knowledge seems to me a good starting point for the definition of knowledge base. It should be remarked, however, that Aristotle's definition is not generally accepted. For example, Michael Polanyi has argued at length that knowledge is *not* always explicit (Polanyi, 1962). The title of this book is "Personal Knowledge", which, for Aristotle, is almost a *contradictio in terminis*, since knowledge, as knowledge of causes, is universal. However, for computer science, working with *symbols*, Aristotle's definition applies very well.

A knowledge base is a database that contains knowledge, in the Aristotelean sense. I do not want to say that all data stored there is "knowledge"; there are also particular facts. But the presence of knowledge is what makes the database into a knowledge base.

1.1.4. Knowledge base research

Having defined knowledge, the next question is what knowledge base research is. An answer to this question can be given by a reference to the famous *Critique of pure reason* of Immanuel Kant. Kant was not a psychologist or empirical scientist studying sensation, cognition of perception. As a philosopher, he was interested in the necessary conditions for cognition. In order to perceive a chair, we must have certain perceptual facilities, the concept of a chair, etc.. But in order to perceive at all, we must already have an idea of "object" and of time and place, because we can only perceive a certain chair at a certain time and on a certain location. Time and place are called *transcendental* structures. Kantian philosophy is transcendental philosophy in that it deals not with particular experiences (c.q. reason), but with the necessary conditions of experience (reason) in general.

It is beyond the scope of this thesis and my own capabilities to do any justice to the Kantians thought. For our discussion, two lessons will be taken from Kant, one positive and one negative. Let me start with the positive one; the negative one will be dealt with in the next section. It occurs to me that *mutatis mutandis* Kant's critical method sets an example for research on knowledge representation. *A scientific approach to knowledge representation is not merely aimed at building the best knowledge base or designing the best knowledge representation language, but at a critical explanation of the principles and presuppositions underlying any knowledge representation language.* Such a principle may for example be the a priori recognition of a temporal structure. Many traditional database languages do not obey this principle, as we already noted above. Another principle has to do with the difference between syntax and semantics. A knowledge representation language is a formal language with a certain syntactic structure. The meaning of the language has to be given by means of a compostional interpretation in semantic structures. Moreover, this semantic interpretation must make up the complete formal meaning of the syntactic expressions. In the following section I will argue that the transcendental character of natural language is another often overlooked but fundamental principle of knowledge representation.

1.2. FROM KNOWLEDGE BASE TO LANGUAGE BASE

1.2.1. The transcendental character of language

Kant is also important for our present project in a negative way. In his rational rigidity, Kant concentrated on the knowing subject only and abstracted away from the context, including history, society and language. The German philosopher J.G. Hamann was one of the first to recognize this over-abstraction. The "Magus vom Norden" pointed out that it is not possible to know something without a given (natural) language and a history in which the subject is already present before he starts thinking. This criticism of Kant has been taken up by many twentieth-century philosophers such as Wittgenstein, Heidegger and Apel. Other philosophers that have recognized the inevitability of language include Gadamer in Germany, Merleau-Ponty, Derrida, Ricoeur and Foucault in France and Charles Peirce, Austin, Davidson and Rorty in the Anglo-American world. Some citations:

> "Man makes the word, and the word means nothing which the man has not made it mean, and that only to some other man. But since man can think only by means of words or other external symbols, these might turn around and say: You mean nothing which we have not taught you, and then only so far as you address some word as the interpretant of your thought ... the word or sign which man uses is the man himself". (Ch. Peirce, 5:313-314)

> "It is only in language that one can mean something by something". (Wittgenstein, 1953)

> We do not first learn what to talk about and then what to say about it (Quine, 1961:71)
>
> "Human experience is essentially linguistic". (Gadamer, 1976)
>
> "In sharing a language, in whatever sense this is required for communication, we share a picture of the world that must, in large features be true. It follows that in making manifest the large features of our language, we make manifest the large features of reality. One way of pursuing metaphysics is therefore to study the general structure of our language" (Davidson, 1977/87)
>
> For Frege, as for all subsequent analytical philosophers, the philosophy of language is the foundation of all other philosophy because it is only by the analysis of language that we can analyze thought. Thoughts differ from all else that is said to be among the contents of the mind in being wholly communicable: it is the essence of thought that I can convey to you the very thought I have, as opposed to being able to tell you merely something about what my thought is like. It is of the essence of thought, not merely to be communicable, but to be communicable, without residue, by means of language" (Michael Dummett,1975/87)

To this philosophical chorus, we can add voices from linguists and psychologists. The hypothesis of Sapir and Whorf is well-known: peoples speaking different languages may be said to live in different worlds of reality in the sense that the languages they speak affect, to a considerable degree, both their sensory perceptions and their habitual modes of thought. There is some discussion about the question what the phrase *considerable degree* means, but under a weak interpretation, the hypothesis is generally accepted by most linguists.† Fodor (1975:156), who assumes an innatively known "inner code", conjectures that this inner code cannot be too much different from (external) language:

> the resources of the inner code are rather directly represented in the resources of the codes we use for communication. [If true, this] goes some way toward explaining why natural languages are so easy to learn and why sentences are so easy to understand: the languages we are able to learn are not so very different from the language we innatively know, and the sentences we are able to understand are not so very different from the formulae which internally represent them.

In psychology, Harré (1987) proposes to enlarge the psychological paradigm by taking language serious. An example concerns the study of emotions. Much current psychological research is built around "tacit examplars in the manifestation of

† Besides Fodor, see also (Nida, 1975), (Dik, 1987) and (Wierzbicka,1989). Wierzbicka goes further than Fodor in equating the inner code (or at least our representation of it) with the lexicon. This is not to deny that some concepts are universal. But the bulk of the lexicon is language-specific and intertwined with the culture. And of course, some languages are closer to each other than others.

Not all linguists agree on this. Some maintain "that the conceptual resources of the lexicon are largely fixed by the [innate, universal HW] language faculty, with only minor variations possible" (Chomsky, 1983; see Rieber, 1983). Such assertions seem to be more inspired by theoretical dogma than by empirical research.

which gross physiological perturbations (anxiety) or socially important behavioral displays (anger/aggression) are prominent". Hope, shyness, sadness, chagrin and remorse, for instance, do not get much of a run. Harré posits that the study of such emotions, and also more exotic ones like the Japanese *mono no aware* or the extinct English *accidie* can only be studied by taking serious how the *word* is used. Sellars (1967) defends a psychological nominalism, according to which *all* awareness of sorts, resemblances, facts, etc., in short all awareness of abstract entities - indeed all awareness even of particulars - is a linguistic affair. Harnad (1986) describes an abstract cognitive system that is intended to model the categorization process. In this system, categorization of perceived objects is assumed to be independent from language. However, language is indispensable for *labeling* the categories and for building higher categories on top of the grounded ones.

Most of the thinkers cited thus far deal with the lexicon and its influence on thought (some of them also include grammar). Von Humboldt already had remarked that language is very much a world which the spirit must put between itself and its objects ("die Sprache ist eine wahre Welt, welche der Geist zwischen sich und die Gegenstände setzen muss"). It does not necessarily mean that there is no external world (idealism), but at least that the external world is always known through mediation of language. *Karl-Otto Apel* does also consider the rules of language performance (for an introduction, see Apel, 1987). His most significant contribution is the discovery of what he calls "transcendental pragmatics". Charles Morris (the founder of three-dimensional semiotics, the distinction between syntax, semantics and pragmatics) already recognized that the *semantic* function of signs presupposes an "interpretant" (introduced in the *pragmatic* dimension of sign usage). Rules of logic, (for example, modus ponens), cannot be motivated independently from the pragmatic dimension, but presuppose the pragmatic argumentation in everyday language. This can be illustrated by the following example. When Descartes formulates his famous universal doubt: "I doubt hence I exist", cogito ergo sum, then it must be remarked that this doubt is not truly a universal doubt, or it is only a paper doubt, because apparently Descartes does not doubt the meaning of the word "doubt" and does presuppose fellow humans to which he communicates his conclusion. In that sense, the conclusion "I exist" follows indeed from the presupposed pragmatic context, not by way of logical derivation, but because the "I doubt" presupposes an existing language game in which the Speaker participates (see also Hintikka, 1962). Apel also gives special attention to formal languages. It is sometimes suggested that a formal language, such as the "mathesis universalis" of Leibnitz or the logical language of Wittgenstein's *Tractatus*, could be used to overcome natural language. However, as Apel shows, these languages always presuppose natural language and they need it for their interpretation.

Let us keep in mind that we are talking about *knowledge*, which is, as we defined it, communicable. This is not to deny that there are other cognitive processes, such as visual perception and motoric control, that have more to do with *experience* than with *knowledge*. I do not want to suggest that the representation and processing of visual information (percepts, sensory icons) depends on language. On the contrary, I assume that these experiences are typically not expressible in language. In some sense, these experiences make up the unexpressible "background" of the symbolic system (cf. Winograd & Flores, 1986; Searle, 1983). My argumentation is about knowledge, not about the background of knowledge.

The transcendental character of natural language as far as knowledge is concerned has far-reaching consequences for knowledge base research. This will be worked out in the next section.

1.2.2. Linguistically motivated knowledge representation

In the previous section, we found that from a philosophical point of view, everyday language has a transcendental character. This means in concrete that any knowledge representation language explicitly or implicitly presupposes (is grounded in) natural language. At first sight, this is not very revolutionary. For example, an important knowledge representation language is first-order logic which has been designed by Frege and Russell on the basis of natural language and whose terminology (the quantifiers "for all" and "there exists", the notion of "predicate", logical connectives like "and" and "or") is directly inspired by its natural language counterpart. Several extensions to first-order logic, in particular modal logics, usually take up a linguistic modality (necessity, possibility, obligation etc) and build this into the calculus by means of an operator. That natural language offers a kind of "horizon" for knowledge representation has been formulated explicitly by Russell Abbott in an article in the Communications of the ACM:

> We will never be able to claim the knowledge representation problem is solved until we have a reasonably complete knowledge representation system for natural language, which we do not have now" (Abbott, 1987:670).

In view of this, one wonders why so much research on conceptual models and knowledge representation proceeds "as if natural language does not exist". It is imported occasionally, but often with bad conscience. For example, Smith & Smith, in their famous article on generalization and aggregation (1977), require that aggregation must yield a concept namable by a simple (English) noun, but this requirement is dismissed again by Codd (1979) as being "too imprecise". Most designers (of Entity-Relationship models) make use of the fact that entities are designated by nouns and relationships by verbs. However, there is no systematic motivation for this and, if pressed, they would say it is merely a "heuristic".† Apparently, a "naive metaphysics", including for example the assumption that the reality is neatly carved up in "entities" and "relationships" etc (that no one has been able to define) is preferred. In the ISO report on conceptual models (van Griethuysen, 1982), the following picture illustrates the idea of a conceptual model in relationship to a Universe of Discourse (Fig. 1.2):

† In the Binary Relationship approaches (Abrial, 1974; Bracchi et al, 1976; Nijssen, 1984) linguistics has clearly played an important heuristic role.

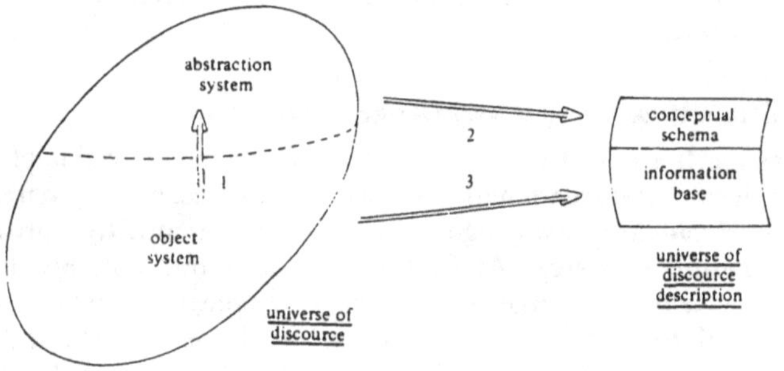

Fig. 1.1 Universe of Discourse and conceptual schema (ISO,1982)

However, the very notion of "Universe of Discourse" suggests that there is some discourse that is "about" this Universe. Without a discourse, there is no Universe of Discourse either. Thus the situation is not as simple as in the above picture; the Universe of Discourse is not an independent object, but presupposes a language through which users and designers perceive this world. For example, the fact that "fuel consumption must not exceed a certain maximum" (one example of a constraint in the report), cannot be discovered by examining a certain physical situation, but only by realizing the "in-between world" (von Humboldt) that is built up in the social discourse. For a similar critique of naive assumptions in conceptual modeling, see also Stamper (1985;1987).

In this thesis, I want to draw radical consequences of the transcendental character of language. If the knowledge representation problem involves the ability to describe the semantics of natural language, then we can better start with natural language instead of muddling with "naive metaphysics". This approach is not only more satisfactory from a philosophical point of view, it has also clear scientific-methodological advantages: it provides an objective criterion for testing knowledge representation functions that does not need vague amateuristic-philosophical conjectures (such as what an entity *really* is, or whether types exist). Instead we can check to what extent a certain language permits translation in natural language and vice versa. This is what Jackendoff (1984) calls the Grammatical Constraint on semantic formalisms (often violated in logic and AI), and Wilensky (1987) the "transducability" constraint.

Furthermore, we must realize that the grammaticality constraint is not a mere burden. A knowledge representation language that is based explicitly on the grammatical form of natural languages has several practical advantages. In the first place, it offers a conceptualization that evidently comes close to the one of the user (one requirement we noted above). A second reason can be given by reference to the

Japanese Fifth Generation Project that explicitly requires the ability to communicate in natural language (Moto-Oka, 1982). Research on natural language interfaces has made clear that representation and interface must be designed in close harmony. It is not only very costly, but also counterproductive to design a natural language interface independently from the database itself.† The use of a language-based knowledge representation language, facilitates the interface design and takes away the need for an intermediate level of representation.

Another advantage can be illustrated from our own research on CPL. The CPL system (Dignum et al, 1987) is a tool for building conceptual models (for a formal description of the semantics of CPL, see Dignum, 1989). It takes a natural language description of a certain Universe of Discourse and extracts structural information as well as integrity constraints. In analyzing the structural information, it makes use of conventional dictionary information, such as the subcategorization of verbs (the number and kind of terms they take). The integrity constraints are a direct translation of deontic sentences, such as "a member can borrow a book if it is available". The result is a number of CPL sentences that can be interpreted in the CPL system (written in Prolog). This can be used as a prototyping system. The user can enter facts (data) that are stored in the database as long as he uses words defined in the conceptual model built up by the system. The data can be checked against the integrity constraints.

Although the CPL system is still in a prototyping phase, it suggests that in some cases a considerable part of the domain model can be extracted from linguistic information (text plus lexicon). Thus a CPL system can be used profitably in knowledge acquisition. We need not only think of information system environments (the present scope of CPL), but also of more qualitative data such as found in encyclopediae and handbooks. A system that can read these texts automatically and translate them to a formal knowledge representation format (perhaps in interactive mode), would be a nice tool to have.

1.2.3. Antithesis

Although the advantages of a language-based knowledge representation formalism are clear, there are also objections to make. One strong objection is that natural language is provably not very suited for knowledge representation. It is often too vague and haunted by ambiguities. Present-day models may be simplistic, but natural language is at the other extreme: its syntactic and semantic structure are too

† For example, Small and Weldon (1983) compared the performance of SEQUEL and (restricted) English on a number of data retrieval problems and found that "there were no significant differences in solution accuracy, but subjects worked faster using SEQUEL". This result was largely caused by the fact that the underlying model was a relational database. The English query "find the doctors whose age is over 35" elicited an error message because the table was not specified and should be worded as "use the staff table to find the doctors over 35 years of age". Obviously, this is not a comparison between a structured query language and natural language but only tests whether it is easier to produce SEQUEL statements in SEQUEL than in English.
Small and Weldon's research is a negative confirmation of Kaplan's (1978) general conclusion on the differences between natural language and high level query languages that "a direct translation to a currently available formal query language is an inadequate model of the process of human question answering". See also (Pirotte, 1977; Lacroix & Pirotte,1977).

Sample Universe of Discourse description for CPL

We have a library which contains 2000 works and 750 members. A member can borrow or return one or several works by applying to one of the library wickets. He also has the possibility to reserve a work if none of its copies are available. In that case, his reservation is placed at the end of a queue of reservations made for the same work. As soon as a copy is returned, the first member in the queue is informed that the work is available. He has one week to come and borrow the work.
A library member cannot have more than 3 books at a time and each loan has to be returned at the end of 3 weeks.

Some CPL sentences derived from this text are:

```
*  PERMIT: borrow(ag = A in member)(go = B in book).
   {a member may borrow a book}
*  PERMIT: reserve(ag = A in member)(go = B in book)
           (sit: ~ available(B)).
   {a member may reserve a book if it is not available}
*  MUST: return(ag = A in member)(go = B in book)
         (sit: PERF: borrow(ag =A)(go = B)).
   {a member must return a book if he has borrowed it}
```

Fig. 1.2 Example from CPL

complex.

Another objection accepts the transcendental character of everyday language, and uses this argument *against* a linguistic approach. If everyday language is truly transcendental, then we cannot expect that a formal language can ever exhaust it. Even if one takes a linguistic approach, as we suggest, we cannot expect that the process of formalizing and defining will be finished at some day. In slightly different wordings, this is also the conclusion of Winograd and Flores (1986). In their Heideggerian terminology, each formal system "breaks down" at some point.

Let us start with the second objection. I agree that the knowledge engineer can never abstract completely from the social and linguistic context. But this is not to dismiss the whole project of knowledge representation. And if we continue, we can better do this recognizing the transcendental character of everyday language instead of ignoring it.

That the transcendental character of ordinary language is not an objection against but rather an argument in favor of a linguistic approach is also the conclusion of Gardner(1987). Her research is on knowledge representation in the legal domain. She acknowledges the so-called *open texture* of many legal predicates (cf. Hart, 1961). Although the technical legal predicates are rather sharply defined, at some point they must be grounded in ordinary language. The law may contain a rule about dogs, but it does not define a dog. The law may specify what it means that someone *owns* a dog, but this definition is parasitic on the ordinary meaning (cf. our section 3.10). However, her conclusion is not that the project is doomed to fail. Recognizing the open texture problem implies, according to Gardner, that the knowledge representation formalism must be grounded in natural language rather than on semantic primitives (as in earlier systems for legal reasoning).

1.2.4. Language versus linguistic theory

We now turn to the first objection. Natural language is often vague and ambiguous. Therefore it seems not a good candidate for knowledge representation. My answer is that it is not necessary to take natural language as such. The grammaticality constraint requires that the formalism must be directly translatable to natural language, but it does not forbid formalisms. A language-based approach to knowledge representation does allow for formal abstraction, and even favors it, as long as the formalism is motivated by linguistic arguments. Fortunately, such a motivation need not be made by knowledge engineers themselves. They can make profitable use of past and ongoing linguistic research. Our suggestion is that knowledge base theory builds on linguistic theory, not that it tries to replace it. A reasonable "interface" between linguists and knowledge engineers is the "deep structure" of the sentence. Linguists have hypothesized such a deep structure and have described how it relates to surface form. Knowledge engineers (in casu, information system designers) can take this deep structure and use it in conceptual modelling. They can also examine the logical properties of this deep structure. And finally, computer scientists can relate this structure to data structures in the computer (implementation questions).

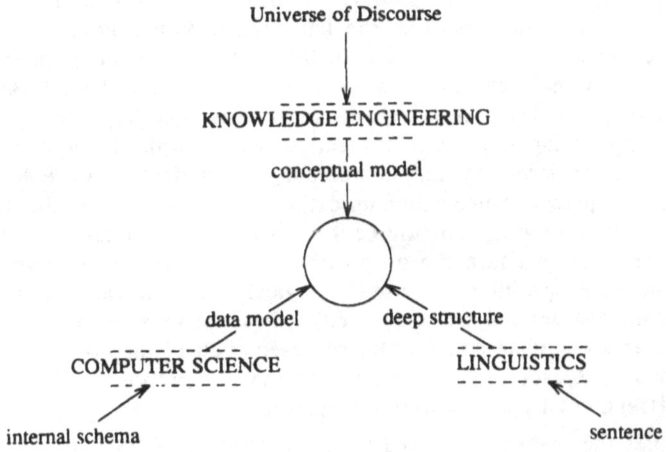

Fig. 1.3 Linguistics, computer science and knowledge engineering

Figure 1.3 is a schematic representation of how the scientific disciplines of linguistics, computer science and knowledge engineering interrelate. Computer science is separated here from knowledge engineering, the former dealing with implementation and the latter dealing with modelling. The "deep" structure of the linguist coincides with the conceptual model of the knowledge engineer. The same structure comprises the highest (external) level of the implementation built by computer scientists. Presently, each one of the three disciplines has its own formalism. If they have to cooperate, for example, if the conceptual model has to be implemented or if a natural language interface must be provided, one structure has to be translated to another. In our proposal, the different formalisms are unified so that translation is no longer necessary.

Finding the "deep structure" of natural language is not a trivial task. It is hardly surprising that several competing theories co-exist. In this thesis, I have chosen for one theory, Functional Grammar (FG; see Dik, 1978; Dik, 1987; Dik, 1989fc). The underlying structure used in FG, also called *predication* achieves a high level of expressiveness in a formal framework. At the same time, it is closely bound to surface form since Functional Grammar puts heavy restrictions on the expression rules (no transformations, no filters). The predication is described as a *frame* (or functional structure) where the slots are semantic functions, such as *agent, recipient* etc, or other functions (syntactic, pragmatic, grammatical). In this respect, FG shares a lot of ground with Artificial Intelligence. Both FG and AI took inspiration from Fillmore's case grammar (Fillmore, 1968) and Halliday's systemic-functional grammar (Halliday, 1984; cf. Winograd, 1983). An important advantage of Functional Grammar is expressed by its name: it considers grammar to be functional. This is not only a matter of using functional structures, but means in particular that the form of the underlying structure as well as the expression rules are related to the functions that the language is supposed to fulfil. In FG, language is not just a formal system, but in the first place an instrument of social interaction between human beings, used with the primary aim of establishing communicative relations between speakers and addressees. FG linguists try to reveal the instrumentality of language with respect to what people do with it. In other words, the underlying structure should not only attain descriptive adequacy, but also functional adequacy. Since communication can be viewed as the sharing of propositions, FG's underlying structure contains a propositional structure as well as illocutionary operators that turn the proposition into a question, a command, or a report for example. Propositions are used in logical reasoning (another function of language, presumably derived from the first). Descriptive adequacy requires that the proposition is a complete and faithful representation of the content of the sentence. Functional adequacy requires in addition that the propositional structure can be processed effectively by a reasoning mechanism.†

For related work, the reader is referred to recent trends in GPSG, in particular the work of Pollard and Sag. In *Information-based syntax and semantics* (Vol.1), the authors defend an "information-based approach to the study of natural language

† Note that the name "functional" refers to a range of properties (not unrelated). Whether Functional Grammar is also "functionalist" in the psychological sense (Fodor, 1983), is an open question. It is functionalist as far as it tries to build a functional model of the linguistic agent (Dik et al, 1989). But this does not necessarily mean that all cognitive and emotional phenomena of man are open to a functionalist interpretation.

syntax and semantics that considers the objects that make up human language as bearers of information within the community of people who know how to use them". Although the authors sometimes end up with different conclusions than FG, there is also a lot in common. We will make profitable use of this.

To be honest, I must also notice a possible disadvantage of Functional Grammar. It is relatively young and not worked out to the same degree as for example Transformational Grammar. At some points, the theory shows gaps. Few computational tools have been developed yet (but see Dik & Connolly, 1989). In my opinion, this disadvantage is outweighted by the positive advantages. I also hope the research presented here can contribute to the further development of FG.

Let us summarize the advantages of a linguistic approach mentioned thus far:

(1) a linguistic approach has a more realistic philosophical foundation (less naive than the simple positivism adopted in most other approaches);

(2) a linguistic approach can help making knowledge base theory more scientific by giving observable criteria for evaluating the representational power of a formalism;

(3) a linguistic approach is indispensable if we ever want to achieve the goals of the Fifth Generation project, communication by means of natural language (as well as bilingual translation, and knowledge acquisition from natural language documents);

(4) a linguistic approach has heuristic value; it can prevent us from making naive assumptions or reinventing the wheel;

1.2.5. The language base

Taking a functional-linguistic approach to databases also influences our view of what a database is. Instead of viewing a database merely as a model of some Universe of Discourse, we view it first of all as a communication device. People can communicate by means of speech. Once humans invented writing and printing. Communication in written form uses the same language as oral speech, but the written form makes it possible to store discourse, and send it over a physical distance. Compared with oral speech, written language is not bound anymore to a certain time and location. In our days, we also communicate by means of computers. Sometimes this communication is for social purposes only, but more often the communication is part of some cooperative enterprise. An important goal of communication in companies is the *coordination of actions* (cf Winograd & Flores, 1988). The computer has the same advantages as the written form (bridging time and space, cheaper and faster), and some others beside. One is the possibility of integrity checking and the possibility to combine different predications according to pre-established deduction rules (logical reasoning). Another advantage is the possibility of multiple indexing. A written document, such as a book or a ledger, is always organized in one way. Stored in a computer, it can be accessed in multiple ways.

In spite of these obvious advancements, the information system still remains a communication tool. The information in it has some purposes, it is put there by someone for someone. As we noted above, the meaning of the symbols can never be described exhaustively. In the beginning of this chapter we suggested that a knowledge base is a database that contains a separate domain model. Now we can add that a *language base* is a knowledge base that contains not only a domain model, but also an *environment model* describing the communication context. A language base contains not just facts and propositions, but *messages*. These messages are frames that contain propositions. The propositions embedded in the messages are not considered to be "objective representations" of some world, but evaluations of the part of a Speaker who is presumably pretty much involved with the domain in question. He does not want to give an "unbiased view" (if it would exist), but he wants to communicate his viewpoint and his desires. He wants to coordinate his actions and appointments with another agent. In other words, a language base does not represent an objective view, but messages from specific agents in the context of coordinate activities (cf. Taylor, 1987). In some sense, this also holds already for traditional databases. The data items stored there stem also from some Speaker. But it is pretended that they represent atomic and eternal facts. Specifying the Speaker and Addressee can be viewed as another level of data independence: instead of leaving the pragmatic information implicit (so that a user must find out himself who originated the message, and cannot ask for it) it is made explicit and retrievable.

1.3. SUMMARY AND CONCLUSION

In this chapter we have tried to give content to the phrase "knowledge base". We considered the goal of data independence, and the meaning of "knowledge" by Aristotle. From Kant, we borrowed the idea of transcendental critique in order to characterize knowledge base theory as a scientific discipline. Using the idea of transcendental critique, we considered in particular the status of natural language. This led us to conclude that knowledge presupposes language. As a consequence, we proposed a linguistic approach to knowledge engineering, that is, an approach that builds on linguistic theory. We suggested several practical advantages of such an approach. Finally, we coined the term "language base" for a knowledge base system that is explicitly designed for supporting meaningful communication between humans.

As far as linguistic theory is concerned, we selected Functional Grammar as a promising starting point. The task that lies before us is the formal specification and logical interpretation of the Functional Grammar underlying predication. Although we cannot expect to give a complete semantics for all aspects of the predication, we have been able to do so for a reasonable fragment. This fragment is at several points more powerful than most formalisms presently in use or proposed. At other points, it recapitulates what has been achieved already by others. In the latter case, it still has the advantage of a linguistic motivation. That does not mean that it is always right, but assures at least that it can be criticized on empirical grounds. This property - rarely found with other approaches in this domain, unfortunately - seems to me a *sine qua non* for long-term progress.

1.4. OUTLINE OF THESIS

Chapter 2 gives a systematic overview of Functional Grammar from the perspective of the knowledge engineer. It also introduces a certain kind of data structure, f-structures, as a formalization of the frame concept. In chapter 3, we present a model-theory that is based on the Domain Theory of Scott, in particular, the idea of information systems. This theory allows for an elegant treatment of partial information which is desirable both in linguistics and knowledge engineering. We give a semantic interpretation of simple FG structures using this model-theory. The chapters 4, 5 and 6 can be seen as extensions. In chapter 4, we discuss the structure of the lexicon. We argue that a lexicon, provided that it is set up properly, embraces the various parts of the conceptual schema - so central in knowledge engeneering - in a single coherent and motivated framework. Chapter 5 is about terms (referring expressions) and chapter 6 about propositions. We define the syntactic structure as well as the semantics of various term and predication operators, such as number, aspect, and modality. We also point out the applicability of these structures and operators for knowledge base theory. For example, in chapter 5 we compare the FG definition of terms with recent ideas about complex objects, and in chapter 6 we show that operators of deontic modality are profitable for the specification of integrity constraints. Finally, chapter 7 describes the message level which is perhaps still the most neglected subject in knowledge base theory. We present a simple communication model and investigate the use of speech act theory in information system design.

If the reader is still with me at the end of the thesis, I hope he has been convinced of the following three claims:

(1) FG predications can be endowed with rigourous logical semantics;

(2) FG predications make up a formal knowledge representation language that can be used for specification, retrieval, deduction and communication;

(3) for a disciplined theory of the principles of knowledge bases, linguistics is extremely fruitful and in fact indispensable.

2

Outline of functional grammar

2.1. INTRODUCTION

In this chapter I will present a summary of the theory of Functional Grammar. We are particularly interested in the use of FG in knowledge engeneering, so readers more interested in the linguistic motivations and applications are strongly encouraged to consult the FG literature, in particular (Dik,1978; Dik,1989fc). The present summary is explicitly made from a computational perspective, but this is not the only possible perspective.

The theory of Functional Grammar contains two main formal components. The first component describes the structure and semantics of the **knowledge representation language**. The central knowledge unit is called the *proposition*. Propositions are put forward in *messages* and contain *predications*. We could say that predication, proposition and message are different levels of some "underlying clause structure".

The second component of FG is formed by the various kinds of **expression rules** which map underlying clause structures onto linguistic expressions. The expression rules must determine the form of each part of the expression, their relative ordering, and, in the case of speech output, the prosodic contour (accent and intonation).

The FG knowledge representation language is described at four levels. We start at the bottom:

PREDICATE

Predicates designate entity types, relationship types or attribute types. They are stored in the lexicon. Predicates are contained in predicate frames which specify among others the *semantic* functions applicable to the predicate (such as Agent, Goal, Recipient etc).

PREDICATION

A predication is a structure created by inserting terms into predicate frames, and instantiating the frame at a spatio-temporal location. It denotes a State of Affairs in the Universe of Discourse.

PROPOSITION

A structure made up of one or more predications (connected by means of conjunction, implication, embedding etc). A proposition may also contain modal operators. It designates a possible fact. It can be true or false with respect to a certain State of Affairs.

MESSAGE

A message consists of a frame of a certain illocutionary type that contains a proposition. Besides, the illocutionary frame has entries for Speaker, Addressee, Speech Time, Theme, etc. Functions at the message level such as discourse topic are called *pragmatic functions*.

This layered description is supplemented by the notion of a term.

TERM

An expression designating some entity in some (mental) world. A term is a structure consisting of a head (the type of the term, being a noun predicate frame from the lexicon) and an optional set of restrictors.

Terms are part of the central knowledge unit, the proposition. The entity referred to by the term in the mental model is called the *referent*. Being part of the predication, terms are also included in the message, as (potential) *topics*. Term types (the nominal predicates) are included in the lexicon.

The four levels of the clause correspond to four functions of language in general:

(1) **conceptualization**: words provide us with a conceptual schema through which we can know the world and find sense in it;

(2) **representation**: by means of language structures, we can build models of (part of) the world, or imagine ones of our own;

(3) **information:** symbolic representations can be stored, processed and used to derive new information;

(4) **communication**: through a common language, we can communicate propositions, relate socially and do things with words.

Alternatively, the four levels correspond with four modules of a general knowledge base architecture (see Fig. 2.1): The *data dictionary* contains, among others, the conceptual schema which is used throughout the knowledge base system. The *data base* (in the model-theoretic view, cf. Reiter 1984) is a set of atomic representations of the Universe of Discourse. A knowledge base system may maintain several databases at the same time, corresponding to alternative views of the world. The *knowledge base proper* (logical database, rule base) is a set of facts, inference rules and constraints.† Together these make up a logical theory. The *message base* provides an interface with the external world, the users or other knowledge bases.

† Note that we distinguish both a knowledge base proper and a database. In many approaches, either one of the two is chosen. However, we believe that both must be sustained together. The database provides a *model* of the Universe of Discourse and its structure is relatively simple so that processing can be done efficiently. The propositions in the knowledge base are more complex, but they are to be taken as assertions (c.q. constraints) *over* the database. Knowledge base processing corresponds to general theorem-proving; database processing to "surface semantics". For the difference between surface semantics and deep semantics, see (Levesque,1988) and (Johnson-Laird,1983).

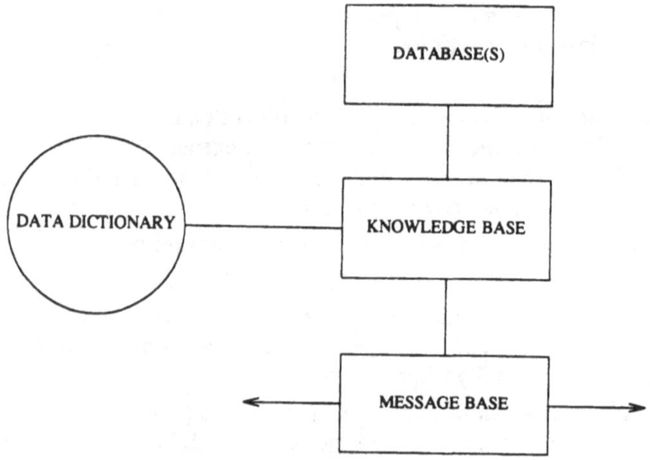

Fig. 2.1 Knowledge base architecture

It stores the exchanged messages. The constraints on the message base are stored in a section of the knowledge base.

The FG underlying clause consists of lexical and abstract elements. The lexical elements are defined in the lexicon which is language-specific. The abstract elements can be further categorized as follows:

(a) **functions**: semantic, syntactic and pragmatic.

(b) **operators**: taken from a universal set of operators and working on the expression as a whole.

(c) **connectives**: such as conjunction and disjunction.

The *semantics* of the underlying clause is not homogeneous but depends on the function we are looking at. The core of the semantics is model-theoretic, in accordance with the referring function of propositions. However, not for every element of the underlying clause a model-theoretic semantics gives an adequate account of its meaning. Therefore the model-theory is supplemented with lexical semantics, propositional logic and illocutionary logic.

We will now consider each part in some more detail.

2.2. LEXICON

In Functional Grammar, the lexicon is an integral part of the grammar. For each word, it contains at least three different types of information:

(1) grammatical information: a functional structure specifying the category of the predicate (Verb, Noun, or Adjective), the stem, grammatical features such as gender or declination, and irregular forms. Example:

```
(cat => v; stem => "see";
 forms => (past => "saw"; pap => "seen"))
```

Each predicate is given as part of a predicate frame which specifies its valency (the number and types of arguments it takes). The argument positions are further specified by semantic functions and selection restrictions. Example:

```
pregnant(x woman)
kiss(ag x  human)(go y thing)
give(ag x human)(go y)(rec z human)
```

`ag`, `go` and `rec` are semantic functions (roles) Agent, Goal and Recipient. The selection restrictions take the form of terms or predications, whose structure is spelled out below.

(2) structural information: relating predicates to one another. The most important one is the taxonomic relation, designating subsumption or subtype relationships. Examples:

```
car < vehicle
kiss < touch
five < number
```

Other possible structural links are for instance converse and antonymy relationships. Structural links are also used to represent meaning conditions such as the pre- and postconditions of dynamic predicates (`pre`, `post`). If F is a predicate frame and G is one of its meaning conditions, then when F is asserted of *x*, G may also be asserted of *x*, or: "when a speaker asserts F as holding of *x*, he is committed to accept that G holds of *x*" (cf. Dik et al,1989).
Examples:

```
a.  kiss(ag x human)(go y) <
        touch(ag x human)(go y)(instr [m]z lip(z))
b.  father(x animate) < parent(x animate)
    father(x animate) :- male
```

The definitions can be expressed as "kissing something implies touching it with the lips" and "a father of someone is a male parent of that one". The ":--" connects a definiendum to some definiens.

(3) conceptual information: the lexicon also contains a set of predicate *schemata* that can be thought of as stereotypical predicate frames. The conceptual information attached to predicate frames includes the meaning definitions describing essential (but not necessary) characteristics of the concept.

As an abstract structure, the lexicon consists of a set of predicate frames, a set of structural relations, and a set of scripts. The latter sort of information is incorporated in the frame. For example, the lexical entry of *to give* may be:

```
(pred => (cat => v; stem => "give";
          forms => (past "gave"; pap "given"));
 type => transfer;
 sem => (ag  => x animate;
         go  => y thing;
         rec => z animate);
 cond => (pre => have(pos x)(go y);
          post => have(pos z)(go y));
 conv => receive)
```

The terms and conditions in this structure are abbreviated for convenience. A more formal treatment will be given later with the use of f-structures (cf. 2.7.2). Note the following properties of lexical entries:

(1) All the predicates involved are actual predicates of the object language described. They are not to be considered as abstract predicates of some language-independent meta-language (cf. Dik, 1987a; Nuyts, 1989 for a critique; section 4.5.3 of this monograph for some motivation).

(2) All the functions and lexical relations are abstract elements and should be considered as language-universal.

(3) In the case of meaning conditions and definitions, the formal structure of definiens and definiendum is the same, and is wholly compatible with the structure of the predication. This means that is easy to convert a predication containing for example the verb *kiss* into one containing the expression *touch with the lips* by substituting the definiens structure for the definiendum.

(4) A certain predicate may correspond with several frames. If the grammatical information is different, we have to do with homonyms. It is also possible to list several frames for one homonym. And each predicate frame usually subsumes several predicate scripts.

(5) Predicate formation rules. The lexicon represents the stock of basic predicates which language users must know in order to be able to use them, while the predicate formation component reflects what they may form by themselves. Thus, derived predicates are those predicates which can be formed by means of some synchronically productive rule. An example is English agentive nominalization rule:

INPUT: `F-v(ag X t)`
OUTPUT: `F++"er"-n`

which applied to the predicate `work` yields:

INPUT: `work-v(ag X human)`
OUTPUT: `worker-n`

This rule can be paraphrased as: if there is a verbal predicate F with an agent slot, then we can form a nominal predicate assembled by suffixing 'er' to the predicate F. The ++-operator in `x++'er'` stands for suffixation and is the ordinary string append. In the present thesis, I will ignore the divergence of spelling and pronunciation. In principle each predicate stands for its phonological form, and spelling is secondary.

2.3. TERMS

A term is an expression which can be used to refer to an entity in some world. The general format of a term is as follows:

$$\Omega\, x\; P : \phi_1(x) \ldots \phi_n(x)$$

where Ω stands for one or more term operators, x is a variable used as reference marker, P is the head of the term, and each ϕ_i is a restrictor.

An *operator* specifies properties that apply to the term as a whole, such as definiteness (i,d) and cardinality ([n], where n is an integer or an integer type such as singular or plural). The reference marker is used to express co-reference of terms and takes the form of a one-character variable (optionally followed by an index number). Each term is of a certain category indicated by the head which must be a nominal predicate. The restrictors are predications specifying some additional property which the entity must have in order to qualify as a potential referent of the term. Restrictors will be realized as attributive modifiers or relative clauses.

Both the head and the restrictors are frames that may contain other arguments besides the term variable. Most nouns occurring in the head are atomic, but there are nouns, such as *father* that take an argument. Some examples:

```
(d[m] x dancer : russian)
(d[s] y father(d[l] z john))
(i[7] z dwarf)
(i[_] x1 _ : concrete)
(*[s] x2 man)
```

(the underscore at head position signals that the head is empty). These terms will be expressed in English as:

the russian dancers
the father of john
seven dwarfs
something concrete
every man

From a functional point of view, referring is regarded as a pragmatic, cooperative action of a Speaker S within a pattern of verbal interaction between that Speaker and some Addressee A. The entities E referred to are mental representations (leaving deictic reference aside). Since they are things that can be construed in the mind, we can distinguish two main usages of terms (Dik, 87:3):

(i) S may use a term T in order to help A construe a referent E for T, and thus introduce E into his knowledge base

(ii) S may use a term T in order to help A retrieve a referent E for T, where E was already present in his knowledge base

The construction of referents is typically achieved through indefinite specific terms, and the retrieval of referents by definite terms.

Note that a referent is not necessarily singular; it may also be a set of any cardinality. It may also be neither a set nor an individual but a "mass", as in the terms "*some water*" or "*much gold*". A mass has parts and can be measured but it is not countable. Bunt (1985) has proposed the notion of *ensemble* to unify the concepts of set, individual and mass (see also Dik, 1987).

There is a close interdependence between referents and terms, or between our ontology and linguistics. Only those referents can be created and distinguished that are identifiable by means of (linguistic) terms. On the other hand, the correspondence with the "real" world is indirect, and one physical object can be termed in several ways in the knowledge base. That is to say that terms are *intensional* objects for which identity does not coincide with extensional identity. For more details, see chapter 5.

Adjectives, which can be used as restrictors, are scalar (by default) or polar. An example of the former is *big*, of the latter *English*. For scalar adjectives, the property attributed to the term referent is based on a comparison with some norm (relative to the domain stipulated by the category of the term). The norm is either a category prototype or an explicitly introduced second term. For example, *John is quicker than Peter* (comparative), or *Mary is the most blessed of all women* (superlative). Explicit comparison is marked as an adjective operator. Some examples:

(a) `[< d[s] x Paul] strong`
"less strong than Paul"

(b) `[>y] long`
"longer" (than y)

(c) `[[2] inch] deep`
"2 inches deep"

Example (a) shows an adjective whose measure is smaller than that of another term (*Paul*). In example (b), the comparison term is assumed to be topical and in that case does not need to be expressed. In (c), the measure is equal to that of some generally accepted yard stick.

In FG, all restrictors, including the adjectives, are represented as one-place open predications. However, since adjectives always apply to the referent of the term in which they are contained, and this referent can hardly be said to have a specific semantic function with respect to the property expressed by the adjective, we prefer to write adjectival restrictors as ϕ rather than as $\phi(x)$.

2.4. PREDICATION

Predications consist of predicate frames where the slots have been filled with terms. Terms refer to entities in some world and predicates designate properties of or relations between such entities. A predication as a whole designates a State of Affairs (SoA), something which can be the case in some world. FG makes a distinction between propositions and predications (cf. Davidson, 1967). Propositions are the bearers of truth-values, that is, a proposition is the sort of thing which may be true or false. Propositions can be the objects of verbs such as *know* and *believe*. SoAs, on the other hand, are spatio-temporal entities much like ordinary physical objects. They occupy intervals of time and space. They can be the objects of perceptual verbs such as *see* and *hear*, and they can be said to "occur".

SoAs can be divided into different kinds, according to the values which they can have for a number of distinguishing parameters. The most important semantic parameters defining a typology of SoAs are Control, Dynamism, Telicity and Momentaneousness. Part of the typology is represented in picture 2.2.

	+dynamic EVENT	**-dynamic** SITUATION
+controlled	action	position
-controlled	process	state

Fig. 2.2 Typology of States of Affairs

The semantic parameters are inherited from the predicate frame as it is specified in the lexicon. For example, *to give* is an action, *to sit* is a position, *blowing* (of the wind) is a process, and *to lie* (in bed) is a state.

A predication which results from the insertion of term structures into the argument slots of some predicate frame is called a *nuclear predication*. A nuclear predication corresponds to a SoA type. The nuclear predication may be extended with additional slots called secondary semantic functions (also called *level 1 satellites*), such as `instr` (instrument), and with restrictors. The result is called a *core predication* which has the following form:

$P\ (\alpha)\ (\sigma_1)\ :\phi_1$

where P is the head of the frame (typically a verb), α is a set of arguments, and σ_1 a set of the secondary semantic functions, also called level 1 satellites. The secondary semantic functions are optional. ϕ_1 stands for zero or more restrictors. Each argument is headed by a semantic function and surrounded by brackets.

Example:

```
touch(ag x person)(go i[s] y person)(instr d[p] z lips)
```

Here, the Head is the verb *touch*, with two semantic functions "agent" and "goal" and a secondary semantic function "instrument".

A core predication can be *instantiated* to represent a particular SoA so that we get structures of the form:

$[n]\ e\ \Phi\ (loc\ l)\ (tmp\ t)$

where e is the SoA variable, l the location, t the event time, n the quantity and Φ the core predication. The result is called an *embedded* predication, since the predication is embedded under the SoA variable. The event time can be further specified as to its type, its duration or its relationship with other time variables. Location and event time are sometimes called *implicit* arguments, because SoA instances necessarily exist in space and time. If they are not expressed (in the sentence, in the predication), this means that their value is unspecified rather than absent. Quantification is only possible if the event is discrete (telic). In the majority of cases, there is no quantification at all. The quantification is an operator that may be omitted.

Embedded predications can now be extended by means of predication operators, restrictors and satellites. Predication operators represent grammatical means by which the SoA can be located with respect to a reference frame, notably a reference time. Predication satellites, such as *yesterday* represent lexical means for specifying the reference frame. The final result is an *extended predication*, or *predication* for short, which takes the form:

$$\pi_2 \; E \; (\sigma_2) : \phi_2$$

where π_2 stands for the predication operators, E is the embedded predication, and σ_2 and ϕ_2 are the (level 2, i.e. predication) satellites and restrictors respectively. The predication operators may include:

$$[t]$$

to represent the reference time.

Expanding the predication to predicate level, we get the full structure:

$$\pi_2 \; [n] \; e \; P \; (\alpha) \; (\sigma_1) \; (\sigma_2) : \phi_1 : \phi_2$$

An extended predication denotes what we call a *fact*. A totally ordered set of extended predications is called a *course of events* (cf. Barwise & Perry, 1983:56). The difference between a fact and a SoA is that the latter is not located in time yet. A fact is basically a SoA plus a reference time.

At the level of the (extended) predication, syntactic (or "presentative") functions can be assigned. Syntactic functions are Subject and Object. Formally, they are functions from facts to terms. They specify the perspective from which the State of Affairs is presented in the linguistic expression (Dik, 78:13). An example of a predication with Subject function assigned is:

```
(e kiss(subj ag d[7] z dwarf)(go d[s] y snowwhite) : tender(e))
```

"*the seven dwarfs kiss snowwhite tenderly*"

Let us now look more closely at the predication operators. According to (Dik, 1989), two main groups can be distinguished: one dealing with aspectuality, and one dealing with (objective) modality. Modality is a borderline case between the predication level and proposition level, and we treat it in the next section. We concentrate now on aspectuality only.

Aspectuality is a field consisting of various subareas for which it is difficult to find a common denominator. The subareas are:

- *Perfectivity*. This type of aspectuality hinges on the question whether the SoA is presented from an outside point of view, as one complete, indivisible whole (Perfective) or from an inside point of view, as being non-complete or in progress (Imperfective). This is a feature of the SoA type that may be overruled by means of a predicate operator.

- *Phasal aspect*: These operators serve to describe what can be said at the reference time about the occurrence of the SoA. If the reference time overlaps with the event time, this is expressed by predicate operators like PROG (progressive), INGR (ingressive), and EGR (egressive). Otherwise the operators express either the pre- or postcondition of the event, that is, either PROSP (prospective) or PERF (perfect). See Fig. 2.3. In English, operators from the second group can be combined with those in the first group, as in *John has been reading a book*.

Phasal aspect must be sharply distinguished from tense. Tense locates a fact with

(a)

```
                         SoA
            ------------------------------------->


          ----->          ----->            ----->
     START            MIDDLE              END
```

(b)

```
                         SoA
PRE-STATE ---------------------------------------> POST-STATE
```

Fig. 2.3 Phasal Aspect operators in schematic form

respect to the time of the speech event or some other reference moment: whether it is past, present or future. On the contrary, Aspect deals with the inclusion and precedence relationships between event times and reference times.

- *Quantificational aspectuality* deals with the "quantity" of the SoA, whether it occurs just a single time, or repeatedly, or habitually etc. This is expressed by means of the [*n*]. If n = "+", we have the "repetitive" reading.

As an example of an extended predication with Phasal aspect operators, consider:

```
PERF PROG e4 kiss(subj ag d[7] z dwarf)(go d[s] y snowwhite)
```
"the seven dwarfs have been kissing Snowwhite"

SoAs can also be connected:

(1) *subordination*: one SoA can be an argument or satellite of another SoA. Examples of the latter are `circ` (circumstance) and `purp` (purpose) satellites, as in: *The prince kissed Snowwhite in order to wake her*. An example of the former, where one SoA is an argument of another SoA, is: *John saw Jacky bite Molly*.

(2) *junction*: if e_i and e_j are SoAs, then so is:
e_i `&` e_j - conjunction
e_i `or` e_j - disjunction
e_i `xor` e_j - exclusive disjunction

To conclude this section, we summarize the "levels" of the predication and their intended meaning:

STRUCTURE	MEANING
nuclear predication	lexical (atomic) SoA type
core predication	compound SoA type
embedded predication	SoA instance
extended predication	fact

2.5. PROPOSITION

The next and central level of the underlying clause is called the proposition (cf. Hengeveld, 1988). A proposition represents a *judgement* that is true or not with respect to facts. It is a piece of information that can be shared by linguistic agents and stored in their knowledge bases. In the functional perspective, a language is conceived of in the first place as an instrument of social interaction between human beings, used with the primary aim of establishing communicative relations between speakers and addressees. In view of this, the proposition, as being the message content, has several functions:

(a) it provides information about some State of Affairs (by means of the predication(s) it contains)

(b) it characterizes some intentional state of the Speaker

(c) it provides the Addressee with clues for building or updating a mental model

A basic proposition denotes a *possible fact*. An extended proposition is a basic proposition with additional proposition operators and satellites.

The general structure of a proposition is:

$$\pi_3\ p\ \pi_m \Phi\ (\sigma_3)\ :\ \phi_3(p)$$

where p is a proposition variable, and π_3 is a proposition operator. π_m denotes an optional modal operator allowing for modal judgements, Φ is a predication, σ_3 stands for (level 3) satellites, and ϕ_3 for restrictors at the propositional level. As an example, consider:

```
p4 POS (PERF e3 poison(subj go d[s] x apple))
```
"The apple may have been poisoned"

where p4 is a proposition variable and POS a modal operator.

Let us now first consider the modal operators and then the propositional operators.

A proposition can be used to express a simple fact. In that case we call it an *atomic proposition*. Atomic propositions may be combined with a modal operator resulting in a modal proposition. We restrict the phrase "modal" to what FG calls objective *modality*. Objective modality expresses the Speaker's evaluation of the likelihood of occurrence (the "actuality") of the proposition. Examples are POS (possible) and NEC (necessary). Objective modality can be divided into two sub-areas: (i) *epistemic modality* in which the Speaker evaluates the actuality of the SoA in terms of his knowledge of SoAs in general; (ii) *deontic modality* in which the actuality of the SoA is evaluated in terms of a system of moral, legal or social norms. Potential distinctions of each subarea are:

(i) certain - probable - plausible - possible - improbable - impossible
(ii) obligatory - acceptable - permissible - unacceptable - forbidden

Examples

(i) `NEC (PERF e poison(subj go d[s] y snowwhite)`
"Snowwhite must have been poisoned"

(ii) `OBL (e kiss(subj ag d[s] z prince)(go d[s] y snowwhite) : tender)`
"the prince should kiss Snowwhite tenderly"

The semantic interpretation of deontic modality (obligation, permission, prohibition) is based on the notion of commitment. An agent is committed to an action iff he has supported it in some discourse situation. A commitment thus has at least a content (the action to be performed), a responsible agent (the one who is committed to perform the action), and a third party (the one to whom the agent is responsible). Commitments exist in principle independently from facts; a commitment can be satisfied or not, or not yet. If a commitment is unsatisfiable, there is no logical inconsistency, nor are we in some unspecific "sanction state". Rather we are in a state that is characterized by the fact that the commitment in question in unsatisfiable. Usually, the agent will undertake some appropriate action, for instance apologizing or paying a fine. Note that it is also possible that each commitment in itself is satisfiable, but that a set of them in insatisfiable.

To capture the meaning of deontic sentences, our database should contain not only representations of actual SoAs ("acta"), but also of commitments ("agenda"), some of which are satisfied and others unsatisfied or unsatisfiable.

Modal operators are contained in propositions. When the proposition itself is the object of further specification, we talk about propositional operators. These operators are also covered under the term modality or mood sometimes, but to distinguish them from the modal operators, we call them *evidential*. Evidentials mark the truthfulness of the proposition in terms of the way the speaker has ascertained this (Foley & Van Valin, 1984:218). Is it based on visual perception? Or hearsay information from other linguistic agents? In English, a similar function is performed by certain sentential adverbs like *obviously, evidently, seemingly*. In our representation evidentials are represented by explicating the model from which the proposition is derived.

`EXP` according to the model based on sensory data (experiential)

`QUO` according to the model based on information from others (quotative)

We assume that the Speaker holds several models simultaneously. A certain proposition may be true in one model and not in another. By explicating the model he can qualify this commitment to the proposition.

The *subjective* is a special case of evidential mood. "The very essence [of subjective modality] is to express the speaker's reservations about giving an unqualified "I-say-so" to the factuality of the proposition" (Lyons, 1977:799). The Speaker suggests rather than states a proposition. He can express more or less support to the proposition. This is indicated by an operator [c] which could be either a numerical value of belief support (certainty factor) or some support type (like `CERT` for certain). A somewhat complex example (we ignore irrelevant SoA markers):

(a) `([0.7] p4 (e streptococcus(subj d[s] x organism))`

"Probably (CF=0.7) the organism is streptococcus"

(b) `([0.7] p4 (e streptococcus(subj x))`
`(cond p3 ([t] gram-positive(subj i[s] x organism))))`

"If an organism is gram-positive, then probably (CF=0.7) it is streptococcus"

The proposition may be extended by means of satellites and restrictors. The satellites may specify the reference time,† a condition, a reason, or some epistemological evaluation. Restrictors at this level also have to do with the epistemological status. An example is *allegedly*:

```
(PAST p (e run(subj ag d[s] x john) : fast)
        (tmp t2 yesterday) : alleged(p))
```

"*Allegedly, John ran fast yesterday.*

To distinguish propositions with and without propositional operators, we could say that the latter denote judgements and the former denote statements. In other words, a statement is a judgement plus an epistemological reference point (optional).

2.6. MESSAGE

The highest level of the predication is called the message. It designates an actual speech event. Since it designates an event, we can use a frame similar to the predicate frames used in the predication. We distinguish at least four types of messages:

(a)	ASSERT	the Speaker presents a proposition with his own support
(b)	ASK	the Speaker presents a proposition without his support
(c)	DIRECT	the Speaker presents an action with his own support
(d)	PROPOSE	the Speaker presents an action without his own support

In each case, the expected response of the Addressee is cooperative support:

AGREE	take over the proposition
ANSWER	lend support to (one of) the unsupported propositions
COMPLY	take up the commitment
COMMIT	commit to the proposed action

The message type must be distinguished from the sentence type. In FG, sentence types are DECL (declarative), INT (interrogative), and IMP (imperative). It is possible to use a sentence of type INT to express a DIRECT, for example, in polite requests: "Could you open the door please?".

The general format of a message is:

[<ST>]<ref><m-frame>(1P <term>)(2P <term>)(cnt <proposition>)

where ST is the speech time, ref the reference marker and m-frame the message frame with slots for `1P` (first person), `2P` (second person) and `cnt` (content).

The following example assumes a Latin lexicon and grammar:

† The reference time specified at the proposition is the time of the proposition, which can be regarded as a timeless entity, but as the time that is chosen as a reference point for the evaluation of the fact described in the predication. See chapter 6.

```
([t58] m1 DECL(1P d[s] x caesar)(2P d[p] y senator)
            (cnt PRES p
            (PERF e1 venire(subj ag x)(dir z1)) &
            (PERF e2 videre(subj exp x)(go z2)) &
            (PERF e3 vincere(subj ag x)(go z3))))
```

which is expressed by the speech event:

```
([t58] m1 DECL(1P caesar)(2P senators)
            (cnt "veni vidi vici")
```

The FG underlying clause is not a speech event, but a speech event type (not an utterance, but a sentence). The speech event type omits the contextual participants and operators. The underlying clause of *veni vidi vici* is:

```
DECL(PRES p (PERF e1 venire(subj ag 1P)(dir z1)) &
            (PERF e2 videre(subj exp 1P)(go z2)) &
            (PERF e3 vincere(subj ag 1P)(go z3))))
```

This structure gives enough information to generate the accompanying sentence. Linguistically, it is complete. But in the message base we store *actual* speech events, including the contextual information.

At the message level, two pragmatic functions can be assigned. They fall outside the scope of the clause. The *Theme* presents a "domain or universe of discourse with respect to which it is relevant to pronounce the following predication" (Dik, 1978:130). A constituent with *Tail* function presents, as an 'afterthought' to the predication, information meant to clarify or modify some constituent in the predication. *Theme* and *Tail* are optional slots of the message frame.

Operators at the message level are called *illocutionary operators*. The most important ones are *mitigation* and *aggravation* which determine the degree of politeness or indirectness of the message.

Terms at the message level are called (potential) topics. A topic can be Given, New or Resumed. Topics are interrelated in a relevance structure: one topic can be a subtopic of another one (Yule 1981; Hannay, 1985). This topic structure can be used as an index for information retrieval on the message base.

2.7. NEGATION

In general, an underlying clause is a complex structure consisting of several layers. The layers of this structure are represented by the reference markers. For example, in the sentence we just saw from Caesar, the reference markers are:

message:	m1
proposition:	p
SoA	e1, e2, e3
term	x, y, z1, z2, z3, t, t58

Each of these reference markers are supported by the Speaker. In normal communication, the aim is that the Addressee supports them too. This is also the expected response. But there are several ways in which the Addressee can fail to meet the expectation. First, he can fail to support the *message*. If he is not interested in the topic, or could not understand the sentence, he will not support the message. By implication, he does not support the proposition and other reference markers either. Now suppose that he accepts the message. Then he can still disagree with the proposition. In a similar vein, he can accept the proposition as such, but disagree about the SoA that is contained in it, or about one of the terms. For example, 2a-c show various ways of non-support:

(1) John Brown has married a Swedish princess

(2a) Nonsense.

(2b) No, he DATED her.

(2c) No, she is NORWEGIAN

In (2a) the Addressee does not give support to the proposition, although he apparently has accepted the message. In the words of Austin, he has understood the message but not taken it up (Wunderlich makes a similar distinction between Verstehen and Akzeptieren). In (2b), he accepts the proposition but not the SoA. In (2c), he also accepts the SoA, but not the last term. In the last two cases, he presents a modified referent (with Focus) that he does support.

In general, we assume that the discourse participants can show their attitude to each level and that this attitude can be of three forms:

(a) positive support

(b) negative support

(c) no support

Negative support can mean different things, depending on the level:

(i) (message) rejection

(ii) denial (or outer negation)

(iii) exclusion (or inner negation)

In case (iii), the negation is relative to some world: whether the SoA is actual in that world or not, or whether the term referent exists in that world or not. In case (ii), the negation is relative to some theory, and in case (i) the context of the negation is the present discourse.

If we trace a particular discourse, things become even more complicated because we have to keep track of Speaker and Addressee. Some SoAs (resp. propositions, messages) will be supported by both, whereas others are under discussion.

For the sake of completeness, we should also mention a fifth type of negation, namely predicate negation. This is a lexical rule. An instance of this rule is:

```
(cat => a; stem => "uninhabited") <=
        (cat => a; stem => "inhabited")
```

The rule derives the adjective "uninhabited" from the adjective "inhabited". At the lexical level, negation takes the form of antonymy relations.

Negation and lack of support are expressed as operators. If x is a reference marker, then NEG x indicates negative support and ? x indicates lack of support. The support operators usually have all other operators in their scope. Some examples (in abbreviated form):

(a) `(PRES p NEG (OBL e come(ag d[x] mary)))`
"mary needn't come"
the Speaker denies the proposition "mary must come"

(b) `(PRES p OBL (NEG e come(ag d[x] mary)))`
"mary must not come"
the Speaker wants to exclude the situation that "mary comes", but supports the proposition that "Mary must not come".

(c) `(PRES p (e have(po d[s] x john brown)(go NEG i[p] y kid)`
"John Brown has no kids"
the Speaker excludes the existence of "kids of John" (in the relevant world)

```
(d)  INT( PAST p (e beat(subj ag y)
                   (go d[s] wife(y))
                   (tmp ? t))))
```

"when did you beat your wife?"
The "beating" itself is supported, but the Speaker indicates that he lacks support for the time of the event.

2.8. FORMAL REPRESENTATION

The predication (frame) is a formal structure written in linear notation. Other notations are possible as long as the structures are homeomorphic. Some structures are more apt for some operations, and others for different ones. The linear notation is easy to write down, but not so easy to comprehend when several layers have to be considered. Another disadvantage of the linear notation is that it obscures the internal structure. When we are aiming at knowledge base applications, we are not bound to strings. Structured datatypes are more easy to work with internally. We have considered two possible formalizations: conceptual graphs and f-structures. Graphs have been used extensively in data modeling (Chen, 1976; Nijssen, 1980) and in Artificial Intelligence (Sowa, 1984). F-structures originated from work in computational linguistics.

Fig. 2.4 shows how a predicate frame can be written graphically as a what I call a *predication graph*. Nominal terms are represented by rectangles, verbal predications by means of diamonds and adjectival restrictors by means of circles. A fully-specified predication graph is constructed by merging several graphs together (see Sowa,1984).

Although predication graphs can be used to represent FG predicate frames, they can become quite cumbersome when multiple layers have to be distinguished. Just as diagrams in data modeling (Entity Relationship diagrams, NIAM diagrams), they seem to be at their best at the conceptual level. For propositions, they are less useful. Moreover, the rules operating on graphs (for example, predicate formation rules) favour a procedural specification rather than declarative. For these reasons, I use the predication graphs only for the presentation of lexical structures. For the formal representation of predicate frames I will use a particular form of *frame*. Frames were originally introduced as data structures without a precise mathematical

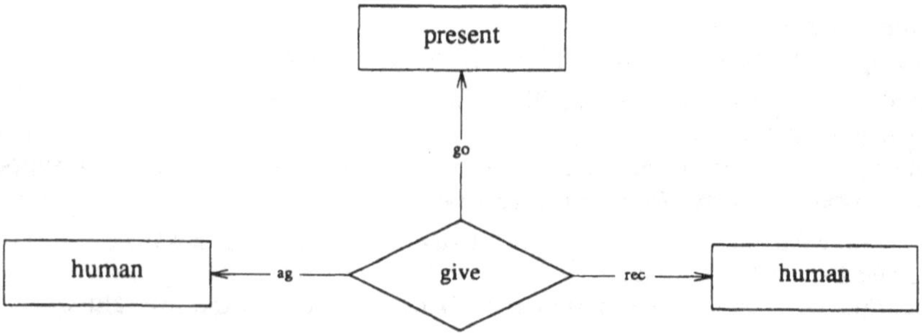

Fig. 2.4 Predication graph for the frame
`give(ag x human)(go y present)(rec z human)`

meaning (Minsky, 1974). The slots could contain data, but also procedures which might have side-effects. In the course of time, a particular form of frames called *f-structure* (feature structure, or Attribute Value Matrix) was introduced which allowed a precise mathematical definition. F-structures are used in Lexical Functional Grammar (LFG) and all kinds of unification based grammars such as HPSG (Pollard & Sag, 1988), but have not been used for the representation of FG underlyinbg clauses before. In this thesis I will follow the definitions of Ait-Kaci (1986ab) who makes heavy use of typing and type subsumption. Let us start with a small non-linguistic example.

```
student(id => name(last => X:string);
        lives_at => Y:address(city => philadelphia);
        father => person(id => name(last => X);
                         lives_at => Y))
```

Here we have a frame "student" with three slots, one labeled "id", one "lives_at", and one "father". Each slot contains another frame. For example, the "id" slot contains a frame with head symbol "name" and with a slot "last" pointing to an "atomic" frame with head "string". The X at this place is a *tag symbol* used by the co-reference constraints. The last name of student must co-refer with the last name of the father of student. If a certain substructure does not co-refer with another structure, it is not necessary to attach a tag symbol to it. For example, the substructure "philadelphia" has no tag symbol.

It is possible to define a typing on these structures recursively as follows. Suppose that we have a typing relations on atomic frames, for example:

```
philadelphia < cityname
student < person
```

Suppose, moreover, that in general, A is a subtype of B if and only if

(i) the type denoted by the head of A is a subtype of the (type of the) head of B

(ii) all the slots of B are also in A (but not necessarily the other way round!) and for each slot, the argument in A is a subtype of that one in B

(iii) all co-reference constraints binding in B are also binding in A

Then the following structure is a supertype of the preceding one:

```
person(id => name;
       lives_at => address(city => cityname);
       father => person)
```

Formally, an f-structure consists of a list of addresses, where an address is a string of labels (for example, id, id.last), and a symbol function ψ that attaches to each address a certain symbol. The symbols may be predicates, like person, or values, like philadelphia (in the example, it happens that heads of subframes are predicates and the "leaves" are values). For the moment, we assume one (ordered) domain Σ of symbols. If we want, we can type Σ and let it consist of various subdomains.

An f-structure can be *tagged* with variable symbols. This is a useful feature when we define rules on predicates, such as predicate formation rules and agreement rules. A tagging is nothing but a function from addresses to variable symbols. In the following definition, we include tagging although we will forstall the explanation of its use.

We put some requirements on the set of addresses A. In the first place, it must be prefix-closed, i.e., if $u,v \in L^*$, and $u.v \in A$, then $u \in A$. Secondly, A must be finitely branching, i.e., if $u \in A$ then the set $\{u.a \in A \mid a \in L\}$ is finite. If A obeys these requirements, we call it an *address tree* (on L).† We now define the f-structure, alternatively called "frame".

Definition 2.1 Let Σ be a typed set of symbols, with a subsumption ordering $\leq$ and including a top element Δ. Let L be a partially ordered set of labels. Let T be a set of tag symbols.

An *f-structure* is a triple (A,ψ,τ), where A is an address tree on L, ψ is a symbol function from L^* to Σ such that $\psi(L^* - A) = \{\Delta\}$ and τ is a tag function from A to T.

end 2.1

The symbol function ψ is defined in such a way that it maps all addresses not occurring in A to the top element Δ.

The tag function τ is defined as a function from addresses to T. In the examples above, we used some "syntactic sugar": we omit writing explicitly tags for addresses that do not share. Hence not every address has an explicit tag symbol.

Addresses in a tree which are not the prefix of any other address in the tree are called *leaves*. The empty string ϵ is called the *root* address.

An f-structure (A,ψ,τ) is finite iff A is finite. In what follows, I will consider only

† Ait-Kaci (1986:119) calls it a *term domain*, but that would be rather confusing in our context. For a precise definition of an address tree, see Appendix A.

finite f-structures. A *subtree* of A at address w is the tree $A\backslash w = \{w' \mid w.w' \in A\}$. Given a frame $f = (A,\psi,\tau)$, and an address w in A, the subframe of f at address w is the frame $f\backslash w = (A\backslash w, \psi\backslash w, \tau\backslash w)$ where $\psi\backslash w$ and $\tau\backslash w$ are defined by:

$$\psi\backslash w(w') = \psi(w.w') \quad \forall w' \in L^*$$
$$\tau\backslash w(w') = \tau(w.w') \quad \forall w' \in A\backslash w$$

For example, in the following frame of sheep:

```
(pred => (stem => "sheep"; cat => n; forms => (plur => "sheep"));
 cat => t;
 type => [animate])
```

the addresses are:

$A = \{\epsilon$, pred, pred.stem, pred.cat, pred.forms, pred.forms.plur, cat, type$\}$

The *leaves* in A are

{pred.stem, pred.cat, pred.forms.plur, cat, type}

A subtree of A at address "pred" is the tree with addresses:

{stem, cat, forms, forms.plur}.

For more details on f-structures, see Appendix A. The *subsumption ordering* on frames will be defined in section 4.4.1.

2.9. EXPRESSION RULES

The fully specified underlying clause structure is supposed to contain all those elements and relations which are essential to the semantic and pragmatic interpretation of the clause on the one hand, and to the formal expression of the clause on the other. In this section, we go into the second aspect, that is, the generation of sentences from underlying clauses by means by expression rules.

As far as the expression rules are concerned, these take care of three main features of linguistic expressions:

- the *form* of constituents
- the *order* in which constituents are to be expressed
- the *prosodic contour* (accent, intonation)

As for the form of constituents, note that the FG predication contains only basic and (lexically) derived predicates. All the "grammatical" elements of linguistic expressions, such as inflectional affixes, adpositions, and grammatical particles, will be spelled out by the expression rules as the result of the application of operators and (semantic, syntactic, and pragmatic) functions on these predicates. All these elements which have some influence on the form of the constituents will be treated as *morpho-syntactic operators* (both operators and functions). Formal expression rules are in general of the following form:

operator (input form) = output form

where the input form may either be a predicate from the underlying clause structure or an output of an earlier formal expression rule. The output may contain auxiliary morpho-syntactic operators which are introduced by the rule. For example, consider the expression of Past Perfect verbal phrases, as in:

John *had cooked* the potatoes

The underlying predication has the form:

DECL(PAST p (PERF e cook(ag d[s] x john)(go d[p] y potato))

The relevant expression rules are (the ^ stands for word concatenation):

```
PERF( X-v ) = have ^ PaP (X)
PaP( X ) = X++"ed"
Past( have ) = "had"
```

So

```
PAST(PERF(cook-v))= PAST(have ^ PaP(cook-v)) = "had" ^ "cooked"
```

Using f-structures, these rules come out slightly different. The technique we use is *unification*. We start with the underlying clause structure and derive new information by applying subsumption rules. A pecularity of this approach is that it is incremental: no information is thrown away. The unification can only extend the f-structure. The process stops when we have enough information to generate the corresponding English sentence as output. It is beyond the scope of this chapter, in fact of this thesis, to give a complete description of this technique. The following example is meant to convey only the flavour of it; I intend to work it out in a separate paper.

Let us assume that the underlying f-structure takes the following (simplified) form:

```
{underlying f-structure}
past perf(pred => (stem => "cook"; cat => v);
          cat => p;
          sem => (ag => john; go => potatoes))
```

The functor of the predicate frame consists of the symbol "past perf" which is to be taken as a *set* value {past, perf}. The predicate frame is a predication (cat=> p), rather than a term (cat => t), and the predicate is verbal (cat => v).

Consider the following subsumption rules (these rules are formal expression rules for English):

```
[1] perf(cat=>p) ≤ (pred => pap; head => have)
[2] pap(forms => -) ≤ (stem => X; head => X ++ "ed")
[3] pap(forms => (pap => Y)) ≤ (head => Y)
[4] past(cat => p) ≤ (head => past)
[5] past(forms => -) ≤ (stem => X; head => X ++ "ed")
[6] past(forms => (past => Y)) ≤ (head => Y)
```

where have stands for the lexical structure of the verb *to have*. To get an intuitive idea of the meaning of these rules, let us consider rule [1]. This rule says that if we have an f-structure with symbol perf and address cat pointing to p — that is, we have a predicate frame with a Perfect operator in front of it — then, we can infer by means of subsumption the following things. First, the grammatical head of the frame is have. Second, the symbol of the substructure addressed by pred entails pap. Informally, this says that the predicate is in the scope of a Past Participle operator and that the auxiliary *have* is the grammatical head of the whole structure. This follows from the presence of the `perf` operator.

Let us now exemplify the workings of the rules together. Applied to the f-structure of "John has cooked potatoes", we get (ignoring irrelevant material):

{applying rule [1] to the predicate frame}

```
past perf(pred => pap(stem => "cook"; cat => v);
          cat => p;
          head => (stem => "have"; cat => v; forms => (past => "had"));
          sem => (ag => X:john; go => potatoes);
          syn => (subj => X))
```

{applying rule [2] to the predicate}

```
past perf(pred => pap(stem => "cook"; cat => v; head => "cook"++"ed");
          cat => p;
          head => (stem => "have"; cat => v; forms => (past => "had"));
          sem => (ag => X:john; go => potatoes);
          syn => (subj => X))
```

{applying rule [4] to the predication}

```
past perf(pred => pap(stem => "cook"; cat => v; head => "cooked");
          cat => p;
          head => past(stem => "have"; cat => v; forms => (past => "had"));
          sem => (ag => X:john; go => potatoes);
          syn => (subj => X))
```

{applying rule [6] to the auxiliary}

```
past perf(pred => pap(stem => "cook"; cat => v; head => "cooked");
          cat => p;
          head => past(stem => "have"; cat => v;
                       forms => (past => "had");
                       head => "had");
          sem => (ag => X:john; go => potatoes);
          syn => (subj => X))
```

It must be kept in mind that the order of derivation is not essential in itself, since the rules are never destructive. In the final result, all the formal constituents of the sentence are present. What remains to be done is to determine the order in which these elements have to be expressed.

In Functional Grammar, the linear ordering of constituents is governed by a combination of universal principles and language-specific rules. Some important universal principles are the following. These rules may conflict. In that case, we may expect a certain tension in the grammar that can be the cause of some language change.

(1) *Functional pattern*. The following general schema for functional patterns can be shown to have considerable language-independent validity:

P2, P1 (V) S (V) O (V), P3

In this schema, S and O indicate the Subject and Object position, and the V's possible positions for Verbs. The P positions indicate "special positions". P2 indicates the position of left-dislocated constituents (typically Themes), P3 the position of right-dislocated constituents (typically Tails). P1 is clause-internal, the initial position of the clause. P1 is not used for one function, but is typically used for pragmatic functions (Topic or Focus), such as question-words. The functional pattern combines a number of subprinciples, such as: Theme < Proposition, Subject < Object, and P1 < X (X being any constituent of the same level). The expression A < B means that the preferred position of A is before the position of B.

(2) *LIPOC* There is a language-independent preferred order of constituents (LIPOC) according to which constituents are preferably placed from left to right in increasing order of complexity.

PROcl < PRO < NP < NPP < V < NP < PNP < SUB

Here PROcl stands for clitic pronouns, PRO for pronouns, NP for noun phrase and SUB for subordinate clause. NPP and PNP are complex noun phrases and stand for postpositional NP and prepositional NP respectively. For evidence on LIPOC and the way it can be applied, see (Dik, 1978:192). LIPOC includes also the observation that, for any category, conjunction, or adding a preposition, or increasing the internal complexity, has the effect of moving the preferred position to the right.

(3) *semantic structure*. In FG, operators are specified at several layers. The predicate operators π_1 (such as perfectivity) are at a lower or more central level than the predication operators π_2 operators (such as modality). The propositional operators π_3 (mood) are at a higher level than both of these. According to Hengeveld (1988), the preferred order of the expressions these operators take (morphemes, clitics, auxiliaries) is in accordance with the ordering of the layers:

The preferred order of operators is
$\pi_3 \pi_2 \pi_1$ Pred or
Pred $\pi_1 \pi_2 \pi_3$

Cf. also Rijkhoff(1986)'s principle of head proximity. Loosely speaking, we can say that the more close constituents are in the underlying clause, the more close their expressions will be in the output sentence.

We repeat that these principles can be very well in conflict with each other, and actual grammars are typically locally stable solutions to these conflicts. Nevertheless the principles have an important explanatory value.

In FG, the ordering of constituents for a given language is given by means of templates. In (Weigand, in prep) I will defend a different solution that makes use of *linear precedence rules*. This solution is inspired by the fact that the FG ordering principles often take the form of a (partial) ordering between constituents. Linear precedence rules are used also in certain unification-based languages, such as the ID/LP version of GPSG (Uzkoreit, 1987). Advantages of LP rules are:

- LP rules can be easily augmented ("persistency")
- LP rules need not be complete, which is a pro for languages with relative free word order
- LP rules can be formulated at several layers, which makes them more economic than rules that take the whole predication in their scope

For example, for the example above we can formulate LP rules such as:

```
head < pred
syn.subj < head
(cat => v) < sem
```

When we now transform the address tree of the f-structure of *John had cooked the potatoes* into a finite graph (cf. appendix A), we can determine the expression by making a graph traversal starting at the empty address and applying the LP rules. In this case, this means that the subject is expressed first ("john"), then the head ("had"), then the predicate ("cooked") and finally "the potatoes". I hasten to add that this example is grossly simplified. But for a more realistic grammar, we also need to define the f-structure more precisely. This will be done in the subsequent chapters.

I have dwelled relatively long on the expression rules. This is because the rest of the thesis is focused on the semantic interpretation of f-structures. Therefore this section is all I have to say on them for the moment. The interested reader is referred to the FG literature for more specific problems.

2.10. CONCLUSION

Functional Grammar offers a general framework for knowledge bases. The underlying clause structure (proposition) seems to be a good candidate for a knowledge representation language. There are natural mappings from parts of the predication to modules of the knowledge base. The lexicon enables us to store conceptual schemata consisting of predicate frames. The propositions can be endowed with a logical interpretation. In contrast to most present-day knowledge bases, the FG knowledge base contains also a message base in which we can model and implement the Environment of Discourse.

If anything, this overview suggests strongly that linguistics and knowledge engineering are in many respects working at the same project. Without ignoring the differences in research aims and methodology, we also conclude there is enough common ground for an integrated approach. Such an integration, if ever achieved, will be fruitful for both.

3

Semantics

3.1. INTRODUCTION

In this chapter I will set up a model-theory necessary for the semantic description of the FG constructs. The interpretation is a function that maps theories, thought of as "syntactic" objects, to models, thought of as "semantic" objects. I prefer a linguistic, or perhaps "mentalistic" interpretation of the model-theory, but the model-theory itself is purely formal and can be read without accepting the linguistic background. Janssen (1981) earlier gave a compositional tranlation from FG predications to a Montague-like extension of predicate logic. In my approach, the interpretation is given directly in terms of models. This has the advantage that we can tailor our models more closely to the "ontology" of FG.

From a linguistic point of view, propositions are put forward by linguistic agents in the context of an encompassing language game. The propositions are evaluated relative to mental models created and updated by the linguistic partners (Dik, 1987; Johnson-Laird, 1983). Such a mental model meets the following requirements:

- consistency: it is not possible to build a model in which both p and $\neg p$;
- lexical entailment: each model presupposes the lexical knowledge shared by the linguistic agents. Each model satisfies the meaning postulates.

Moreover, since the mental model is always "work-in-progress", we must assume that the mental models are *partial* (some predications are true, some are false, and the other ones are unspecified) and we require:

- persistency

which means here that partial information need not be retracted or rewritten when it is combined with other (new) partial information. Partial models have been studied as situations by Barwise & Perry (1983), a book that has been one important source of inspiration for this chapter.

Given a model M, and a proposition ϕ, we can ask the question whether ϕ is true or false with respect to M. Since M is a partial model, ϕ can also be assigned the truth-value "unknown". Following the general custom in logic, this truth-evaluation is defined in two steps:

(a) for each atomic formula p, check whether $I(p)$, is true in M (where I is an interpretation function)

(b) for complex formulae, such as $p \wedge q$, the truth-value depends on the truth-value of the parts (compositionality principle)

Let ϕ be a proposition. If ϕ is true in M, we write $M \models \phi$. If ϕ is false, we write

$M \dashv \phi$.

To be complete, we remark that, besides the truth-functional meaning of a proposition, we may also consider the *constructive* meaning of a proposition. The constructive meaning of a proposition is the update effect of the proposition on the mental model under consideration. The constructive meaning can be formalized as a relationship (function?) between models and models. Constructive meaning is only partly covered in this thesis.

The *language* of our model-theory is the language of FG predications. We can simplify our task by using the *normal form* of a predication rather than the predication itself. The normal form (defined precisely in definition 3.19), consists of the decomposition of the predication in its functional equations. For example, the predication

(1) `(p4 (PERF [t] e2 kiss(subj ag d[s] x prince)(go d[s] y snowwhite)))`

can be decomposed as follows. First consider the functional dependencies between `e2` and `x` and `y`. These can be written as:

```
ag(e2) = x
go(e2) = y
```

The nominal and verbal heads are interpreted by means of a function *TYPE*. For example, TYPE(`e2`)=`kiss`. In the normal form, we write these equations as one-place predications:

```
kiss(e2)
prince(x)
snowwhite(y)
```

It is inherent to Functional Grammar that the proposition can be decomposed in a set of functional equations and predications. However, there are several kinds of functions, and hence the normal form contains a variety of equations. For example, we have pragmatic functions, semantic functions, syntactic functions, operators, predicates, etc. For our model-theory, we are especially interested in what we may call the *semantic* normal form. This subset contains, first of all, equations about the semantic functions (arguments as well as satellites). Furthermore, we include (equations about) the predicate, the restrictors, and COUNT (see below). But syntactic and pragmatic functions are not included. They play a role in structuring the proposition (and hence in the logical interpretation), but they are not reflected in the model itself.

Restrictors are properties linked to the node they specify without a function indication (we could also say, with an "empty function"). We will use a function "QUAL" from entities to properties for their interpretation. In the normal form, we write them in the same way as the nominal heads, that is, as predications. For example, a term like "the white snow" is represented as:

```
snow(x)
white(x)
```

The function COUNT specifies the cardinality of a referent:

```
dwarf(z)
COUNT(z) = 7
```

In some cases, we need also inequalitions. These will be discussed later.

So far for the syntactic part of the model-theory. Instead of the traditional set-theoretic model of first-order logic, we prefer to represent a model by a topological structure in which the requirements stated above are explicit. The kind of structure is the Scott information system that will be introduced in section 3.2. In the subsequent sections, some extensions are introduced. We conclude by presenting the truth-conditions for a subset of the propositional part of FG.

3.2. SCOTT INFORMATION SYSTEM

The Scott information system was introduced in (Scott,1982) in order to study the category of (algebraic) domains, as part of a Theory of Domains. The main purpose of this theory was to give a mathematical model of a system of *types* - including function-space types - and to explain a notion of computability with respect to these types - especially when they are recursively defined. Or put moie simply: how can infinitary mathematical entities be represented within finite computers.†
Intuitively, an information system is a set of "propositions" that can be made about "possible elements" of the desired domain (the actual elements will be a subset of the possible elements). We will assume that sufficiently many propositions have been supplied to distinguish distinct elements; as a consequence, an element can be constructed abstractly as the set of propositions that are true of it. But then we can make a switch: instead of assuming that two distinct elements are distinguishable, we simply postulate that two elements are distinct only if their sets of propositions are distinguishable. Let us first explicate the structure between the propositions.

Definition 3.1 An *information system* is a structure

$(D, \Delta, \mathrm{Con}, \vdash)$

where D is a set of data objects, where Δ is a distinguished member of D (the least informative member), where Con is a set of finite subsets of D (the consistent sets of objects), and where $\vdash$ is a binary relation between members of Con and members of D (the entailment relation for objects). Concerning Con, the following axioms must be satisfied for all finite subsets $u,v \subseteq D$:

(*i*) $u \in \mathrm{Con}$, whenever $u \subseteq v \in \mathrm{Con}$;

(*ii*) $\{X\} \in \mathrm{Con}$, whenever $X \in D$; and

(*iii*) $u \cup \{X\} \in \mathrm{Con}$, whenever $u \vdash X$.

Concerning $\vdash$, the following axioms must be satisfied for all $u,v \in \mathrm{Con}$, and all $X \in D$:

(*iv*) $u \vdash \Delta$;

(*v*) $u \vdash X$, whenever $X \in u$; and

(*vi*) if $v \vdash Y$ for all $Y \in u$ and $u \vdash X$, then $v \vdash X$.

end 3.1

In words, we can say of Con that, as set of sets, (i) it is closed under subsets, (ii) it contains all singletons, and (iii) adjunction of an entailed object to a consistent object preserves consistency. The entailment has the following properties: (iv) Δ is

† See (Laymon,1987) for a philosophical discussion of Scott domains and its applications to the epistemology of science. For applications in logic, see also (Landman,1986).

entailed by anything, (v) $\vdash$ is reflexive, and (vi) is transitive.

Example 1 We first give an example from the domain of natural numbers. Let D be the set of all pairs (n,m) such that $n \leq m$. Intuitively, a pair stands for the proposition $n \leq x \leq m$, where x is a yet-to-be-determined element about which the proposition gives only a little information. A set of propositions is consistent iff there is an x for which all propositions are true. Then the set $\{(2,4)\}$ is consistent, and so is $\{(2,5),(3,6),(1,4)\}$. The set $\{(0,2),(3,7)\}$ is inconsistent. The top element Δ is simply $(0,\infty)$. The entailment $u \vdash X$ can be defined in such a way that whenever an integer satisfies all the propositions in u, then it must satisfy X. For instance, we can state that $\{(x_1,y_1), (x_2,y_2)\} \vdash (z_1,z_2)$, for all x_i,y_i, where $z_1 = max(x_1,x_2)$ and $z_2 = min(y_1,y_2)$, provided that $z_1 \leq z_2$ (otherwise the set is inconsistent).

Example 2 Let Noun be the set of English nouns. Suppose that D = Noun $\cup$ $\{\Delta\}$, every set is consistent and the entailment is defined by means of the subtype relationship:

student < person
king < monarch
person < Δ

Then a set of nouns, such as

{taro, student, baseball player, japanese}

stands for an entity for which each of the predicates is applicable (unification). The axioms of entailment apply well to the subtype relationship: top element, reflexivity, transitivity are natural features of subtyping.

3.2.1. The elements of a system

We assume that the information system contains enough data objects to distinguish between distinct elements. That is why we can identify the elements with their finite approximations, the sets of propositions true of them; formally we can assert:

$$x = \{X \in D \mid X \text{ is true of } x\}$$

Elements are sets of data objects. But not every set is an element. First, the set must be consistent in itself, otherwise it can't denote an element. Secondly, entailment is, by the very meaning of the word, truth-preserving. Hence we require an element to be deductively closed. In classical terms, this implies that elements are defined as *proper filters*.

Definition 3.2
The *elements* of the information system A = $(D, \Delta, \text{Con}, \vdash)$ are those subsets x of D where:

(a) all finite subsets of x are in Con; and

(b) whenever $u \subseteq x$, and $u \vdash X$, then $X \in x$.

We write $x \in |A|$ to mean x is an element of A. $|A|$ is called the *domain set*.
end 3.2

The two axioms ensure that an element is (i) consistent in itself, and (ii) deductively closed. An element that is not included in any strictly larger element in the domain set is called a *total* element. When $u \in$ Con, $[u]$ stands for the smallest element of the information system that contains u.

Example 3 Suppose

{student, graduate} $\vdash$ staff-member, and

{student} $\vdash$ person

are entailments in our information system, where D is {student, graduate, staff-member, person, Δ}. Then {student, graduate} is a consistent set, but it is not yet deductively closed. The closure is

[student, graduate] = {student, person, graduate, staff-member, Δ}

which is an element of the information system. In this case, it is also a total element, in fact the only total element. It is not the only element. For example, {person,Δ} is also an element.

Proposition 3.3 Let A be an information system. For each $u \in$ Con, there is exactly one element $x \in |A|$ such that $[u] = x$.

Proof Suppose that u itself is not an element. Then it is not deductively closed. This means that there is some strictly larger consistent set u' in which u is contained. If u' is again not deductively closed, we can repeat the same trick until we have arrived at a consistent set which is deductively closed.†

In order to prove that there is not *more* than one smallest element containing u, we suppose there are two elements, x_1 and x_2, such that $u \subseteq x_1$ and $u \subseteq x_2$. Clearly, the intersection of x_1 and x_2 is not empty. It is also consistent. Moreover, if the intersection entails some Y, then $Y \in x_1$ and $Y \in x_2$ also. In other words, the intersection is deductively closed, and hence it is an element. This means that when u is contained in several elements, we can simply take the intersection of them to arrive at $[u]$. □

end 3.3

Since we have defined the information system as consisting of *sets*, we immediately have the set inclusion $\subseteq$ between elements. In this context, $x \subseteq y$ can be read as: "x approximates y". So without further axiomatization, we have that $|A|$ is a *partially ordered set*. It is easy to see that $|A|$ is also closed under intersection: $x \cap y$ is again consistent and deductively closed. This means that $|A|$ is what is called an *inf semilattice*.

If an information system has only one total element, then it is always the case that this element coincides with the data set itself. We call it the *top* or maximal element. We can also define the bottom element $\perp$ of the system as the least element contained in all other elements. Formally:

$$\perp = \{X \in D \mid \{\Delta\} \vdash X\}$$

It is easily seen that not every informations system has a top element, but every information system has a bottom element. In the example above, $\perp = \{\Delta\}$. Note that Δ is the top of the dataset (it is entailed by any consistent set of data objects),

† If the dataset is infinite and this process does not end, then we have at least an monotonically increasing chain of consistent sets. From proposition 3.4 we can derive that this chain has a limit. This limit is an element of the information system.

but that $\{\Delta\}$ (or its deductive closure) is the bottom element of accompanying the domain set.

It is also worthwhile to ask ourselves the question whether $|A|$ is a complete lattice. To this end, we must define the supreme of a family of sets. The set-theoretic union is not sufficient, since it is not necessary that $x \cup y$ is consistent nor that it is deductively closed. Let us write the sup (supposing it exists) as $x \underline{\cup} y$. It must be the least element in $|A|$ which includes both x and y. So $x \underline{\cup} y$ exists exactly when there is at least one element z in $|A|$ such that $x \subseteq z$ and $y \subseteq z$. This turns out to be a way to say that $x \cup y$ is consistent. In that case the sup is the deductive closure of the set-theoretical union. If the system has a top, then we always have sups, and $|A|$ is a *complete lattice*. When the top is missing, the partially ordered structures corresponding to domains are called *conditionally complete, algebraic cpo's* (see Gierz *et al*, 1980 for a more extended discussion)

There is, however, an important case in $|A|$ where the union is consistent, and is in fact the sup in the domain set. This is formulated in the next proposition:

Proposition 3.4 Suppose we have a sequence of elements such that

$$x_0 \subseteq x_1 \subseteq \dots \subseteq x_n \subseteq \dots$$

then there is a *limit*

$$y = \bigcup_{n=0}^{\infty} x_n$$

which is an element of the information system.

Proof We have to prove first that every finite subset of y is in Con. But any finite subset of y must be a subset of one of the x_i, because the sequence of elements x_i is increasing. Every x_i is an element, and so, consistent. Therefore, every finite subset of y is consistent.

The second requirement is that whenever $u \subseteq y$ and $u \vdash X$, then $X \in y$. The $\vdash$ relation is defined between finite subsets of D. So we only have to check for *finite* u. But then we can use the same trick as in the first part of the proof, since an eligible u must be a part of some x_i, and each x_i is deductively closed. So y is deductively closed. □

end 3.4

Convention In the following, we will sometimes use the following notation. If $u,v \in$ Con, then

$$u \vdash v$$

means that $u \vdash X$ for all $X \in v$.

In this notation, the axioms (*iv*) to (*vi*) of definition 3.1 take the form (u,v,w being arbitrary members of Con):

(*iv*) $u \vdash \{\Delta\}$;

(*v*) $u \vdash v$, whenever $v \subseteq u$; and

(*vi*) if $u \vdash v$ and $v \vdash w$, then $u \vdash w$.

3.2.2. Consistency by entailment

The definition of an information system always includes the definition of *Con*, the set of consistent subsets. In principle, *Con* can be defined in different ways. We now show how it can be defined by making use of the entailment. The basic idea is to add a "rogue" element ∇ to D, in addition to the top element Δ. Whereas the top element is entailed by anything, according to axiom (iv):

$u \vdash \Delta$, always,

bottom entails everything:

$u \vdash X$, for all $X \in D$, whenever $\nabla \in u$

Let V be a domain including ∇. Then we can construct a domain V' in which ∇ is thrown out as "inconsistent". We need the following axioms (Scott, 1982:606)

(1) $D_{V'} = D_V - \{\nabla\}$

(2) $\Delta_{V'} = \Delta_V$

(3) $Con_{V'} = \{u \subseteq D_{V'} \mid u \text{ finite and not } u \vdash_V \nabla\}$

(4) $u \vdash Y$ iff $u \in Con_{V'}$, $Y \in D_{V'}$ and $u \vdash_V Y$

A set is inconsistent if it contains or entails ∇, and consistent otherwise. It is easily checked that V' is indeed an information system. In fact, it is not necessary that ∇ is a bottom element, if only it is identified as a "rogue" object.

3.2.3. Functions

An information system A specifies one domain. For our semantics, we have several domains, such as:

- entity domain
- SoA domain
- integer domain
- time domain

The domains are connected by means of functions. For example, the semantic functions ag and go mediate between the domain of SoAs and the domain of entities. In this section, we will see how functions on information systems can be defined.

Because of the special nature of the information system domain, we must be explicit of what a function on domains is. Let us first cite Scott(1983):

> Consider two domains. To map from one to another, some information about a possible element of the first is presented as *input* to the function f. Then as *output* the function f starts generating an element. If the input were u, a consistent set, then *part* of the output in the second domain might be a consistent set v. We could say that there is an input/output relationship set up by f, and indicate by $u\ f\ v$ that this relation holds going from u in the first domain to v in the second. Of course to get the full effect of f, it is necessary to take *all* the v's related to a given u, because even a small finite amount of input may cause an infinite amount of output. But every element of a domain is just the sum total of its finite subsets (finite approximations), so it is sufficient to make the mapping relationship go between finite sets.

Here is the formal definition with the exact conditions that the relation f must satisfy:

Definition 3.5 Let A and B be two given information systems. An *approximable mapping*

$$f: A \rightarrow B$$

is a binary relation between the two sets Con_A and Con_B such that:

(*i*) $\varnothing \, f \, \varnothing$

(*ii*) $u \, f \, v$ and $u \, f \, v'$ always imply $u \, f \, (v \cup v')$; and

(*iii*) $u' \vdash_A u$, $u \, f \, v$, and $v \vdash_B v'$ always imply $u' \, f \, v'$.

We say that A is the *source* of f and B is the *target*.

end 3.5

The view of a function as some input/output passage that gives you some information about domain B provided you are willing to give some information about domain A, is consistent with the intuitive idea about information systems. The function does not directly assign some value to some argument: it gives (partial) information about the value on the basis of (partial) information about the argument. Condition (i) means that no information about the input merits no information about the output. Condition (ii) implies that all the contributions to the output from a fixed input are consistent, and in fact the union of two output sets is again an output set. Output corresponding to a fixed input is *cumulative*. Condition (iii) assures us that the mapping f works in harmony with the two entailment relations.

We now consider what this means for elements and first define the *image* (function value) of a function.

Definition 3.6. If f: A → B is an approximable mapping between information systems, and if $x \in |A|$ is an element of the first, then we define the *image* (or *function value*) of x under f by the formula:

$$f(x) = \{Y \in D_B \mid u \, f \, \{Y\} \text{ for some } u \subseteq x\}$$

Alternatively, we could use the equivalent formula:

$$f(x) = \bigcup \{v \in Con_B \mid u \, f \, v \text{ for some } u \subseteq x\}$$

end 3.6

Under this definition, it has to be *proved* yet that the image of an element in $|A|$ lies in $|B|$ in order to justify the use of ordinary function-value notation. This is taken care of by the next proposition:

Proposition 3.7 Let f,g: A→B be two approximable mappings between two information systems. Then

(i) f always maps elements to elements under definition 3.4;

(ii) $f = g$ iff $f(x) = g(x)$ for all $x \in |A|$; and

(iii) $f \subseteq g$ iff $f(x) \subseteq g(x)$ for all $x \in |A|$.

Moreover, the approximable mappings are monotone in the sense that

(iv) $x \subseteq y$ in $|A|$ always implies $f(x) \subseteq f(y)$ in $|B|$.

All these results follow from the observation that for all $u \in Con_A$ and all $v \in Con_B$

(v) $u f v$ iff $[v] \subseteq f([u])$

end 3.7

(proof is straightforward and omitted)

Functions can be taken as objects themselves. In that case, they happen to form an information system.

Definition 3.8 Let A and B be two information systems. By A→B, the *function space*, we understand the system where:

(i) $D_{A \to B} = \{(u,v) \mid u \in Con_A \text{ and } v \in Con_B\}$

(ii) $\Delta_{A \to B} = (\emptyset, \emptyset)$; and where,

for all n and all $w = \{(u_0,v_0),\ldots,(u_{n-1}, v_{n-1})\}$, we have:

(iii) $w \in Con_{A \to B}$ iff whenever $I \subseteq \{0,\ldots,n\text{-}1\}$ and $\bigcup\{u_i \mid i \in I\} \in Con_A$, then $\bigcup\{v_i \mid i \in I\} \in Con_B$; and

(iv) for all $u' \in Con_A$ and $v' \in Con_B$.

$$w \vdash (u',v') \text{ iff } \bigcup\{v_i \mid u' \vdash u_i\} \vdash v',$$

end 3.8

The first conditions say that the function space consists of *pairs* of consistent sets. One pair (u,v) can be read as meaning that if the information in u is supplied as input, then at least v will be obtained as output. If the function would contain just one pair (u,v), for each u, it would be enough to check whether v is consistent. But if the function may contain several pairs, we have to require consistency. This is done in (iii). It says, informally, that whenever you give a consistent amount of input, then the combined output must be consistent too. If so, the function is consistent. Finally, in (iv) entailment is defined on function elements. Let w be fixed and determine some function f. Then for each u', $\bigcup\{v_i \mid u' \vdash u_i\}$ is a consistent set, by (iii). But if this set entails v', then it is clear that, whatever the way we further extend f, it will ultimately contain (u',v') too. In this sense, (u',v') is entailed by w. The three conditions on entailment (definition 3.1) are easy to check. Now we can prove the following theorem:

Theorem 3.9 If A,B and C are information systems, then so is A→B, and the approximable mappings f : A→B are exactly the elements $f \in |A \to B|$. Moreover, we have an approximable mapping *apply*:(B→C)×B→C such that whenever g:B→C and $y \in |B|$, then

$$\text{apply}(g,y) = g(y)$$

end.

Proof See (Scott,1982) □.

end 3.9

In definition 3.5, we defined the function space in such a way that the axioms of consistency and entailment are respected. An approximable mapping is closed under entailment (3.5, part iv), that's why approximable mappings are exactly the *elements* of the information system.

The approximable mapping *apply* can be constructed easily. The input of *apply* is a mapping, that is, pairs of consistent sets, say $w \in Con_{B \to C}$, and a consistent set of $|B|$. Now the relation we want from such pairs to consistent sets $v' \in Con_B$ is nothing more or less than $w \vdash (u', v')$.

$$\langle\langle w, u'\rangle, v'\rangle \in apply \text{ iff } w \vdash (u', v').$$

The theorem justifies us in using $g(y)$ and $apply(g,y)$ as equivalent forms. We also have a function *Comp* for composition of functions. We can write

$$Comp\colon (B \to C) \times (A \to B) \to (A \to C),$$

where for functions of the right types we have:

$$Comp(g,f) = g \circ f$$

It can be proved that *Comp* is itself approximable too. In mathematical terms, this means that the domains together with the approximable mappings form a *category*. We don't go into that. One interesting thing can be remarked, however, which says that the entailment relationship is interchangeable with an approximable mapping:

Proposition 3.10. Let A be an information system. Then the following formula defines an approximable mapping $I_A\colon A \to A$:

(*i*) $u \; I_A \; v$ iff $u \vdash_A v$,

for all $u, v \in Con_A$. And we have:

(*ii*) $I_A(x) = x$

for all $x \in |A|$.

end 3.10

(Proof is obvious).

Anticipating a bit on the application of this theory to FG models, this result is interesting, because it implies that it does not make much difference whether we define the TYPE relationship between instances and types as an entailment or as an approximable mapping. In an earlier version of this chapter, instances and types were defined in one domain, with an entailment between them. Now they are separated, and TYPE is a function between the instance domain and the TYPE domain, which gives room for another interpretation of the entailment. Proposition 3.10 may help us to explain why the choice may seem arbitrary.

3.2.4. Product systems

In the category of sets, the (Cartesian) product of two sets is by definition just the set of ordered pairs of elements. We could use the same definition if we start with the elements of the two domains. The disadvantage is that the determination of the product domain from data objects is obscured. Therefore a definition tailored to information systems is preferred. The idea is that elements of the product system are sets of pairs, where each pair gives partial information perhaps only about one of the coordinates.

Definition 3.11. Let A and B be two information systems. By A × B, the *product system*, we understand the system where:

(i) $D_{A \times B} = \{(X, \Delta_B) \mid X \in D_A\} \cup \{(\Delta_A, Y) \mid Y \in D_B\}$

(ii) $\Delta_{A \times B} = (\Delta_A, \Delta_B)$;

(iii) $u \in Con_{A \times B}$ iff **fst** $u \in Con_A$ and **snd** $u \in Con_B$

(iv) $u \vdash_{A \times B} (X', \Delta_B)$ iff **fst** $u \vdash_A X'$; and

(iv') $u \vdash_{A \times B} (\Delta_A, Y')$ iff **snd** $u \vdash_B Y'$;

where, in (iii), u is any finite subset of $D_{A \times B}$, and in (iv) and (iv'), $u \in Con_{A \times B}$, and we let:

$$\textbf{fst } u = \{X \in D_A \mid (X, \Delta_B) \in u\}, \text{ and}$$

$$\textbf{snd } u = \{Y \in D_B \mid (\Delta_{A,Y}) \in u\}.$$

end 3.11

It has been proved (Scott, *ibid*) that if A and B are information systems, then so is A × B.

3.2.5. Entailment bases

Another useful construct is the subsystem, the analogue of the subset in set theory (cf. Larsen & Winskel, 1984). If a domain A represents possible elements, we may be interested also in the actual ones. It is reasonable to require that the actual ones are possible. It is also desirable that the subsystem itself is an information system. These two requirements motivate the following definition. The definition goes in two steps. First, we define what is an *entailment base*, and then we show how this entailment base can be used to form a subsystem.

The idea of an entailment base can be captured by the following small example. Suppose that we have an information system containing, among others, the "predicative" data objects *Student, Person, Graduate Student, Staff member*, as well as data objects for individual tokens *john, mary, peter*. Now a distinction can be made between entailments that always hold, such as {*Student*} ⊢ *Person*, and entailments that happen to hold in some application at some time, for example, {*john*} ⊢ *Student*. The first idea is then to define a "minimal" information system *A* that contains only those entailments that always hold. *A* can be regarded as a universal system. Then a particular application at some time can be viewed as the *addition* of certain entailments to the universal system *A*. There are of course many additions possible, leading to as many "subsystems". Note that subsystems inherit all the information from *A*. Whatever is true in *A* holds also in each subsystem.

A certain application can be specified then as a set of entailments. Preferably, we only give the relevant entailments. For example, we only specify that {*john*} ⊢ *Student*, and we take it for granted that this implies that {*john*} ⊢ *Person*. But that means that we cannot simply unite the entailment set of the specification with the general entailments; what we need is the "deductive closure" of this union. For this reason, we call the specification an *entailment base*. The corresponding subsystem is formed by taking the deductive closure of this base.

Note that the derivation of new entailments from a given entailment base is itself another entailment process, as we will show in the next definition by describing this relationship in such a way that it can be converted directly to the axioms in definition 3.1. For the specification of entailments, we make use of the convention stated at the end of 3.2.1 that defines entailments as a binary relation of consistent sets rather than as a relation between consistent sets and members of the data set.

Definition 3.12 Let A $(D, \Delta_A, Con_A, \vdash_A)$ be an information system .

[1] An *entailment base* E on A is a set of pairs (u,v), written also as $u \vdash v$, where $u,v \in Con_A$. The pairs are called entailments. The set of all entailment bases is called *Ent*.

[2] Entailment *on* entailment bases in *Ent* is defined as follows. For every entailment base E and F:

(i) $E \vdash_{Ent} \{\Delta_{Ent}\}$

(ii) $E \vdash_{Ent} F$ whenever $F \subseteq E$

(iii) $E \vdash_{Ent} F$ whenever $E = \{(u,v), (v,w)\}$ and $F = \{(u,w)\}$

where Δ_{Ent} is a distinguished least informative element of *Ent* that entails every entailment in A:

$\{\Delta_{Ent}\} \vdash_{Ent} \vdash_A$

[3] An entailment base E in *Ent* is said to be *consistent* iff $u \cup v \in Con_A$ whenever $E \vdash_{Ent} \{(u,v)\}$.

[4] The *possible worlds* of an information system A are the entailment bases E such that:

(i) every finite subset of E is consistent;

(ii) if $F \subseteq E$ and $F \vdash_{Ent} G$, then $G \subseteq E$ (i.e, E is deductively closed)

plus a "rogue element" denoted by [∇], containing all possible entailments. Ordering on possible worlds is the subset ordering between entailment bases.

If E is a consistent entailment base, then [E] is the smallest possible world containing E.

[5] The *subsystem* A(E) of A with entailment base E is a system $(D_A, \Delta_A, Con_A,$ [E]), provided that E is consistent, or the empty information system otherwise.

end 3.12

The empty information system is the system where Con = ∅. Since there are no consistent sets, the domain is empty too.

We do not prove that the entailment on entailment bases is indeed an entailment in the sense of definition 3.1, and that this entailment, together with the consistency requirements, make *Ent* into an information system. This result is seen directly from the definition.

Proposition 3.13 Let A be an information system. If E is a consistent entailment base on A, then A(E) is an information system and $|A(E)| \subseteq |A|$.

Proof We check the axioms of the information system, starting with the axioms of entailment. Since [E] contains all entailments of A, axiom (iv) and (v) are trivially fulfilled. Axiom (vi) follows from requirement (iii) above. The consistency axioms are easy too. If [E] is consistent, then, whenever $u \vdash X$, we know that $u \cup \{X\} \in Con_A$. This fulfills axiom (iii). Axiom (i) and (ii) follow from the consistency axioms of A and the definition of A(E). So A(E) is an information system.

To prove that $|A(E)| \subseteq |A|$ we must prove that every deductively closed consistent set in $|A(E)|$ is also in $|A|$. If $u \in Con_{A(E)}$, then $u \in Con_A$. Moreover, if u would be deductively closed in A(E) but not in A, there would be an entailment in A that could enlarge u. But every entailment in A is also in A(E), so this is impossible. □

end 3.13

Note that we impose a natural ordering of inclusion on entailment bases, and that the closure operation is monotonic, that is, if $E_1 \subseteq E_2$, then $[E_1] \subseteq [E_2]$. All inconsistent entailment bases are "smashed" to $[\nabla]$. If we look at the domains of $A(E_1)$ and $A(E_2)$, then we get an inverse inclusion: $|A(E_2)| \subseteq |A(E_1)|$. The more entailments we add, the more chance that two elements "merge". The lower limit is achieved when A(E) is the empty information system and $|A(E)| = \varnothing$.

The set of possible worlds not only has a top element, $[\nabla]$, but also has a bottom element, made up by the set of entailments of A itself. The corresponding domain is the top element of the possible domains. Let us derive an ordering on subsystems A(E) as the inverse of the ordering on possible worlds, that is,

$$A(E_1) \leq A(E_2) \text{ iff } E_2 \subseteq E_1 \text{ (or } E_1 = \Delta).$$

Then it follows that the set of subsystems of A form a complete lattice, with the meet and join operations defined as follows:

(i) $A(E_1) \wedge A(E_2) := A([E_1 \cup E_2])$, (*unification*), and

(ii) $A(E_1) \vee A(E_2) := A([E_1 \cap E_2])$ (*generalization*).

This result deserves a separate proposition. We use the notation $\mathcal{R}(A)$ for the set of subsystems of information system A.

Proposition 3.14 Let A be an information system, and let the ordering $\leq$ and the operations $\wedge$ and $\vee$ on subsystems be defined as above. Then the structure $(\mathcal{R}(A), \leq, \wedge, \vee)$ is a complete lattice.

end 3.14

Although this is a nice result, it must be remarked that the structure is still weak. The lattice is not even distributive. This can be shown as follows. Suppose we have non-empty entailment bases E, F, G such that E is strictly larger than A and has a non-empty overlap with $[F \cup G]$, but not with [F] nor with [G]. This is not impossible, since the deductive closure of F united with G may contain new combinations. But then

$$A([E \cap [F \cup G]]) = A(E) \vee (A(F) \wedge A(G)) \neq (A(E) \vee A(F)) \wedge (A(E) \vee A(G)) = A([E \cap F]) \wedge A([E \cap G]) = A(\varnothing) \wedge A(\varnothing) = A$$

The left hand part of the inequality has a non-empty entailment base (strictly larger than the entailment set of A), but the right hand part, by definition contains just the entailment base of A (bottom). So the meet and join are not distributive.

We must also consider the effect of the "consistency by entailment" construction on the domain of subsystems. We can suppose that in A, every subset of D is consistent. Let E be a consistent entailment base on A. Now suppose we add an "inconsistency entailment", of the form $u \vdash \nabla$ to E, producing E'. Of course, we still have that $[E] \subseteq [E']$, and $|A(E')| \subseteq |A(E)|$. But what happens when we remove the inconsistent sets? It turns out that this does not affect the inclusion relations. In the example, if $u \vdash \nabla$ was not already in [E], then $[u]$ is an element of $|A(E)|$. It is not an element of $|A(E')|$. In other words, the "inconsistency entailment" only *removes* elements. Every consistent set in A(E') is also consistent in A(E). So we still have that $|A(E')| \subseteq |A(E)|$.

The relevance of this discussion for our model-theory is that the entailment bases seems to offer a pleasant implementation of the three requirements we put forward in section 3.1, summarized by the keywords consistency, entailment and persistency. The subsystems permit a situation calculus akin to the one of Barwise & Perry(1984). We will work this out shortly.

3.2.6. Data algebra

We have now enough machinery to introduce our substitute for the logical definition of a model. The model consists of domains, representing the referents and the information about them, and functions between these domains. Together this makes up a data algebra.

Definition 3.15 A *data algebra* $\mathcal{A}$ is a pair (Dom,Func) where Dom is a family of domains and where Func is a set of functions over the domains. The *signature* of a data algebra is a set of domain names S, also called *sorts*, and a set of function symbols Σ. A particular function symbol f has an *arity* w and *sort* s, where w is an ordered subset of S and $s \in$ S. The elements of Dom are represented as A_{s_1}, A_{s_2} etc.

On the set of sorts S, a subsumption ordering may be defined. In that case, it is required that, for any two sorts s_i and s_j, if $s_i < s_j$, then $|A_{s_i}| \supseteq |A_{s_j}|$.

A *data algebra specification* of signature (S,Σ) is a pair (I,P), where I is a set of information systems and P a set of approximable mappings between them. Each data algebra specification corresponds to a data algebra $(\{|A| \mid A \in I\},\{|f| \mid f \in P\})$.

end 3.15

Our definition follows closely the general definition of a many-sorted algebra. The particularity is that our domains are specified by means of information systems and the functions by means of approximable mappings. The fact that the sorts can be ordered is not essential, but it facilitates some definitions.

The lattice structure of subsystems defined in the previous section carries over to data algebras, but some small extensions must be made. Consider a fixed data algebra specification $\mathcal{A}$(I,P). Then we can, for each information system $A_s \in$ I consider its subsystems. Keeping the approximable mappings fixed, we arrive at a set of data algebra specifications $\mathcal{A}$() by substituting each A_s by some subsystem A_s(E). The ordering on this set is simply the induced ordering, that is, $\mathcal{A}_1 \leq \mathcal{A}_2$ iff for each s, $A_s(E_1) \leq A_s(E_2)$.

For the approximable mappings an ordering was defined in 3.2.3. This ordering can also be lifted to the data algebra specification level. Combining this with the $\leq$ ordering above, we arrive at a general partial ordering. The lifting goes in such a way that, we require, for two functions f_1 and f_2 both with source A_s and target A_t, that $f_1(x) \subseteqq f_2(x)$ for each $x \in |A_{s,2}|$. A *mapping base* with respect to a given approximable map f is a set M of pairs (u,v) such that $f \cup M$ is an approximable mapping. The definition of a mapping base goes in the same way as that of an entailment base.

Consistency of data algebras includes the following. In the first place, every domain must be consistent. This means in particular that every singleton set $\{x\}$, where x is a data object, must be consistent, and that the entailment bases are consistent. Furthermore, every function must be consistent, that is, map consistent sets of the source to consistent sets of the target.

Given a data algebra specification $\mathcal{A}(I,P)$, we can consider all data algebra *sub*-specifications $\mathcal{A}(E,M)$, where E is a family of entailment bases, one for each information system in I, and M a family of mapping bases, one for each function in P.

Proposition 3.16 The set of data algebra subspecifications $\mathcal{A}$(E,F), with respect to a given data algebra $\mathcal{A}$, and with special bottom element ∇, has a lattice structure, where

(i) $\mathcal{A}$(I,P) $\simeq \nabla$ when one of the domains, entailment bases, or functions is inconsistent;

(ii) $\mathcal{A}(I_1, P_1) \leq \mathcal{A}(I_2, P_2)$ iff $A_{i,1} \leq A_{i,2}$ and $f_{i,1} \subseteq f_{i,2}$, for each domain $A_i \in I$ and function $f_i \in P$.

(iii) meet and join are defined by pairwise meet and join of the entailment bases and mapping bases.If the meet of two data algebras is inconsistent, the result is ∇.

Proof Follows from lattice structure of entailment bases and mapping bases. □
end 3.16

Since models will consist of data algebra subspecifications, the fact that these have a lattice structure is convenient from the point of modularity and persistency. We will now turn to the application.

3.3. APPLICATION

We now arrive at the application of our theory. Our model will consist of a type level and an instance level. The type level is closely bound to the lexicon. In this chapter, the two even coincide. Later, it will turn out that the lexicon is part of the type level, but that some other types must be recognized as well.

3.3.1. Type level

We first introduce some basic sets, in accordance with the general outline of FG presented in chapter 2. We start from the assumption that types *are* lexical predicates. In other words, we do not have to a stipulate an abstract concept DOG, for dogs, because this concept is already given by the predicate "dog" (for English speakers).

Assumption 3.17

• The lexicon consists of predicates. Each predicate is of some sort. The set of lexical sorts *Psort* contains:

x (first-order) entity predicates;
e SoA predicates;
q qualifier predicates (adjectives)
n integer predicates
u universal type (top element of *Psort*)

• The set *Semf* of semantic functions (given by the FG theory) is provisionally given by:

{ag, go, rec, ref, instr},

• *Psort* is a flat lattice such that $s \leq$ u, for each $s \in$ *Psort*

end 3.17

That *Semf* is provisional means that we do not claim this set to be complete. However, additions can be made without affecting the interpretation given here.

The set of predicates *Pred*, specified in the lexicon, is sorted. For the sake of discussion, we use a sample minilexicon containing the following predicates:

$Pred_x$	{prince, dwarf, princess, person, snowwhite}
$Pred_e$	{sleep, eat, kiss, touch, act}
$Pred_q$	{male, little, female, human, furious}
$Pred_n$	{1, 2, 3, ...}

By means of the sets *Psort*, *Semf* and *Pred* (with sorted subsets $Pred_s$) we can define a data algebra. Let us call it *T* (for "types").

The *signature* of *T* is as follows:

S = *Psort* (domain names)

Σ = *Semf* (function symbols)

where {ag, go, rec, instr} $\subseteq \Sigma_{e,x}$

and {ref} $\subseteq \Sigma_{x,x}$

In words, it says that ag is a function from SoA predicates to entity predicates, etc.

A data algebra specification of signature (S,Σ) consists of a family of information systems and approximable mappings between them.

For sort x,q and e the information systems A_x, A_q and A_e are defined as follows:

$D_x = Pred_x \cup \{\Delta_x, \nabla\}$

The entailment base is:

{prince} $\vdash_x$ person

{princess} $\vdash_x$ person

{prince,princess} $\vdash_x$ ∇

{dwarf,person} $\vdash_x$ ∇

$D_e = Pred_e \cup \{\Delta_e, \nabla\}$

{kiss} $\vdash_e$ touch

{touch} $\vdash_e$ act

{eat} $\vdash_e$ act

{act,sleep} $\vdash_e$ ∇

$D_q = Pred_q \cup \{\Delta_q, \nabla\}$

{male,female} $\vdash_q$ ∇

The dataset of D_u is the union of these datasets including Δ.

Using the construction of "inconsistency by entailment" we can, for each lexical domain D, construct an information system in which we allow only those sets that do not entail ∇. Sets of predicates that are inconsistent are called *incoherent*. The lexicon is a data algebra of coherent domains.

For the *functions* of the data algebra (Func) we use the same symbols as for the function names, for example ag. Functions are specified by approximable mappings. A possible pair in such a relation is:

{kiss} ag {person}

saying that the agent of kissing must be a person. The force of this specification is that of a selection restriction. It implies that an agent of some kissing event must at least be of type person.

Finally, we also have entailments in A_u that cannot be specified in some specific sorted information system A_s because they involve predicates of different sorts. These entailments represent selection restrictions on qualifiers. For example,

{human} $\vdash_u$ person

saying that the application domain of the qualifier *human* is the entity type *person*. Qualifiers can also apply to SoA types:

{furious} $\vdash$ act

This equation says that the domain of application of *furious* is restricted to actions. This implies that *furious* cannot be applied coherently to *sleep*. The set {sleep,act} is incoherent, and so is the deductive closure of {sleep,furious}.

The signature of T can be given without reference to the specific predicates and types in the example. The signature is a universal property of lexicons and defined by the linguistic theory. Lexicons may differ in the particular domains and functions (a lexicon for English, a lexicon for Dutch, a lexicon for scientific English, etc).

The formalization of the lexicon by means of an information system captures two important aspects: it formalizes the *generalization* relationship between predicates and it formalizes the *inconsistency* or incoherence relationship between predicates. Although the lexicon has more to offer than this, these two aspects are very basic from the point of view of conceptual modeling (cf. 4.3.3).

3.3.2. Instance level

The lexicon consists of types. Let us now turn to the instance level. Instances are represented by means of referents. As we may expect, the instance level is in many respects a mirror image of the lexical data algebra, but there are some small additions.

In the first place, we assume sorted sets of referents:

Assumption 3.18

The set *Ref* of referents occurring in our model is partioned as follows:
Ref_x = {x1, x2, ...} is an infinite set of entities;
Ref_e = {e1, e2, ...} is an infinite set of SoAs;
and Ref_u is the union of these sets.
end 3.18

Note that we do not have instances of integers. The cardinality function COUNT discussed later maps referents to integers.

For each sort s, the set Ref_s is mapped to an information system:

$$(Ref_s \cup \{\Delta_s, \nabla_s\}, \Delta_s, \text{Con}, \vdash)$$

where Con contains all subsets of the dataset and the entailment relation is the minimal one, that is, $u \vdash \Delta_s$, for each u, and $u \vdash X$ whenever $X \in u$. As before, the ∇ is the rogue element. We notice that the symbol Δ_x is ambiguous now, standing for both the top symbol of the lexical domain of sort x and the top symbol of the instance domain of sort x. If necessary, we use Δ_{xT} and Δ_{xI} to differentiate between them.

In this section, we will work out the data algebra of instances. A data algebra of instances will be called a situation. Situations will be connected to T, the lexical data algebra. The bridge between these two systems is provided by the functions *TYPE*, *QUAL* and *COUNT*. These functions map each referent to an element of T. The elements of the domains Ref_s are called *instances*. Fig. 3.1 gives a schematic overview:

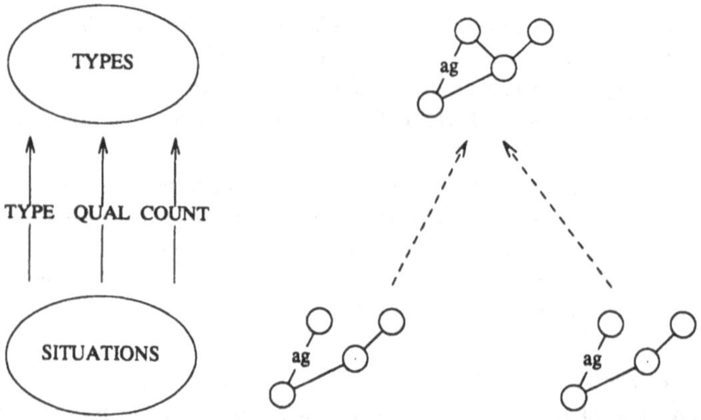

Fig. 3.1 Model structure: types and instances

In a knowledge base system, there is usually one lexicon, but situations may be numerous. It is profitable to introduce the notion of a situation in stages. The first stage is to define a "universal" data algebra of instances called I. The signature of I is as follows:

$S = Psort$ (domain names)
$\Sigma = Semf$ (function symbols)
where {ag, go, rec, instr} $\subseteq \Sigma_{e,x}$
{ref} $\subseteq \Sigma_{x,x}$

The domains of I are specified as information systems on the referent sets Ref_e and Ref_x. The functions in I are specified as approximable mappings, such as ag.

The function *TYPE* from instance level to type level is defined by means of an approximable mapping (the deductive closure of a binary relation between consistent sets):

$$\text{TYPE}: Ref_u \rightarrow Pred$$

such that referents of sort s are mapped to predicates of sort s. This can be axiomatized as:

A1 $\text{TYPE}(\Delta_{xI}) \vdash \Delta_{xT}$
A2 $\text{TYPE}(\Delta_{eI}) \vdash \Delta_{eT}$
A3 $\{\Delta_{xT}, \Delta_{eT}\} \vdash \nabla$

The function *COUNT* from instance level to type level is defined by means of an approximable mapping:

$$\text{COUNT}: Ref_u \rightarrow Pred_n$$

Finally, the function *QUAL* from instances to qualifiers:

$$\text{QUAL}: Ref_u \rightarrow Pred_q$$

The structure of *I* is best illustrated by means of a small example. Consider the following predication:

(1) `[t1] e1 kiss(ag [2] x7 prince: little)(go [s] x8 snowwhite)`

In section 3.1, we introduced a simplified version of the normal form of the predication. Having defined the lexicon and the data algebra, we can make this more precise. The normal form of predication (1) consists formally of the TYPE specifications:

{x7} TYPE {prince}
{x8} TYPE {snowwhite}
{e1} TYPE {kiss}

the QUAL specification:

{x7} QUAL {little}

and the COUNT specification:

{x1} COUNT {2}

plus the function specifications:

{e1} ag {x7}
{e1} go {x8}

In principle, the normal form of the predication may also include entailments inside of one domain. We will see some examples shortly. Note that we adopt the convention to write TYPE and QUAL specifications in predication format For example, {x7} TYPE {prince} is written as prince(x7).

Definition 3.19 Let p be a predication, with referent markers x_i for terms and e_i for SoAs. We say that x_i (e_i) is *dependent* on e_j iff x_i (e_i) is the reference marker of a term (predication) which is an argument or satellite of e_j. The *normal form* of the predication is the set of equations defined exhaustively as follows:

(a) If x is dependent on e, and the function of x is f, then the expression $\{e\}\ f\ \{x\}$ is well-formed and called a function specification in the normal form;

(b) If r is a referent marker of a term or SoA with head P, then the expression $\{r\}$ TYPE $\{P\}$ is well-formed and called a TYPE specification in the normal form.

(c) If r is a referent marker of a term or SoA with qualifier Q, then the expression $\{r\}$ QUAL $\{Q\}$ is well-formed and called a QUAL specification in the normal form.

(d) If r is a referent marker of a term or SoA with number operator n, then the expression $\{r\}$ COUNT $\{n\}$ is well-formed and called a COUNT specification in the normal form.

(e) If p is an identification (the predicate part of the predication is a term), and x and y are the referent markers of subject and predicate term respectively, then the expression $\{x\} \vdash y$ is well-formed and called an inclusion equation; if p is negative, then $\{x,y\} \vdash \nabla$ is an exclusion equation.

end 3.19

Using the normal form, a data algebra I is defined as follows:

Dom The domains are specified as information systems whose datasets are made up by the referent sets introduced in assumption 3.2. If the normal form of the predication contains entailments between referents, then the domain is specified by subsystem A(E), where E is the entailment base made up of the inclusion and exclusion equations now read as entailments.

Func The functions (ag, go, etc) are defined by the approximable mappings, induced by the functional equations from the normal form (now read as elements of approximable mappings).

The data algebra I contains the referents and their functional structure, but not the *type* definition. The next step is to combine I with T. Let us call the new algebra U. $U = I + T$. To avoid confusion, we rename the sort symbols and function symbols from I by means of an accent, so we have x as the sort of entity types and x' as the sort of entity instances. Similarly, ag is a function between lexical domains and ag' is a function between referent domains. If there is no risk of confusion, we may omit the quote sign.

Now U is defined by:

S $= S_T \cup S_I$

Σ $= \Sigma_T \cup \Sigma_I \cup$ {TYPE, QUAL, COUNT}

Dom $= Dom_T \cup Dom_I$

Func $= Func_T \cup Func_I \cup$ {TYPE, QUAL, COUNT}

where TYPE $\in \Sigma_{u',u}$, QUAL $\in \Sigma_{u',q}$, COUNT $\in \Sigma_{u',n}$.

Note that the data algebra U is made up of an invariant lexical part and a variant instance part. "Invariant" means that we assume the lexical definitions do not change during the life of the knowledge base. The variant parts are then the entailment bases and functional equations. This means that it is not necessary to specify U completely for each different predication. In the beginning of the knowledge base, we have a data algebra "shell" consisting of the lexical part and an empty instance part. "Empty" means that only the trivial entailments on the domains are specified, and the approximable mappings are the minimal ones. The each predication (each normal form) corresponds to a *subalgebra* of the shell. A subalgebra is called a *situation*, which is thus fully specified by means of a family of entailment bases and functional equations.

3.3.3. Situations

We suppose that *U* is a universal data algebra shell. We define a situation as follows:

Definition 3.20 A *situation* in *U* is a tuple (E,F,G) where *E* is a family of entailment bases on Ref_{sI}, *F* is a family of function specifications (for each $f \in$ Semf) and *G* a family of function specifications, for TYPE, COUNT and QUAL.
end 3.20

The structure of a situation is actually quite simple and we can easily picture it as a set of tables:

G

TYPE	
ref	pred
x7	prince
x8	snowwhite
e1	kiss
x9	dwarf
x4	dwarf
...	...

COUNT	
ent	num
x7	2
x9	7
x4	1

QUAL	
ent	qua
x7	little

F

AGENT	
soa	ent
e1	x7

GOAL	
soa	ent
e1	x8

E

ENTAIL	
ent	ent
x9	x4

For each semantic function, we have a separate table. Here we only pictured those of AGENT and GOAL. The derivation of the situation above from predication (1) is straightforward. The only subtle point is that the predication contains reference markers and the situation contains referents. The reference markers are not necessarily identical with the referents, since the predication can be verified (made true) in various situations, as many as there are different interpretations. The exact truth-definition will be given in 3.12. However, given a certain interpretation function on reference markers, the construction of a situation is simple.

The entailment base E_s contains the entailment $\{x4\} \vdash x9$. This is to be interpreted as saying that x4 is one of the seven dwarfs represented by x9. This entailment is not derived from predication (1), because it is not found there. I added it just for getting a more complete example. The interpretation of the entailment on instances is postponed to chapter 4.

It is possible to combine situations with one another. For example, we can expand the situation above with another situation s2 with referents {x8,e2}, and containing the equation:

```
{x8} TYPE {princess}
```

corresponding to the predication:

```
([s] princess)([s] x8)
```
"She is a princess"

Situations have been studied by Barwise & Perry (1983). The main difference with the model-theory of classical logic is that whereas the state of some world fixes the actuality of each fact, and hence is unique, situations can be numerous. One motivation Barwise and Perry present for believing in more than one real situation has to do with embedding. A sentence like *Joe saw Jackie bite Molly* describes a relation between Joe and a certain event, one in which Jack was biting Molly. This event is not a world (in the logical sense), but a partial world. A partial world is called a situation and within a world, there are numerous situations. If we accept the existence of several situations, then it is also useful to see what relations can exist between them. One is the relationship of "part-of": one situation can be part-of another situation. It is also possible that two situations are *incompatible*, which means that their union is not consistent. Furthermore, we can say that one situation classifies another. The picture that emerges here to the attentive reader is that the situations themselves are part of an information system. For example, consider the following situations (characterized here by their predications):

s1 `{ e1 bite(ag [s] x jack)(go [s] y molly),`
`([s] dog)([s] x jack),`
`see(exp [s] z joe)(go e1)}`
"Joe sees Jack bite Molly. Jack is a dog"

s2 `{ ([s] dog)([s] x jack)}`
"Jack is a dog"

s3 `{ ([s] cat)([s] x jack)}`
"Jack is a cat"

Here we have three different situations, but they are not unrelated. Situation s1 contains situation s2. Situation s3 is incompatible with situation s2 (and s1), since Jack cannot be both a cat and a dog. That situation s2 is "part-of" s1 simply means that the entailment base E, the type set (G), and the function set (F) of s2 are contained in s1. In the same way, "incompatible" means that the union causes an inconsistency, either at type level or at instance level.

Let us first see what it means that a situation is inconsistent. A situation can be inconsistent in three ways. The first possibility is that there is something wrong with the types or qualities. This is the case in the example in the union of s2 and s3. A second possibility is that one of the approximable mappings at the instance level does not accord with selection restrictions imposed at the lexical level. A third possibility is that there is something wrong with the instances, that there is an inconsistent instance. An example of the latter is the following:

```
sl = { (x [s] jack)(y [s] molly), NEG (x [s] jack)(y [s] molly)}
```
"molly is jack and molly is not jack"

which is translated to the specification:

```
{x} TYPE {jack}
{y} TYPE {molly}
{x} ⊢ y
{x,y} ⊢ ∇
```

Now we have an instance [x] = {x,y,Δ,∇} that is inconsistent. In general, this kind of problem arises when two referents are said to be the same and different at the same time.

The following definition summarizes when a situation is inconsistent. Note that only the second case distinguished above need to be specified explicitly, since the other two cases are already met in the consistency requirement of data algebra subspecifications.

Definition 3.21 Let s = (E,F,G) be a situation, in universal data algebra U.

We say that s is *consistent* iff

(i) $\mathscr{A}$(E, F $\cup$ G) is a consistent data algebra subspecification of $\mathscr{A}(U)$;

(ii) for each function $f \in Semf$

$$TYPE(f'(r)) \vdash f(TYPE(r));$$

Otherwise s is *inconsistent*

end 3.21

Note that the expression "$TYPE(f(r))$" is well-formed since r is an element, so $f(r)$ is an element, and so is $TYPE(f(r))$. The same holds for the dual expression $f(TYPE(r))$. Condition (i) requires that the properties of a term or predication are mutually consistent. Condition (ii) guarantees that the selection restrictions are met. For example, if e is an instance of paying, then $ag(e)$ must be of type *human*, in other words, $TYPE(ag(e)) \vdash ag(TYPE(e))$ (= human).

As we saw above, situations can be part-of another situation or they can be incompatible. This is expressed in the following definition:

Definition 3.22 Let $s_1 = (E_1, F_1, G_1)$ and $s_2 = (E_2, F_2, G_2)$ be two situations.

We say that s_1 is part-of s_2, written as $s_1 \leq s_2$ iff $U(s_1) \leq U(s_2)$, that is, if the data algebra specifications for the two situations are ordered.

We say that s_1 and s_2 are *compatible* iff the pair-wise union of s_1 and s_2 is consistent. This definition can be extended to a set of situations (take the pair-wise union of all elements of the set).

end 3.22

The part-of and compatibility relationship makes the set of situations into an lattice. The *part-of* relationship is reflexive and transitive. We can say that $s_1 \leq s_2$ iff $s_2 \subseteq s_1$. The most uninformative situation, figuring as top element is the empty situation. A set of situations is consistent iff they are compatible.

Theorem 3.23 The structure M (Sit,∅,Comp,$\leq$), where Sit is a set of consistent situations, Comp is the compatibility relation, ∅ is the top element, and $u \vdash v$ iff

$[v] \subseteq [u]$, is an information system. With the meet and join operations, as defined on data algebra subspecifications, the structure forms a lattice.

Proof. Follows from proposition 3.16. □

end 3.23

We have to take Sit as the set of *consistent* situations; if we would allow inconsistent situations also, then not all singleton sets would be compatible (which is a requirement for the information system).

In the sequel, we will usually identify a situation with its deductive closure in the information system. This closure is found by taking the closure of the entailment base and the approximable mappings. One consequence of this is that, for example, the situation *John kissed Mary* includes *John touched Mary* (assuming that *to kiss* entails *to touch*), and includes *someone kissed Mary* etc.

3.4. TRUTH

The data algebra (or more particular, a situation) can be viewed as a partial model structure. Simple propositions (predications) can be mapped directly to a situation, but not every proposition is equivalent to a data algebra; in particular, it is not possible to construe a data algebra for a predication containing universal quantification. However, it is possible to evaluate such a predication against a situation. In other words, it can get a truth-functional meaning, just as in traditional logic.

Upon a little reflection, we see that it is not enough to take one situation, or a set of them, as a model. Since our situations are partial models, they only define what is the case. If something is not entailed by the situation, it is either false or unknown. We can not conclude positively that it is false. So if we take a situation as a model, we cannot make a model for an atomic negative sentence ("John does not kiss Mary").

Under the Wittgensteinian interpretation of a model (a model is a picture of the world), it makes perfectly sense to include only positive facts in the model; quod non est verum neque verisimile non est (cf Russell, 1918/1956; Quine, 1961). It is hard to think of negative States of Affairs (how many of them are there?). But under the Tarskian interpretation of a model (a structure that verifies a theory), interpreting situations as partial models without having the possibility of providing negative information would result in a very weak logic. For an appropriate truth-definition, we therefore need Tarskian models.

A Tarskian model (in our sense) contains not only an *actual* situation (or a set of them), but also a set of *excluded* or *irreal* situations. Excluded situations have the same form as actual situations, but they are used by the Speaker as "counter-examples", situations that he knows can never become true. A proposition p is true with respect to a model iff p can be verified with respect to the actual situation. A proposition p is false iff p can be falsified, that is, if it entails some excluded situation. If p is neither verified nor falsified, then it is neither true nor false.

Note that it does not matter so much for the logical interpretation whether we take one actual situation or a set of them. If we take a set, and they are compatible, then the set is equivalent with the union. Of course, we can't do that with the excluded situations, because here the entailment works the other way round. A situation is falsified if it entails an excluded situation. It need not entail *all* excluded situations.

Definition 3.24 Let A be a domain of situations (including ∇). A *Tarskian model* T (in A) is a pair of the form (Π,Σ), where Π is a subset of A of compatible *actual* situations and Σ is a subset of A of *excluded* situations. $\Pi, \Sigma \subseteq Con_A$ and for each $s \in \Sigma$, it holds that $s \vdash_A \nabla$.

A Tarskian model T is *consistent* iff $\Pi \cap \Sigma = \emptyset$.

For two Tarskian models T_1 and T_2, we say that $T_1 \vdash T_2$ iff $\Pi_1 \subseteq \Pi_2$ and $\Sigma_1 \subseteq \Sigma_2$.

Let p be an atomic proposition (see below).

T verifies p iff the situation induced by p is entailed by some $s \in \Pi$.

T falsifies p iff the situation induced by p entails some $s \in \Sigma$

end 3.24

The definition is inspired by Gabbay and Sergot (1986). Their proposal concerns negation and can be regarded as an extension of the logic programming language Prolog. They define a database as a pair (Π,Σ) where Π is a set of clauses and Σ is a set of goals. The clauses in Π are just the facts and rules of the database, as in Prolog. Σ contains goals which are *not* to succeed. The major difference between their approach and mine is that I define (Π,Σ) as a model, whereas it is a *theory* for Gabbay and Sergot. This difference works through in the fact that the clauses in Σ may contain negative goals in their approach, whereas the elements of Σ in my approach are simple situations.

The general picture looks as follows:

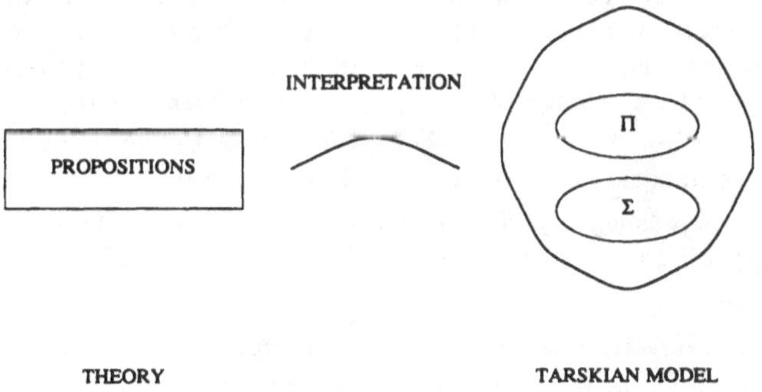

Fig. 3.2 Truth in a Tarskian model

Truth-functions are assigned to propositions. To evaluate the proposition, we must take the structural information into account. One possibility to do this is by using *Discourse representation theory* (DRT; see Kamp, 1981; Heim, 1982; Zeevat, 1989; see also Groenendijk & Stokhof, 1988). What Discourse Representation Theory adds to the normal form of a predication is a division of the specification parts over one or more *data boxes*. For example, the proposition:

If Pedro owns a donkey, he beats him

is translated in DRT to (using our own normal form as primitive propositions) the databoxes in Fig. 3.3

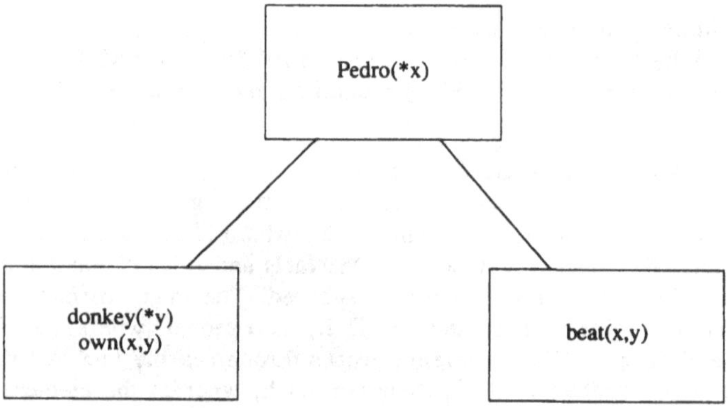

Fig. 3.3 DRS of *"If Pedro owns a donkey he beats him"*

where the term "donkey" gets a universal interpretation because it occurs in a left-splitting box. Loosely speaking, a data box is true with respect to a model iff for every possible interpretation of the referent markers in the left-hand box the right-hand box is true. One advantage of this representation over first-order logic has to do with the scope of the variables and the possibilities of anaphoric reference.

A slightly more complicated example is the FG proposition:

```
p4 ([t] el give(subj ag i[s] x nurse)(go i[s] y apple)(obj rec *[s]
z patient)(top loc *[s] t room)
```

which is expressed as:

In every room, a nurse gives every patient an apple.

which is transformed into the box structure of Fig. 3.4. For this example, we assume that `loc` is also a semantic function from A_e to A_x. This is not quite correct; a better treatment will be given in 5.3.3.

The division over the data boxes is based on information contained in the proposition. We already noted that some of the information makes up the normal form. This is the semantic information. But the proposition contains also structural information that is used as follows:

(1) *quantifier information*. If a term is universally quantified, its normal form equations must be put in a left-splitting box.

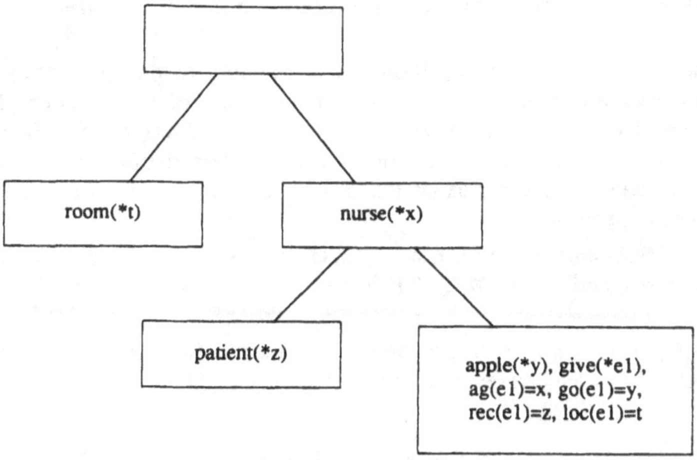

Fig. 3.4 DRS of *"In every room, a nurse gives every patient an apple"*

(2) *syntactic and pragmatic functions*. The box tree is built up from top (the root) to bottom. The order in which we process the arguments corresponds to the layered order of the predication and the logical meaning of the syntactic and pragmatic functions. It is roughly as follows. We start with the propositional topic, followed by the other propositional satellites. Then we process the main predication. In the realm of the predication, we start with the inherent functions (fact time and location), then the *subject* (primary perspective) and then the rest of the arguments and satellites, as well as the predication itself. When several arguments occur at the same level, all universally quantified ones are put together in a left box and the other ones in the right box.

Applied to our last example, the building of the data box runs as follows:

(1) The propositional topic "`*[s] t room`" is processed first. Since this term is universally quantified, we build a left-hand box where we put the equation: "{*t*} TYPE {`room`}". The processing proceeds in the right-hand box;

(2) The next step is to process the predication. Fact time and subject are processed first. Their equations are not quantified, so they are put in the current data box as they are;

(3) Now what is left over are the goal and recipient and the main predication. Since the recipient is universally quantified, it is put in a left-hand box. The rest is put in the right-hand box.

The procedure sketched here does not take into account that terms may be generic, that not all universal quantifiers are the same (compare *every* and *all*), and is simplified in several other ways, but it suffices for our present purposes.

The structural information that is used in building the box tree is a ladder that is thrown away afterwards. It is not reflected in function specifications or entailments. The box tree corresponding to a proposition is called a *structured proposition*.

We now define the simple proposition (corresponding to one data box). We use the term *abstract situation* for the syntactic counterpart of the situation. Instead of functional specifications, it consists of (the corresponding) normal form expressions, and the variables are taken from a set of referent markers *RM* instead of referents *Ref*. Referents are part of the model, referent markers are the variables occurring in the proposition.

Definition 3.25 A simple proposition, or data box, is a pair (M, S) where S is a an abstract situation, and where $M \subseteq RM$ is a subset of the referent markers occurring in S.

An *embedding* for a simple proposition p is a partial function f: $RM \rightarrow Ref$ that assigns a referent to each referent marker occurring in M_P.

end 3.25

A simple proposition p can be evaluated against a Tarskian model T. p is *verified* if there is an embedding f such that the substitution of each referent marker r by its image $f(r)$ leads to a model that is entailed by some s $\in \Pi(T)$. It is *falsified* if its interpretation turns out to entail an excluded situation. With the help of these notions, we can define truth for structured propositions in general:

Definition 3.26 A language of structured propositions p is given by the BNF:

$$\Phi ::= P \mid \neg P \mid \Phi_1 \Rightarrow \Phi_2 \mid \Phi_1 \,\&\, \Phi_2$$

where

- P is a simple proposition;
- $\Phi_1 \Rightarrow \Phi_2$ is a complex proposition whose parts are called the *binding* part and the *predicative* part, respectively;
- $\Phi_1 \,\&\, \Phi_2$ is a conjunction of propositions.

end 3.26

Remarks:

- My motivation for adopting the names "binding" and "predicative" will be clear after the truth definition;

- In general, conjunction is only interesting when one of the conjuncts is simple and the other is complex. The conjunction of two simple propositions can be written equivalently as one simple proposition being the pairwise union of the referent markers and situations. The conjunction of two complex propositions cannot be rewritten to one, but such a conjunction seems to be rare (it does not occur in my examples).

- A proposition can be written as a data box tree by putting the simple propositions of p in a data box, and for each complex proposition we make left-splitting and right-splitting daughter boxes. I adopt the phrase *focal part* for the "right-most descendent" of a proposition p The focal part is a (simple) proposition that can be the predicative part, or the predicative part of the predicative part, etc. Each proposition has one focal part, but a substructure may have a focal part that is different from the focal part of the main proposition.

- The format used here is due to Zeevat (1989). From the same publication, we also take over the use of asterisks to mark the referents is a simple predication that are in M. For example, [ag(e)= x*, go(x)=y)] stands for the simple proposition where M = {x}.

To illustrate the formal definition of propositions, we give the structured form of the proposition *p*: "in every room, a nurse gives every patient an apple" (cf. Fig. 3.4).

```
(room(l*) ⇒ (nurse(x*) & (patient(z*) ⇒ {apple(y*), give(e*),
ag(e*)=x, go(e*)=y*, rec(e*)=z, loc(e*)=l})))
```

This proposition is a complex one with binding part `room(l*)`. This is a simple proposition, with referent set $M = \{l\}$. The predicative part of the complex predication is itself a conjunction of a simple proposition (`nurse(*x)`) and a complex proposition. The binding part of this complex proposition is `patient(z*)` and the predicative part is a simple proposition, containing several equations, and with referent set {y,e}.

Having defined general structured propositions, we extend our definition of verification and falsification:

Definition 3.27 A proposition *p* is verified (falsified) by an embedding *f* and with respect to a Tarskian model T iff

(A) *p* is simple and *f* verifies (falsifies) *p*;

or *p* is not simple, and

(B1) *f* verifies the simple propositions in *p*;

(B2) for all $g \supseteq f$ such that *g* is an embedding for the binding parts of *p* there is an $h \supseteq g$ such that *h* verifies (falsifies) the predicate parts.

A structured proposition *p* is *true* with respect to T iff there is a verifying embedding *f* for *p*. Notation: $V_T(p)=1$.
A structured proposition *p* is *false* with respect to T iff there is a falsifying embedding *f* for *p*. Notation: $V_T(p)=0$.

end 3.27

Example: Let T be a model containing the following actual situation characterized by predications:

```
Π = {e1 own(po x1 Pedro)(go x2 donkey), e2 beat(ag x1)(go x2)}
```

The following propositions are true with respect to T:

```
- e own(po subj x Pedro)(go y donkey)
- e own(po subj x Pedro)(go y animal)
- e beat(ag subj x human)(go y animal)
- e beat(ag subj x Pedro)(go *y donkey : own(po x)(go y))
```

To take the first one (a simple abstract situation): if *f* maps reference marker `x` to `x1` and `y` to `x2`, and `e` to `e1`, then this abstract situation is immediately entailed by the model situation. The last one contains a universally quantified term with a restrictor. The corresponding structured proposition is:

```
{Pedro(x*)} & ({donkey(y*), own(e'*), po(e'*) = x, go(e'*)=y*} ⇒
{beat(e*), ag(e*) = x, go(e*) = y)})
```

We start by verifying the subject. This is done by embedding x on x1. Then we verify the other arguments. Because the goal term is universally quantified, it is put in binding part of a complex proposition. The verifying requires us to embed y to x2 and e' to e1. For this embedding an extension must be found so that the predicative part is verified too. The extension consists of mapping e to e2.

A false proposition with respect to T is for example:

- NEG e own(po x Pedro)(go y donkey)

because the positive counterpart is verified by the situation in T (see below). Not every proposition has a definite truth-value. The proposition "Pedro owns a duckling" is neither true nor false.

To complete the truth-evaluation of propositions, we need a Tarskian procedure to derive the truth-value of a complex proposition, one that includes propositional connectives like $\vee$ (or), $\wedge$ (and), or NEG (negation), from the truth-value of its components;

The following definition (adapted from Veltman, 1985:162) defines truth and falsehood for Tarskian models. We use $T \models_f p$ for "p is verified by f with respect to T and $T \dashv_f p$ for "p is falsified by f with respect to T".

Definition 3.28. Let T be a Tarskian model, f a verifying embedding and p and q be propositions.

- If p is atomic, then

$T \models_f p$	iff $V_{T,f}(p) = 1$
$T \dashv_f p$	iff $V_{T,f}(p) = 0$
- $T \models_f \text{NEG } p$	iff $T \dashv_f p$
$T \dashv_f \text{NEG } p$	iff $T \models_f p$
- $T \models_f p \wedge q$	iff $T \models_f p$ and $T \models_f q$
$T \dashv_f p \wedge q$	iff $T \dashv_f p$ or $T \dashv_f q$
- $T \models_f p \vee q$	iff $T \models_f p$ or $T \models_f q$
$T \dashv_f p \vee q$	iff $T \dashv_f p$ and $T \dashv_f q$

end 3.28

Veltman's (1985) definitions go beyond these, since they are aimed especially on the modal operators *must* and *may*, and on conditionals. We will treat these extensions in chapter 6. For our present purposes, the definitions 3.24-3.28 suffice to give a general account of truth of first-order propositions with respect to partial models.

3.5. SUMMARY AND CONCLUSION

In this chapter, we have introduced the notion of a Scott information system as a general device for examining systems dealing with partial information. Information systems specify domains with an inf semilattice structure. We have applied this theory to the development of a model-theoretic semantics for (non-modal) FG propositions. The model consists of two levels, a type level and an instance level. The type level is made up by the lexicon. At the instance level, the central notion is that of a *situation*. A situation represents a State of Affairs, that is, part of a world. It can be used to represent the contents of a set of "flat" sentences, but also for the denotation of attitude reports, given as embedded sentences. Example of the latter are *John believed that X* or *John saw that X*. The denotation of the X is a situation (or a set of them).

The way from information system up to situation took some steps. Let us look back for a moment to the steps we made. The first step is marked by the definition of *entailment base*. Entailment bases specify subsystems of a fixed information system. In our application, it is not a too strong restriction to have the information system fixed and consider each model as a subsystem of this generic model. We have shown that the set of entailment bases has a lattice structure. This is an important preliminary for systems dealing with partial information.

The next important step is the notion of a *data algebra*, and a data algebra specification. A data algebra is a set of domains and functions between them. A model is not just a bag of objects, but highly structured. This structure can be specified functionally. The data algebra specification, as the name says, specifies a data algebra by means of entailment bases and approximable mapping bases.

The final step is from data algebra to situation. This requires that we fix a certain data algebra and consider all the ways this data algebra can be extended by adding more information. The extensions are specified by means of situations. The way in which situations are built up ensures that the set of situations can be given a lattice structure too. Situations specify the extensions by providing part of a data algebra specification.

So far for the background of situations. Let us now review the application of the situation calculus to truth-functional semantics. I have argued that a situation itself is not sufficient for a model in the Tarskian sense. Rather, a Tarskian model consists of actual and excluded situations. The excluded situations are to be interpreted as "counter-examples", things that are known to be not actual and hence can falsify a certain proposition.

To attach truth-values to propositions with respect to a Tarskian model, we must take the structure of the proposition into account. This structure determines the scope of referent markers. I have given an informal procedure by means of which FG propositions can be transformed to structured propositions. Given a structured proposition, the determination of the truth of atomic propositions comes down to finding a verifying embedding. For complex propositions, the truth-value is given in the standard Tarskian way.

In the following chapters we will work out the general framework in more detail. In particular, we will analyze the internal structure of the lexicon, countability of terms, and models for temporal and modal propositions.

What is not worked out is the procedure by which FG propositions are assigned a propositional structure. The procedure I have given works for a majority of cases, but refinements are still due. It is an open question, to me at least, whether the procedure is universal or may differ from one language to another. Evidently, more linguistic research is needed.

Another shortcoming is the lack of a (syntactic) proof-theory that is consistent and complete with respect to the semantics we have outlined. In chapter 7, we will give some indications on how a proof-theory may look like in a functionalist framework. The dialogue logic developed by Paul Lorenzen suggests itself as a promising starting point.

The most important conclusion I want to draw from this chapter is that FG propositions, at least the "first-order" part, can be given a semantic characterization. For me, this is enough justification for calling FG a knowledge representation language, or a logic. And this means that, in principle, it is not necessary to design a separate formal knowledge base language in which linguistic structures should be interpreted, as it is commonly assumed. FG propositions are linguistic deep structures, but they also provide a full-fletched logical and conceptual device. If someone still wants to distinguish linguistic deep structure and conceptual structure, he may do so, but there is no formal necessity for this duplication. In the light of the philosophical arguments given in chapter 1, I also doubt that there are good psychological/cognitive reasons, but such a claim is beyond the scope of this thesis.

4

The structure of the lexicon

4.1. INTRODUCTION

The lexicon is an indispensable part of the knowledge base. In database theory, it has become generally accepted that a database system should contain a *data dictionary* in which the *conceptual schema* is stored. Although researchers differ on what they include in the conceptual schema, all seem to agree that it includes at least the *structural* information of entity and relationship types. Of course, entity types correspond usually to noun predicates and relationships to verbs, so the Entity/Relationship model can be viewed as a simple lexicon. Usually it does not include converse relations such as between *sell* and *buy* (converse relations are specified in the NIAM approach, Nijssen 1980). The more advanced models make use of subtype relationships, but meaning conditions often have to be specified separately. As far as I know, no model contains lexical rules. If we have a relationship SUPPLY, then we may want to denote the first participants as SUPPLIERs. The same holds for SELL, BUY etc, so obviously there is a general rule involved. In the linguistic approach, this rule is known as a lexical rule of noun phrase formation.

By way of example, we will consider the conceptual schema of the car example introduced in the ISO report on conceptual models (van Griethuysen, 1982). The example is about the registration of cars, their production, transfers and destruction. Figure 4.1 gives the graphic representation of the NIAM model of this universe of discourse.

In the NIAM model, a distinction is made between the non-linguistic object types and linguistic ones. The former include (in this case) MANUFACTURER, CAR-MODEL, FUEL-CONSUMPTION, DATE, etc. The latter include MANUFACTURER-NAME, REG-NO (= registration number), MODEL-NAME, FUEL-CONSUMPTION-AMOUNT, YEAR-NO etc. An example of a subtype relationship is: NON-TRADING GARAGE is-subtype-of GARAGE. Relationships between non-linguistic object types are called "ideas". An example of an idea is "builds" that has two roles: "manuf-by" (which takes a CAR-MODEL) and a role "of" which takes a MANUFACTURER (it is not clear why the relationship is named in the active voice, "builds", whereas the first role is the car model and not the manufacturer). Additional constraints on the model are, for instance, that each MANUFACTURER has only one MANUFACTURER-NAME and vice versa.

This short example of a particular conceptual model suggests that the kind of

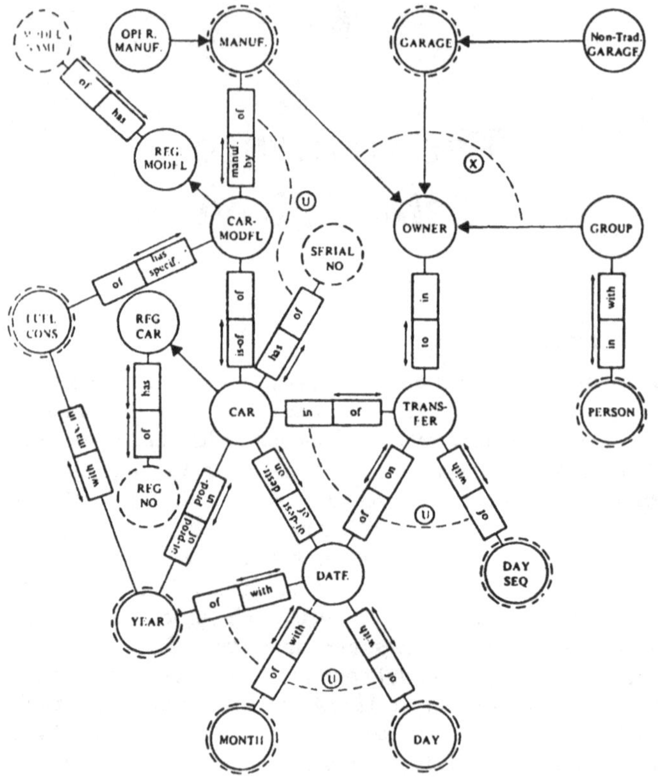

Fig. 4.1 Example conceptual schema (ISO, p.E-18)

information that is represented here, is not much different from what is traditionally stored in the lexicon. An immediate advantage of treating the conceptual model as a lexicon, is that a more disciplined approach becomes feasible. In the first place, we can make use of an existing dictionary as starting-point and try to derive the particular schema for this application as a specialization of the "dictionary schema". The fact that a non-trading garage is a garage, is not something a designer should bother about; he can safely delegate such questions to the linguist. A second advantage is evident if we look at the "ideas" in the schema. Most of them contain prepositions like "to", "in", "of" etc. It is well-known that these prepositions and cases are most often ambiguous. Therefore most linguists would describe such roles preferably by means of so-called "deep cases", or "semantic functions" that are more abstract than the surface forms. These semantic functions can be defined once for all in the linguistic theory so that it is not necessary to reinvent the wheel for every particular discourse.

4.1.1. Objectives

Viewed as a data dictionary, the lexicon fulfils at least the following functions in the knowledge base:

(1) it describes the abstract conceptual structures from which the (or a possible) *internal schema* of the database can be derived (ANSI/SPARC,1975);

(2) it serves as a common *reference point* for different users with different views on the database;

(3) it plays an active role in the question/answering interface by locating semantic errors and providing *help and explanation* facilities;

(4) by constraining the possible uses of the predicates it contributes to maintaining *data integrity*;

(5) it specifies the way in which the data is to be expressed (for instance, what icon to use in the graphical interface). If the system has a *natural language interface*, the lexicon contains the grammatical information necessary for parsing and generating messages, and phonological information for analyzing or synthesizing speech.

(6) the structural and semantic information in the lexicon is also used in *reasoning*, for instance by exploring the inheritance property of taxonomies (Brachman & Schwalze, 1985);

Data dictionaries that fulfill all these objectives satisfactorily do not exist yet. To design such a dictionary is an ambitious project. On the other hand, I do not believe that everything that is sometimes put in the conceptual schema belongs in our lexicon. A typical case is the set of deontic integrity constraints. Deontic constraints are constraints that are not necessarily true in the Universe of Discourse, but only by virtue of some law or convention. In the ISO car example, it is stated that a manufacturer is not permitted to sell cars to private persons. In several modelling approaches, such a constraint is put in the conceptual schema. However, this is not appropriate since the constraint can be violated in practice so it is not necessarily true. Therefore we consciously exclude such constraints from the lexicon.

4.1.2. Organization

Let us now turn to the structure of the lexicon in Functional Grammar and its use in knowledge representation. Loosely speaking, the lexicon is a set of predicate frames containing both syntactic and semantic information. On closer look, it turns out that there is much more structure in it. A useful distinction can be made between vocabulary, thesaurus and dictionary. Dana Scott (1986) defined these parts as follows (cf. Lyons, 1977; I replaced the term "lexicon" by "vocabulary"):

> **The vocabulary** (1) provides the official list of correct forms of words, (2) presents only syntactical features, (3) gives, if necessary, some peculiar (idiomatic) patterns of usage
>
> **A thesaurus** (1) provides the official survey of correct terminology for concepts, (2) presents only basic semantic features, (3) structures the terms into a semantic net, (4) adds to the vocabulary special patterns of usage appropriate to the special concepts.

A dictionary (1) presents the definitions of terms from the thesaurus, (2) gives humans the understanding of specialized words, (3) helps shape the growth of the thesaurus, (4) helps authorities in deciding on the admission of new terms.

We will use the lexicon as an aggregation of these three parts, which can be described alternatively as three sets:

I *predicates*: grammatical information

II *predicate frames*: semantic information

III *predicate schemas*: conceptual information

Entries of conventional dictionaries group all three kinds of information together. For example, consider the following entry for the verb *bar* (Oxford Dictionary):

> **bar**[2] /ba:(r)/ *vt* (-rr-) **1** [VP6A] fasten (a door, gate, etc) with a bar[1]. **2** [VP15B] keep in or out: *He barred himself in*, fastened doors, windows, etc so that no one could enter the building. **3** [VP6A] obstruct: *bar a road/path. Soldiers barred the way and we couldn't go any farther.* **4** ***bar (from)***, prohibit: *bar sb from a competition* order that he shall not take part. [VP6C] (colloq): *She bars smoking in the drawing-room* does not permit it. ... **5** [VP6A] (usu passive) mark with a stripe or stripes: *a sky barred with clouds*

Grammatical information includes the predicate pronunciation and/or spelling, the category (*vt*, transitive verb, in the example), and irregular forms (not in the example above). The grammatical information may also include separable prefixes, such as the prefix *in* in the verb *bar in* (see 2).

A predicate is usually associated with several predicate frames. These frames define the number of arguments and the selection restrictions on them, as well as the genus proximum, the lowest upperbound in the taxonomy (also called a hyperonym). With *bar* we identify the following frames:

```
bar(ag human)(go door)
bar_in(ag human)(go animate)
bar(ag human)(go way)
bar(ag human)(go human)(so soa)
bar(ag human)(go soa)
bar(go thing)
```

We distinguish as many predicate frames as is needed on the basis of the classification and the argument structure. In this case, the six frames above all have a different argument structure and a different taxonomical classification:

```
fasten(ag human)(go door)(instr bar:N))
keep_in(ag person)(go thing)
obstruct(ag human)(go way)
exclude(ag human)(go thing)(so soa)
prohibit(ag human)(go soa)
mark(go thing)
```

The predicate "bar:N" refers to the noun "bar".

The conceptual information attached to a frame consists of a repository of "canned" complex predicate frames called *schemata*. Schemata describe typical usages of the frame and make up the meaning definitions of them. A simple example of typical usage is: *a sky barred with clouds*. We can put this in a schema as follows:

```
bar(go x sky)(instr y cloud)
```

Note that there may be many predicate schemata subsumed under one predicate frame. Only the top element of this structure is called a (lexical) frame, the other ones are called schemata.

The meaning definitions should give a complete characterization of what the speakers mean by using the word. We make a distinction between meaning conditions and meaning definitions. Meaning conditions do not always give a complete characterization of a predicate frame. But they are important as far as they specify conditional relations between predicates. For example, the meaning conditions of the verb *sell* will specify that the seller owns the object afterwards (postcondition). This information is necessary in order to determine the effect of a *sell* transaction on the knowledge base. On the other hand, a knowledge base may manipulate propositions about reptiles without having to know what the word "crocodile" exactly means (for example, without knowing how to distinguish a crocodile from an alligator). The meaning conditions of "crocodile" can be kept sober; its meaning definition may attempt to give a complete characterization.

4.1.3. Some problems

Before we start describing our way of achieving the objectives stated above, it is worthwhile to consider some problems with frame-based languages discovered by previous researchers. The first problem has to do with a fundamental *ambiguity* of frames, the second one with their apparent *arbitrariness*.

In their paper *KRYPTON: A Functional Approach to Knowledge Representation* Brachman, Fikes and Levesque (1985) write:

> While much of the current work in knowledge representation is fraught with disagreement, some trends seem to be emerging. In particular, a great deal of effort has been focused on the development of "frame"-based languages with the following features:
>
> - the principal representational objects - known as *frames* are taken to be non-atomic *descriptions* of some complexity;
> - frames are defined as *specializations* of more general frames;
> - individuals are represented by *instantiations* of generic frames;
> - the resulting connections between frames form *taxonomies*

After recognizing the basic importance of frames, the authors make the following critical observations:

- structures are interpreted in different ways at different times (the principal ambiguity being between definitional and factual interpretations)
- the meaning of the representation language is specified only in terms of the

data structures used to implement it

We don't discuss the second problem (lack of clear semantics) which is obvious enough. The first statement needs some explanation. Woods (1975) already pointed at the distinction between assertional and structural links in a semantic network. Sometimes a node is *defined* by means of its adjacent edges, and sometimes the edge must be interpreted as an *assertion*. To avoid this confusion, Brachman *et al* make a fundamental distinction between T-boxes and A-boxes. T-boxes (terminological) allow us to establish taxonomies of structured terms and answer questions of analytic relationships among these terms, while A-boxes (assertional) are used for describing the domain. The kind of reasoning performed on T-boxes is typically *subsumption*: does term t_1 subsume t_2. The kind of reasoning on the A-boxes is traditional deduction: prove that sentence ϕ is true.

The point made by Brachman and Levesque is a worth noticing. Indeed, it is only possible to make a predication ("assertion") if you have already a set of terms at your disposal. That is why they are called terms. Fregean logic allows only "atomic" terms (constants and variables) thus avoiding the problem. The same can be said about the first-normal form of the relational data model. Such an approach is often too restrictive. Nevertheless, I have the impression that the classification between A-boxes and T-boxes in fact mixes up three different distinctions:

(1) *term vs. predication*: the predication, taken as a basic knowledge unit, must have, at some level, terms "about" which something is predicated. Terms always contain a nominal head (sometimes elliptically) and are represented by a "noun phrase";

(2) *lexicon vs. knowledge base*: some part of the overall knowledge is definitional and part is assertional. Lexical definitions ("terminology") can and should be made for both nominal and verbal predicate frames;

(3) *subsumption vs. deduction*: both terms and predications can be put in a taxonomy, or "isa"-hierarchy. This holds for the lexicon as well as for the knowledge base. Exploring this taxonomy can be called subsumptive reasoning, to distinguish it from general deduction;

In our framework, we want to maintain both the distinction lexicon/knowledge base and the distinction term/predication. However, we use a compatible format for both the lexicon and the knowledge base so that subsumptive reasoning can be used in both.

There is also the problem of lack of foundations for frame representations. According to (Wilensky, 1986), frames are too general. There seems to be no principal answer to the question of which frames can support which slots. Most researchers seem to decide which slots to attach to which frames in accordance with the so-called "belonging" fallacy. The "belonging" fallacy is the idea that a given element should be awarded a particular slot in our representation because, in English, we would be given to say that the slot "belongs to" that element. Thus persons *have* names, ages, and addresses; physical objects *have* weight and height; and so on. Wilensky calls this a fallacy because the underlying concepts of "belonging" have almost no context-free meaning. For example, consider the phrases "John's appartment", "John's car" and "John's girl-friend". While formally similar, these phrases have radically different interpretations. In the first case, the phrase should probably be interpreted as the appartment John rents; the second as the car John owns (or perhaps drives); and the third as the woman he dates. The conclusion is that frame/slot representations assert that there is a relationship between two entities, but the relationship is arbitrary and has no representational status.

The goal of this chapter is to introduce a "frame-based" language that

(a) can fulfil the functions of the data dictionary, as stated above;

(b) exploits the advantages of frames;

(c) is supported by a theory that gives objective and rigid criteria for deciding between different representations. As we argued in chapter 1, this theory must be a linguistic theory, in our case, Functional Grammar;

(d) has a mathematical description. The *f-structure* (see 2.8.2) is the best candidate in this respect. In some sense this structure is less expressive than the original Minsky-frames, for example, it does not allow default values nor procedural triggers. But it is well-defined and sufficient;

(e) can be endowed with a compositional semantics (along the lines sketched in the previous chapter and worked out in subsequent chapters).

In order to concentrate on the semantic aspects, we will largely ignore the discussion of purely grammatical information, such as the representation of irregular forms. This kind of information becomes important in the expression and parser component.

4.2. PREDICATES AND PREDICATE FRAMES

4.2.1. Predicates

In Functional Grammar, predicates are the simple "contentive" lexemes (verbs, adjectives, nouns). Grammatical particles are produced by means of expression rules and are not in the lexicon. An example of a predicate is *bar*. Predicates have several representations, in particular a phonological representation and a graphological representation. In this thesis, I will use the graphological representation, but the expression rules that we will consider usually assume an underlying phonological representation.

We do not identify a predicate with its representation. For example, we have a noun *bar* and a verb *bar* that have the same form. But since they belong to different categories, we treat them as different predicates. It is also possible that there are two predicates of the same category. An example is the Dutch noun *pad* which either denotes a path or a toad. The singular form of these predicates is the same, but the plural form is different: *paden* and *padden*, respectively. They also have a different gender. Because of these formal differences, we treat them as two different predicates.

In this formalization of FG, the predicate is a functional structure that includes the phonological and graphological representation, but also additional grammatical information. Some examples are:

```
(stem => "see"; cat => v; forms => (past => "saw"; pap => "seen"))

(stem => "sheep"; cat => n; forms => (plur => "sheep"))

(stem =>  "bar"; cat => v; sepref => "in"))
```

The two Dutch predicates for *pad* are:

```
(stem => "pad"; cat => n; forms => (plur => "paden"); gnd => neut)

(stem => "pad"; cat => n; forms => (plur => "padden"); gnd => masc)
```

In FUG (Kay, 1979) and HPSG (Pollard & Sag, 1987), this structure is also called an *attribute-value matrix* (AVM) and would be written as follows (assuming that the same slot names would be used):

$$\begin{bmatrix} \text{STEM} & \textit{see} \\ \text{CAT} & \text{V} \\ \text{FORMS} & \begin{bmatrix} \text{PAST} & \textit{saw} \\ \text{PAP} & \textit{seen} \end{bmatrix} \end{bmatrix}$$

The matrix-format can be considered as a notational variant. We prefer f-structures, not because these would be easier to read but because they are at least easier to write down. Definition 4.1 gives the definition, tailored to the intended application. For an explanation of the ordering symbols and other details, see below.

Definition 4.1. Let Σ (the set of symbols), L (the set of labels), and T (the set of tag symbols) be given by:

Σ = String $\cup$ {n,v,a} $\cup$ {masc,fem,neut} $\cup$ $\{\Delta_{str}, \Delta_{cat}, \Delta_{gdr}\}$
L = {stem, cat, forms, sing, plur, past, pap, sepref, gdr ...}
T = {A, B, ...}

where

n $< \Delta_{cat}$, v $< \Delta_{cat}$, a $< \Delta_{cat}$,
$s < \Delta_{str}, \forall s \in$ String
masc $< \Delta_{gdr}$, fem $< \Delta_{gdr}$, neut $< \Delta_{gdr}$, ...

Then a *predicate* or *lexeme* is an f-structure $f = (A,\psi,\tau)$, where A is an address tree on L, ψ is a symbol function from L^* to Σ such that $\psi(L^*\text{-}A) = \{\Delta\}$ and τ is a tag function from A to T, such that:

$f \leqq$ (pred => Δ_s; cat => Δ_c)

The Basic Vocabulary (*Voc*) for some language is a finite set of lexemes.

end 4.1

- The set String presupposes some alphabet for which we can take (a subset of) the ASCII character set, the International Phonetic Alphabet, your favorite national alphabet, or whatever you like. String is supposed to be disjoint of the set of labels, tag symbols and other meta-symbols.

- The "<" is the partial ordering on the domain(s) Σ and the "≦" is the subsumption ordering on f-structures (definition 4.7, also in Appendix A). In this definition, and throughout the rest of this thesis, I use the term f-structure for an f-structure *modulo* alphabetic and permutational variants. Thus each f-structrure stands actually for a ψ^*-type. For the formal details, see Appendix A.
- The periods "..." in the extension of *L* indicate that in practice this definition may need some extensions. This also holds for Σ. For example, in some languages, such as Latin, declinations must be distinguished, in others not. What declinations should be distinguished depends on the language in question. However, we assume that each predicate contains at least a string, and is of either one of the three categories {n,v,a}.

V (verbal)	Predicative: occurrence as the predicate in a predication	event type
A (adjectival)	Qualitative: occurrence as attributive Modifier to the Head of a term	attribute value
N (nominal)	Categorizing: occurrence as the Head of a term phrase	entity type

Fig. 4.2 predicate categories (Dik, 1978)

The category of the predicate poses restrictions on the predicate frames in which it can occur and on its formal expression. To determine the category of a predicate, it is useful to distinguish between the primary use of a category and secondary or derived ones. Primary uses of predicate categories are given in the fig. 4.2. The last column states the corresponding conceptual category.

Although not all verbal predicates denote event types (that is, dynamic States of Affairs), most of them do. In a conceptual taxonomy of Japanese verbs composed by Naoyuki Okada, it was found that from the 1433 standard verbs about more than 1000 denote some kind of change (Okada,1987). More than 300 of these denote a movement.

Adjectives specify a *difference* between two entities. The measure used to detect a difference is important here. For example, to say that an entity is *high*, we need to compare it with another entity or a standard measure. Fig. 4.3 gives some subcategories of a set of 586 standard adjectives in Japanese.

Nouns specify the entity type of the event participants. Typical entities are things existing in space and time (socalled *first-order entities*). There are also second-order entities (being a State of Affairs) and third-order entities (being a proposition, or intensional object). An example of a second-order entity is *Christmas*, or *the destruction of the car*, and of a third-order entity *Newtonian mechanics*, or *penalty law*. Fourth-order entities are symbolic objects like *sentence*, *employee*

CATEGORY	EXAMPLE	DISTRIBUTION
emotion	ureshi(glad)	67
sense	samui(cold)	56
location	fukai(deep)	12
direction	naname-da(skew)	5
shape	marui(round)	79
quality	kutai(hard)	82
quantity	oi(many)	38
light	kurai(dark)	17
color	akai(red)	11
heat	atsui(hot)	22
force, energy	tsuyoi(strong)	16
voice, sound	yakamashi(noisy)	24
appearance	arawa-da(laying upon)	7
start, end	dashinuke-da(sudden)	4
time	hayai(early)	23
continuation	taedae-da(faint)	13
state	uttoshi(dull)	17
abstract	hitoshi(equivalent)	85
others	sayo-da(such)	8
TOTAL		586

Fig. 4.3 standard adjective types in Japanese (Okada, 1987)

record etc (the distinction between different types of entities has been proposed by Hengeveld; see also Dik, 1989).

In FG, the lexicon consists of basic predicates, as defined above, and predicate formation rules. A predicate formation rule can be seen as a partial function from the lexicon into itself. An example is nominalization: given the verbal predicate *sell* we can form the nominal predicate *selling*. A predicate formation rule is synchronically productive, which means that it does not work for a closed set of predicates, but for each predicate of a given type that is added to the language. A predicate that is formed by means of a predicate formation rule is called a derived predicate. Predicate formation rules will be treated in the next section, since they actually map predicate *frames* to predicate *frames*. To be precise, we should say that a derived predicate is a predicate occurring in a derived predicate frame.

4.2.2. Predicate frames

Predicates are used as the head of *predicate frames*. Usually, one predicate is used in several frames. For example, with the verbal predicate bar above, we distinguished five different predicate frames. From a semantic point of view, predicate frames are more central than predicates since different predicate frames with the same predicate may deviate both in the number and type of arguments they take and in their meaning. In contrast, the predicate is more central than the predicate frame from a morpho-syntactic point of view, since the information needed for the expression rules is for the most part stored with the predicate.

Corresponding to the three typical predicate categories - V, N and A - we distinguish the following three basic categories of predicate frames: *P-frames* for predicate frames containing verbal predicates, denoting a predication, *T-frames* for predicate frames containing nominal predicates, denoting a term, and *Q-frames* for (predicate frames containing) adjectival ones, denoting a qualifier. Sometimes predicate formation rules change the basic category of a predicate frame, so the correspondence with the predicate categories is not one-to-one. We will discuss these rules shortly.

We define a predicate frame as an f-structure that embeds the predicate. For example,

```
(pred => (stem => "sheep"; cat => n; forms => (plur => "sheep"));
 cat => t;
 type => [animate])
```

is an f-structure for a T-frame, where the "pred" (pronounced as "predicator") is an f-structure denoting a nominal predicate. The category of the f-structure is 't' and the semantic type is [animate].† For P-frames, the predicate frame typically includes semantic functions:

```
(pred => (stem => "sell"; cat => v;
          forms => (past => "sold"; pap => "sold"));
 cat => p;
 type => [action];
 sem => (ag => (type => [human]);
         go => (type => [thing]);
         rec => (type => [human])))
```

Predicate frames are defined as follows:

Definition 4.2 Let V be the set of (basic and derived) predicates, Sf be a (partially ordered) set of *semantic functions*, and Ptype be a set of primitive types.
Then a *predicate frame* is defined as an f-structure (A,ψ,τ) over the label space

$$L = L_{lex} \cup \{\texttt{pred, type, sem}\} \cup \text{Sf}$$

and symbol domain

$$\Sigma = \Sigma_{lex} \cup \{\texttt{p,t,q}\} \cup \text{Ptype} \cup \{\Delta_{c'}, \Delta_{ptype}\}.$$

such that

$$\texttt{t} < \Delta_{c'},\ \texttt{p} < \Delta_{c'},\ \texttt{q} < \Delta_{c'}$$

$$x < \Delta_{ptype},\ \text{for all } x \in \text{Ptype}$$

that obeys the following restrictions:

(i) $\{\texttt{cat,type,sem,pred}\} \subseteq A$

(ii) in all addresses w with prefix sem, the second element of w is a semantic function:
$\forall w \in A$: $w = \text{sem}.w' \Rightarrow w' = \sigma.w'', \sigma \in \text{Sf}$

(iii) the subframe $f \setminus$ pred is a lexeme:
$f \setminus \texttt{pred} \in \text{V}$

† To distinguish labels from tag symbols in the written version of f-structures, we adopt the convention that symbols, as far as they are not strings, are always in lower-case. Tag symbols are always in upper-case. So a T-frame is a frame where cat is 't', a P-frame is a frame where cat is 'p' and a Q-frame has cat 'q'.

(iv) ψ(cat) ∈ {t,p,q},
ψ(type) ∈ Ptype

The *Thesaurus* (on vocabulary Voc) is a finite set of predicate frames ϕ where V = Voc.

end 4.2

Remarks:

- The sets of semantic functions (Sf) and of primitive types (Ptype) will be introduced later in this chapter.

- The Thesaurus is a finite set of stored predicate frames. The *Fund* will be defined shortly as the set of all predicate frames, either stored or derived. This set can be infinite.

In conceptual modelling, we are primarily interested in the semantic functions. The grammatical information is less relevant. This makes it possible to map a predicate frame to a labelled directed graph. The graph consists of nodes and edges. The predicate frame is mapped to a node labelled with the predicate and the type. The semantic functions are translated to directed edges springing from the predicate node to other nodes corresponding to the selection restrictions. Finally, each node is of a certain category in {p,t,q}. The following picture contains an example of predicate frames. Following conventions in data modelling, we picture T-nodes as boxes, P-nodes as diamonds and Q-nodes as circles.

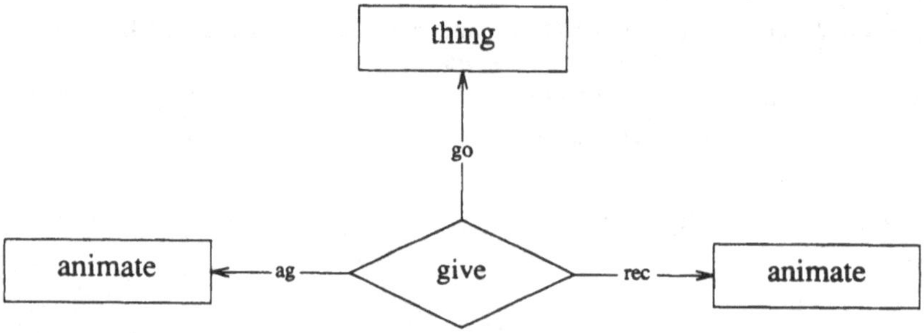

The number of semantic functions in a predicate frame head is called its *arity*. Most terms and qualifiers have arity zero. Examples of zero-arity T-frames are car, person, stock-room. Zero-arity qualifiers are green, high, etc. Frames of arity zero can be used as head of a term (T-frames) or restrictor (Q-frames), but they do not have an internal structure. In contrast, frames with arity one or more represent *aggregated* concepts (cf. Smith & Smith,1977).

T-frames *y* of arity 1 come in two types:

- attribute: name, age, color, mind
- relator: parent, part

(These must be distinguished from possessives:

• possessive: *John's book*

which are treated as *extended* predicate frames; the semantic function poss is here considered as a satellite; cf Mackenzie, 1987).

Attributes and relators are basic T-frames. We use the function ref (referent) for both. The difference between attributes and relators is the following: attributes specify some property of the referent; relators specify a a relationship between two entities. Giving an attribute of an entity is a form of *abstraction*; giving a relatum of an entity is a way to *locate* the entity. Attributes correspond with adjective classes (old of age, green of color, quick of mind, great of name etc), which does not hold for relators. In terms of databases, attributes are existence-dependent on their referent and relators not.

Some examples of attributes and relators with selection restrictions:

```
color(ref thing)
age(ref animate)
part(ref thing)
parent(ref animate)
```

Note that we adopt a version of the so-called Universal Relation assumption (Maier, Ullman, 1984) that says in effect that attributes have a meaning independent of the data structure (relation) in which they are defined. Attributes have equal predicate frame status as other predicate frames. On the other hand, we allow for the possibility that there are several attributes (predicate frames) with the same predicate (homonymy). These attributes will have different selection restrictions or a different type.

Basic T-frames do not have arity higher than 1. Derived T-frames such as destruction may take more than one function which they inherit from the underlying P-frame, as will be explained shortly. Since the arity of basic T-frames is not higher than 1, the semantic function has no discriminatory value, and we may omit it in written form of the predication. For example, color(blood) stands for color(ref blood).

P-frames usually take several arguments. Examples are verbs like *to sell*, but also adjectives used in predicative position (see below). In some rare cases, P-frames have arity zero (examples are meteorological verbs such as *to rain*. The definition of semantic functions for P-frames is not a trivial task and we will devote a separate section to it (4.2.4).

4.2.3. Predicate formation

The Thesaurus is a finite set of basic predicate frames. In general, a language also has rules by which new predicate frames can be derived. Such rules are called predicate formation rules. Therefore the *Fund* of a language is more than the Thesaurus. It is defined as all predicate frames, either basic or derived by means of predicate formation rules from a basic one. In principle, the Fund may be infinite, so it cannot be defined simply by enumeration.

Definition 4.3 A *predicate formation rule* is a partial function that maps predicate frames to predicate frames.

The *Fund* is the smallest set of predicate frames such that Thesaurus $\subseteq$ Fund, and, if $f \in$ Fund and predicate formation rule R applies to f, then R(f) $\in$ Fund.

end 4.3

We use the following conventions for representing functions on frames:

1 The rule applies to each predicate frame that is subsumed by the input frame

2 The rule may be partially specified. If f is some frame that is subsumed by the input frame of R, then R(f) is identical to f except for what is specified in the output frame.

3 The rule may use tag symbols as variables. That is, if the input contains a subframe tagged X, and the output contains X, then the subframe at this address is the same as the one in the input structure. Formally, if i and o are the input and output frames, then $\tau_i \leq \tau_o$.

Let us give some examples of predicate formation rules. The first rule is agentive nominalization and turns a verb into a noun, the second one is verbal nominalization:

```
R1( (pred => (stem => X; cat => v);
     cat => p;
     sem => (ag => (type => T))) =

   (pred => (stem => X ++ "er"; cat => n);
     cat => t;
     type => T;
     sem => -)
```

where ++ is a predefined function "string concatenation". The hyphen at address `pred.sem` marks that it is a leaf (no subframes; see Appendix A).

Example:

```
R1( (pred => (stem => "employ"; cat => v);
     cat => p;
     sem => (ag => (cat => n; type => [human]);
             go => (cat => n; type => [human]))) ) =

    (pred => (stem => "employer"; cat => n);
     cat => t;
     type => [human];
     sem => - );
```

which derives the noun *employer* from the verb *to employ*.

R2 is the rule for gerund formation:

```
R2( (pred => (stem => X; cat => v);
     type => p;
     sem  => (ag => Y; go => Z)) ) =

    (pred => (stem => X ++"ing"; cat => v);
     type => t;
     sem => (go => Z))
```

Example:

```
R2( (pred => (stem => "employ"; cat => v);
     type => p;
     sem => (ag => (type => [human]); go => (type => [human])) ) =

    (pred => (stem => "employing"; cat => v);
     type => t;
     sem => (go => (type => [human])) )
```

As Mackenzie (1986) argues, the gerund preserves the goal-argument, as in: *Employing immigrants* (becomes more difficult). Full nominalization requires the execution of a second rule working on the output of R2 that removes the goal (valency reduction) and makes the predicate category nominal:

```
R3( (pred => (cat => v);
     type => t;
     sem  => (go => Z)) ) =

    (pred => (cat => n);
     type => t;
     sem => -);
```

In general, a predicate formation rule can make one or more of the following alterations to the frame (cf. Dik, 1985).

(1) change a category

(2) rewrite a string (suffixing, prefixing, infixing)

(3) move or remove a subframe

(4) split up a function

We already saw instances of the operations (1), (2), and (3). Removing a subframe occurs in cases of valency reduction, such as the derivation of intransitive *to drink* from transitive *to drink*. An example of splitting up a function node will be given in the next section.

In the rules R1-R3 we have ignored the effects on the meaning definitions. The meaning definition of the derived frame is usually derived from the meaning definition of the input frame. Arguments that are removed may be inherited by the output, not in the semantic functions as such, but in the meaning conditions. We will describe this in section 4.4.3. This can be used for the analysis of phrases like: (he is an) *employer of immigrants*.

4.2.4. Semantic functions

The semantic functions in Functional Grammar indicate the different roles which the entities referred to by terms can play in the states of affairs designated by the predication in which they occur (the term "function" should not be taken in its mathematical sense). They are somewhat reminiscent of those distinguished in Fillmore's case grammar, but their definition puts more emphasis on the semantic aspect. Case roles have also been used extensively in Artificial Intelligence. Although the importance of case functions is generally recognized, there is still little agreement on the exact set of functions. Some AI researchers have given up this task and want the user let them define himself. However, this can easily lead to confusion and uncontrolled diversions when the knowledge base is to be shared by many users. In our view, determining a minimal language-universal set of semantic functions is an empirical issue. It is not a trivial task, but we cannot evade it if we want to give knowledge bases a scientific foundation. We must keep in mind that each proposal is necessarily open-ended.

Let us first review some of the other proposals and then consider Functional Grammar and the criteria adopted there.

In his seminal paper, Fillmore (1968) identified the following case roles: agentive, instrumental, dative, factitive, locative, objective. The *agentive* denotes the animate instigator of the action; *instrumental*, an inanimate force or object involved; *dative* an animate being affected by the action; *factitive*, the object resulting from the action; *locative*, the location or orientation; *objective*: everything else. In Fillmore (1977), this set was slightly changed. New were the *counter-agent*, the force or resistance against which an action is carried out, and the *Experiencer*, the participant undergoing some experience. Despite the fact that Fillmore used names derived from surface case systems, his functions are intended as "deep cases". For example, in the two sentences:

(a) the key opened the door

(b) the janitor opened the door with a key

the term "key" is assigned an *instrument* role in both cases.

In Artificial Intelligence, Schank (1975) developed a representation for meaning called *conceptual dependencies* that is based on language-independent conceptual relationships between objects and actions. His set of conceptual roles bears a strong resemblance to the more linguistically motivated notions of case. Schank distinguishes cases roles filled by objects (actor, object, attribuant, recipient/donor), case roles filled by conceptualizations, that is, other actions (instrument, attribute, attribuant, cause, reason, enablement), and case roles filled by other conceptual categories (time, location, state attribute, state change).

Winograd (1983) presents a version of Halliday's systemic grammar. In this framework, the concept of *process type* plays a fundamental role. Each clause is analyzed as expressing a certain process. These processes can be organized in a system of five basic *process types*. Each process type determines a range of "central participants", as the following table shows:

process type	central participants
material	agent, medium, range, beneficiary
mental	cognizant, phenomenon
verbal	sayer,addressee,verbalization
attributive	carrier,attribute
equative	identified,identifier

Fig. 4.4 Basic process types

Besides these basic functions, there is a range of circumstantial functions that can be specified for each process type. Examples are: location, extent, motion, cause, manner, accompaniment, purpose and matter.

Functional Grammar also makes a distinction between the basic slots of a predicate frame and slots that are added in the process of predication formation. The terms filling the basic slots are called *arguments* and the other ones are called *satellites*. Arguments function in the definition of the SoA type as such, while satellites give further information pertaining to the SoA instantiation as a whole. A general test for distinguishing arguments from satellites is the following: a satellite can be left out without affecting the grammaticality or the meaning of the remaining construction. When arguments are left out, the remainder is either ungrammatical or only interpretable on another reading of the predicate (Dik, 1989fc). Dik warns that this criterion cannot be applied mechanically, since sometimes arguments may be suppressed in specified settings too. But for our present purposes, the criterion is good enough.

Let us now start by considering the semantic functions that can occur in argument position. In FG, the determination of these semantic functions is closely related to the basic typology of States of Affairs. The typology is based on two parameters, *Dynamism* and *Control* (figure 4.5)

	+dynamic EVENT	**-dynamic** SITUATION
+controlled	action	position
-controlled	process	state

Fig. 4.5 Basic typology of States of Affairs

Some simple examples of each type:

(a) John moved the rock (action)

(b) The rock moved (process)

(c) The rock is heavy (state)

(d) John was sitting on the rock (position)

The parameters Controlled and Dynamic are important both semantically and morpho-syntactically. The dynamic/static opposition is well-known in knowledge engeneering and does not need justification. The controlled/uncontrolled opposition is used less often. Nevertheless it is crucial in defining the very notion of an action. So according to Davidson (1966), the logical form of an action sentence is "it was the intention of X to do p". Wierzbicka (1980) puts it as follows: "for someone to do something means for something to become sayable about something because of something sayable about this someone because he wants it". This definition includes the notion of *want*. It is not the case that all actions are intentional. But, as Chisholm (1966) says, "to act is always to endeavour to bring it about that there is some change, but the changes that a man does bring about need not be those that he endeavours to bring about". Therefore, Chisholm himself has proposed the definition: "he made it happen that *p* in the endeavour to make it happen that *q*". For our discussion, it is not necessary to give a complete definition of an action. It is sufficient to observe that it is not possible to define an action without taking recourse to some notion of control (or intention, or want). This is one motivation for the parameter Control. For linguistic motivations, see the work of Dik.

Using the typology given above, the semantic functions can be defined as follows. We distinguish functions that can occur as first argument and those that can occur as second or third argument.

First arguments

Agent	the entity controlling an action "*John* was reading a book"
Positioner	the entity controlling a position "*John* kept his money in an old sock"
Processed	the entity that is primarily involved in a Process "*The rock* moved"
Force	the non-controlling entity instigating a Process "*The earthquake* moved the rock"
Zero	the entity primarily involved in a State "*The cup* was on the table"

Other arguments

Goal	the entity affected or effected by an action or a position "John wrote *the book* in 1965"
Recipient	the entity to which something is transferred "John gave the book *to Peter*"
Location	the place where some entity is located "The cup is *on the table*"
Path	the path along which some entity moves or is moved "The wind blew the leaves *into the kitchen*"

Semantic functions are characterized in two ways:

(1) *semantic*: each function has a certain definition. Note that the definition makes use of the SoA types; a certain function is always defined in the context of a "scenario". The function definitions are intertwined.

(2) *morpho-syntactic*: each function has certain syntactic and morphological properties. For example, the Agent is assigned Subject in a non-passive sentence.

A morpho-syntactic property of the Goal in English is that it takes no morphological or prepositional marking.

In certain cases we shall want to mark a first argument for the function Experiencer, when the State of Affairs is crucially dependent upon the mental faculties of some animate being. Examples of such SoA's are *believe, dream, love*. In FG, Experiencer is treated as as feature of the semantic function (in most cases, the *processed*) rather than a function of its own.

It is sometimes useful to have types of functions. For example, Agent and Force share the property of instigating a certain change. This can be expressed by allowing a function Instigator such that Agent and Force are *subtypes* of Instigator. Still using the parameters of Control and Dynamism, we can distinguish the following types: Instigator, Controller, Affected, Controlled. We also introduce the type Participant as a supertype of all functions that take an entity as their argument (and not a location or path). So Instigator, Controller, Affected and Controlled are subtypes of Participant, and so is Recipient. If an argument is not a Participant, then we call it a Complement.

Another useful function feature is Protagonist (cf. Schachter, 1977). The Protagonist is the semantic correlate of what we have called "first argument" above. It can be seen as a feature of Agents, Forces, Processeds etc. In contrast to the feature Experiencer (which only occurs with certain process types), the feature Protagonist is always attached to *some* function, if a predicate frame has more than one argument (if there is only one argument, the notion of Protagonist as "central" participant looses its meaning). Which one is viewed as Protagonist, is a matter of priority. The following simple priority rules are sufficient:

Controller > Controlled
Instigator > Affected

This says that if we have a Controller or Instigator, this one automatically becomes the Protagonist. If there is neither a Controller nor an Instigator, the next candidate is Affected or Controlled, resulting in a Processed function. Note that we define Protagonist as a derived function, one that is assigned on the basis of other ones. Some advantages of this protagonist assignment procedure are:

(1) It permits an elegant treatment of borderline cases such as certain causatives. Normally, the Controller of an action is the same as the Instigator. However in some cases this does not hold. Consider for example the following causative construction. In English, verbs of locomotion may be causativized by conversion, i.e. without an explicit suffix or copula:

(a) John raced the horse past the barn

(b) He jumped the horse over the fence

(c) Winnetou swam his horse across the river

In these cases, *John* etc is the Controller of action whereas *the horse* is the Instigator and the Controlled. Application of the priority rules causes *John* to be the Protagonist, which is in accordance with the form.

(2) By separating the Protagonist assignment from the definition of the functions themselves, it is easier to specify predicate formation rules. For example, if we want to derive the causative frames above from their non-causative basic frames,

we only need to decouple the Instigator from the Controller. In the basic frame of *race*, these two functions are co-referential. In the derived frame, they are split up. We don't need a new function "Cause". Other examples are certain ergative constructions where the Controller/Instigator is omitted. Then the Affected or Controlled argument automatically becomes the Protagonist.

(3) An advantage of a quite different nature is that we are now also in a position to characterize the semantic function Goal more precisely. The Goal was defined as the entity "affected or effected by an action of position". However, the qualification "affected" is not so appropriate in the case of a position. In that case, the Goal is rather the *Controlled* entity.† So it seems better to define the Goal as a feature that is assigned in a way similar to Protagonist. Whereas Protagonist is the central participant, Goal is the second one. In the case that there is no second one (there is not an affected or controlled entity), then there is no Goal either. From this definition of Goal, we derive the following facts as lemmata:

- there can be only a Goal if there is a Protagonist
- the Goal is either Affected or Controlled
- the Goal can never be the first argument
- the Goal is a participant

Precisely these facts are commonly used to characterize the Goal.

We now define Func, the set of primary semantic functions, as an information system:

Definition 4.4 Sf (F,Δ,Con,⊢) is an information system defined by:

(i) F = { Δ, Instigator, Affected, Controller, Controlled, Location, Path, Participant, Protagonist, Complement, Experiencer, Fro, To, Via }

(ii) Instigator ⊢ Participant
Controller ⊢ Participant
Experiencer ⊢ Participant
Affected ⊢ Participant
Controlled ⊢ Participant
Path ⊢ Complement,
Location ⊢ Complement

(iii) Participant and Complement are mutually exclusive (that is, {Participant, Complement} ⊢ ∇). Location and Path are mutually exclusive. Fro, Via and To are mutually exclusive. All sets not including mutually exclusive functions are consistent.

(iv) Δ is the top element and entailed by each function.

end 4.4

We use the following abbrevations for the most frequent elements of this information system:

---

† One of the morpho-syntactic differences between Controlled and Affected Goals is the ease of passivization. Affected Goals can be assigned Subject function, but Controlled ones only in special cases (cf. Kawamura,1986).

ag	agent	[Instigator, Controller, Protagonist,Participant]
pos	positioner	[Controller, Protagonist,Participant]
fo	force	[Instigator, Protagonist,Participant]
proc	processed	[Affected, Protagonist,Participant]
	zero	[Participant]
go	goal	[Affected,Participant] or [Controlled, Participant]
co	complement	[Complement]
rec	recipient	[To, Participant]
so	source	[Fro, Path, Complement]
dir	direction	[To, Path, Complement]
loc	location	[Location, Complement]
exp	proc-exp	[Affected, Protagonist, Experiencer, Participant]

The system presented here is a kind of micro-analysis of the FG definitions given above. The system permits us to derive that an agent is a controller, since agent ⊢ [Controller]. It is also more fine-grained. For example, instead of having only "goal" as second argument (participant), we also have "complement", and "goal" can be subclassified in "affected" and "controlled". The list of the most frequent elements does not exhaust all possible elements of the system. For example, the use of Fro and To is not necessarily limited to Paths. This can be used profitably in, for instance, the specification of verbs like *to include* or *to exclude*. Consider the frame "exclude someone *from* a SoA". The SoA is not a Path, so the function *source*, in the literal sense, is not adequate. To account for this function, FG would have to invent a new function. In our framework, the function is already present as a possible candidate ([Fro,Participant]).

Another advantage of the typing of functions is that we can exploit the subsumption relation. For example, consider a frame that can both take a force and an agent as first argument (there are numerous examples of these, "to blow", "to destroy", etc). The standard approach in FG requires that we define two predicate frames, one with first argument fo and one with first argument ag. Admittedly, this is not too bad; there are differences in meaning between the two uses. But there is also a lot in common. In our approach, we can account for the shared meaning by having only *one* frame for "destroy", with first argument [Instigator]. The two uses (controlled or not controlled) can then be seen as subtypes of this frame, where the first argument function is more specialized (these subtypes can be modeled as predicate schemata, see 4.5). This makes the representation more efficient.

Note the following things about semantic functions:

- The semantic definition of the functions always refers to the whole frame. It is not the question what role the entity plays "in reality", but in the "projected world", the scene set up by the SoA type.

- Remember that not every argument of a frame has a primary semantic function. We will also introduce secondary functions and satellites. Primary functions are only assigned to the central arguments, those that are necessary for the definition of the SoA. For example, the verb *get(something)* has a predicate frame containing only two functions, proc and comp. In some other theories, *get* has an additional function Donor. Such a function can be defended on semantic considerations, for example, on the basis of the symmetry of *give* and *get*. However, *get* behaves differently from *give* in several respects: (a) it is very difficult to passivize a sentence with *get*, in contrast to *give*; (b) the Recipient can be assigned an Object function (in English), whereas the Donor can not; (c) the Recipient in *give* is always explicitly or implicitly (elliptically) present, whereas the *Donor* seems to be optional in the *get* frame Therefore we conclude that Donor is not a nuclear function in *get*. Now it seems (this is an empirical question) that other frames and frames in other languages apparently never have a *Donor*. That is why Donor is not considered as a primary semantic function. Note that there are no a priori reasons why this should be the case; but neither is the whole issue arbitrary, since there are empirical (linguistic) criteria for favoring one solution over the other.

4.2.5. Places and paths

The location function loc occurs for instance in the frame of *keep*: keep(pos x person)(go y thing)(loc p place). The use of loc as a semantic function should be distinguished from the use of loc as a satellite that can be added to any SoA instantiation.

Examples of dir(ection) and so(urce) can be found in the frames of *send* and *come*. My own account differs slightly from the one in (Dik,1978) in that I prefer to introduce a unifying function type path. One simple reason for this is that most frames that can take a dir can also take a so and vice versa. Other arguments can be found in (Jackendoff,1983). Jackendoff makes a fundamental distinction between the categories PLACE and PATH (besides others, like EVENT and THING). Both PLACE and PATH can be specified further by means of PLACE-FUNCTIONS or PATH-FUNCTIONS. Examples of PLACE-FUNCTIONS are IN, UNDER, ON, or BETWEEN. Examples of PATH-FUNCTIONS are TO, FROM, VIA and AROUND. Translated to our present framework, some examples are (term operators and syntactic functions are ignored):

(a) The lamp is standing on the floor.
    e stand(x lamp)(loc p on(y floor))
    (derived from the frame stand([thing])(loc [place]))

(b) The hunter ran toward the mountain (from the house, through the tunnel).
    e run(ag m hunter)([path,to] y mountain))

(c) The mouse ran from under the table
    e run(ag m mouse)([path,fro] p under(y table)))

In these examples, on() and under() are one-place predicate frames denoting a place. As can be seen from the third example, place-functions can be used in path expressions. The advantage of this approach is that we can confine ourselves to a small set of semantic functions. It is not necessary to have an additional semantic function for each locative or directional function. Consequently, the number of frames for a particular predicate such as *run* can be drastically reduced.

We follow Jackendoff in his treatment of place functions, but we do not see sufficient reason to introduce a special type PATH. Jackendoff's main argument is that PATH's can be referred to, as in the sentence: *John passed (run) there*. However, the reference is always by means of a location or entity: *Where to*, *Where from* etc. Therefore we prefer to have path functions (`fro`, `to`, `via`), but not path referents.

I want to discuss one objection that could be made against my treatment. Verbal predicates expressing some movement - that is, including a `path` function -, differ in the perspective from which the movement is described. The verb *come* describes a movement towards the Speaker or some other given reference point, whereas *go* describes a movement away from the reference point. The verb *run* in the example above is neutral in this respect. We could express the differences between these verb frames by means of the semantic function:

(a) `go(proc x thing)(dir [place])`

(b) `come(proc x thing)(so [place])`

(c) `run(ag x animate)([path] [place])`

The `dir` function in the frame of `go` indicates that the movement is always thought as away from the reference point. But the path inserted in the frame may be both a movement towards and a movement away from an object:

(a1) John went to Mexico
`go(proc x John)(dir y Mexico))`

(a2) John went (away) from Amsterdam.
`go(proc x John)(so y Amsterdam))`

Because of these facts, it seems better to assign a general function `path` to *come* and *go*, and account for the perspective in another way. In only a few instances, such as the verbs *exclude* and *include*, the use of `dir` and `so` seems appropriate.

A further classification of movement predicate frames is possible by putting more selection restrictions on the `path` argument. Jackendoff makes a distinction between *bounded* and *non-bounded* paths. In bounded paths, the reference object or place is an endpoint of the path. In non-bounded paths, or directions, the reference object or place does not fall on the path, but would be if the path where extended some unspecified distance. The difference is reflected in the prepositions, as in the sentences:

(1a) John ran to the house. (bounded path)

(1b) John ran toward the house. (direction)

(2a) John ran from the house. (bounded path)

(2b) John ran away from the house. (direction)

In a third class of paths, *routes*, the reference object or place is related to some point in the interior of the path. An example of a verb requiring a route is *pass*. A car can pass "by the house", or "through the tunnel", but not "to the garage". The predicate frame for *pass* is then:

`pass(proc x thing)([path,via] location)`

For more discussion of movement verbs, see the book of Jackendoff. Before leaving this topic, I have to make one remark considering the place-functions. In the examples given, it is assumed without saying that these place-functions coincide with the English spatial prepositions. Other languages will have different prepositions, hence different place-functions. Some languages do not use prepositions but case marking for location and direction. In these languages, a set of *abstract* place-functions should be defined. In this way a universal set of abstract place-functions can be found on the basis of cross-linguistic research. The same abstract functions can be used in languages like English to *classify* the different (prepositional) place-functions. In some cases, there will be more than one preposition that express the same abstract place-function. This may be due to additional features of the reference object, as in French (whether it is an island, a city, a country, etc.; cf. King, 1987), or to some language-specific irreducible semantic difference.

Summarizing, we can conclude that, using the semantic features {Path, Fro, To, Via}, together with place functions such as `on()`, optional selection restrictions on the argument (typically, `[place]`, but not necessarily so) and additional features such as `bounded`, we can represent quite a range of locative arguments. Place functions have not been used in Functional Grammar before, but, in my opinion, they can bring much relief to the burden placed on semantic functions. The fact that I have used an information system to characterize the semantic functions, is also helpful for keeping the number of different predicate frames as small as possible (the example of *run*).

4.3. LEXICAL STRUCTURES

One of the functions of the thesaurus is to structure the terms into semantic nets. The structural relations are used in deductive and associative reasoning. In this section, we introduce two important ones, namely, *taxonomy* and *contrast sets*. Taxonomy features the inheritance of attributes and selection restrictions, and thus it is a kind of entailment relation. In this way we can define an information system of predicate frames. The notion of contrast sets is used to establish the consistency relation of the information system. Some other lexical structures are also considered.

4.3.1. Taxonomy

The basic lexical structure is the taxonomic structure of *hyponymy* (or *subsumption*) relations. Subsumption is important to the knowledge base because:

(1) subsumption is used in a certain kind of reasoning. For example, if we know that John has seen a robin, then we can infer that he has seen a bird;

(2) subsumption is used to organize the knowledge because of the inheritance property. Information that holds for a supertype is inherited by all its subtypes. This makes it possible to store the piece of information only once. For example, if "name" is an attribute of "person", and a "student" is a "person", then "name" is an attribute of "student" too (attribute inheritance). Moreover, if the age of students is between 18 and 27, and a sophomore is a student, then the age of sophomores is between 18 and 27 too (constraint inheritance).

One of the notorious difficulties with taxonomies is the definition of the upper layers. These are usually quite abstract, like "thing" or "abstract". It is difficult to assign a consistent semantic content to such notions. To solve this problem we assume that the upper layers of the taxonomy are theoretically defined. The elements occurring there are called primitive types and we do not assume that their names necessarily correspond with their usage in natural language (as we do assume with the normal predicate frames). Their definition is given by the linguistic theory.

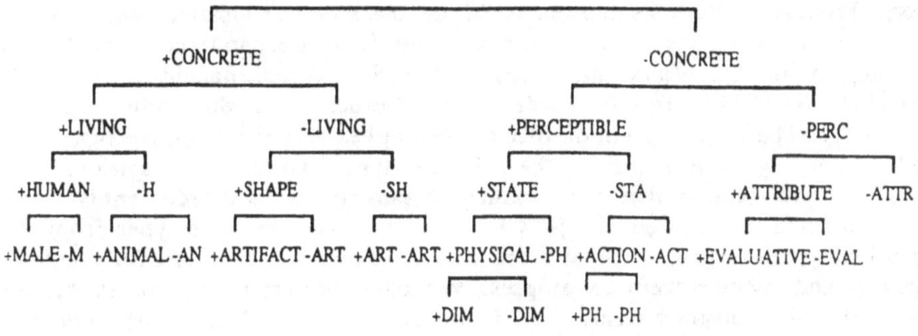

Fig. 4.6 HPRIM features of Aarts, 1976

The distinction between primitive types and specific types has been made also by Aarts (Aarts, 1976) who calls them higher level primary features (HPRIM) and lower level primary features (LPRIM) respectively. One important difference between the two is that the first make up a binary taxonomy while the second ones are often neither binary nor taxonomically ordered. Aarts diagram of high level primary features is reproduced in fig. 4.6.

The Longman Dictionary uses a small number of basic semantic codes that are sometimes more and sometimes less specific than those of Aarts (see Voogt, 1987). The codes are reproduced in fig. 4.7. Some more codes are used for various combinations.

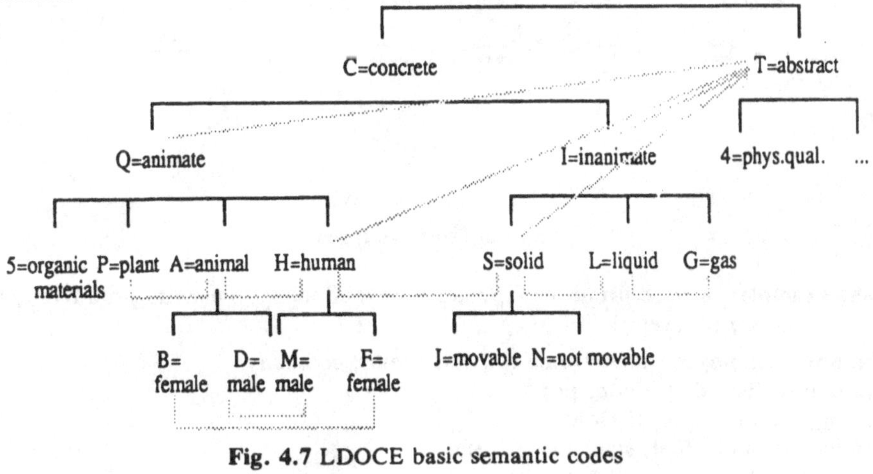

Fig. 4.7 LDOCE basic semantic codes

Our own taxonomy of primitive types is not much different from these two, but we prefer to derive it from the linguistic framework we are working with. We already made a distinction between first-order entities (concrete things), second-order entities (SoA's), third-order entities (intensions, propositions) and fourth-order propositions (utterances). We also noted that SoA's can be further subdivided into Actions, Processes, Positions and States. In the discussion of location functions, we came upon the category PLACE. Time referents form a separate category TIME. The category of Qualifiers introduces three other types, namely QUALITY, MANNER, STATUS (for first-order, second-order, and third-order entities, respectively). The primitive notion of Control implies also the primitive type "animate". Finally, we will also need the primitive type "human" (or "spiritual") to distinguish those entities that can produce or perceive a third-order entity. The resulting schema is modeled in fig. 4.8. To distinguish the basic types from the normal lexical predicates, we write them sometimes between brackets, for example, [animate], and picture them as ellipses. We have preferred to give suggestive names rather than abstract terms like "first-order entity" or "third-order quality". Subtypes at the same level in this tree are mutually exclusive but they do not necessarily cover up the domain of their parent.

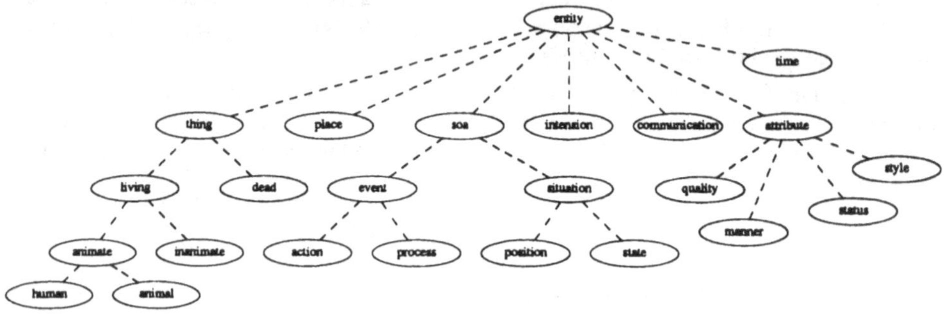

Fig. 4.8 Primitive types

Some examples of each primitive type are (conventionally, we write primitive types between square brackets):

[human]: employee, man, woman, dwarf, child, company
[animate]: fish, dog, dodo, pet
[living]: animal, tree, E.Coli
[material]: rock, fuel, star, house, vehicle
[thing]: circle
[action]: production (produce), transaction (give, sell), comparison, game

[process]: rain, corruption (corrupt), fall
[state]: sleep, anger, existence
[position]: management (manage),
[intension]: desire, idea, belief, theory, concept
[communication]: word, symbol, sentence, language
[place]: in(), between()
[time]: day, hour, winter
[quality]: temperature, number, color, size
[manner]: speed, democracy, intensity
[status]: probability, truth

It goes without saying that far more subdivisions could have been made, but I think this can be done by lexical means without recourse to primitives. The set of primitives should be kept as small as possible. Subtyping between predicate frames does the rest of the job.

In some cases, the primitive types have to be complemented by semantic features. For example, first-order entities can be either non-discrete (fuel, grass) or collective (company) or individual (employee). The respective primitive types are [material,mass], [human,collective] and [human,individual].

Note also that, although the lower primitive features are mutually exclusive, a certain predicate may belong to several types. For example, we distinguish three predicate frames with predicate *government*: one of type [position] (in the sense of governing), one of type [manner] (the manner or system of governing), and one of type [human] (the body of persons governing a State). Positing the existence of three different predicate frames is justified by the fact that they have different types.

Now we have defined the domain Ptype, we can define a more general taxonomic ordering on predicate frames. To be more precise, we define a domain of *types* consisting of primitive types and predicate frames. The taxonomical ordering is transitive, reflexive and anti-symmetric. We define it as follows.

Definition 4.5. Let T be a Fund of predicate frames. Then a *taxonomy* on T is a structure (T $\cup$ Ptype, $\prec$) where $\prec$ is a partial ordering called hyponymy or "isa" with a top element Δ, such that

(i) $p \prec \psi_p(\texttt{type})$, for all $p \in$ Fund.

(ii) if p and q are two predicate frames, with address trees A_p and A_q respectively, and $p \prec q$, then:
$\forall\, \sigma \in$ Sf, if address $\texttt{sem}.\sigma \in A_q$, then sem.$\sigma' \in A_q$, for some $\sigma' < \sigma$.

end 4.5

The first requirement on the taxonomy makes it an extension of the type slot relationship. If p is a predicate frame, and its type is q (where $q \in$ Ptype), then p "isa" q.

Part (ii) says that semantic information (in particular, the semantic functions) is inherited from type to subtype. This is almost definitional for a taxonomic structure. Recall that Sf indicates the set of semantic functions. In definition 4.4, this set was defined by means of an information system. The ordering '<' is the ordering induced by this information system. The second requirement can be compared with the *attribute inheritance* in semantic data models.

Examples of taxonomic relationships are:

```
(pred => (stem => "government");
 cat => t;
 type => [human,collective]) ≺
       [human]
(pred => (stem => "dog"); cat => t; type => [animate]) ≺
       [animate]
```

These two relationships follow from the definition, part (i). However, the taxonomy may contain other links as well, for example:

```
(pred => (stem => "dog"); cat => t; type => [animate]) ≺
       (pred => (stem => "mammal"); cat => t; type => [animate])
```

The taxonomic ordering will be used shortly to define an information system on the Fund.

For an illustration of the second part of the definition, let us take the verbs *to kill* and *to murder*. If *to murder* $\prec$ *to kill*, and *to kill* has an agent and a goal function, then so has *to murder*. Since we have defined a typing on semantic functions, it is possible that the functions σ' and σ are not equal, but just $\sigma' \prec \sigma$ (see 4.2.4).

4.3.2. Semantic fields

Under semantic fields, originally introduced by Wilhelm von Humboldt (*Bedeutungsfeld*), and developed by Saussure, Weisgerber, Trier and others (Schmidt, 1973), we usually understand a "collection of related words" (cf. Grandy,1987). In our framework we restrict the meaning to what are traditionally called contrast sets.

Antonyms are pairs of predicate frames that are the binary opposites of each other (in a certain context), such as *male/female*, *small/big*, *honor/dishonor*. The generalization of an antonym is the *contrast set*. A basic contrast set typically consists of a term L (the covering term) and a set of predicate frames E_1, ... E_n (the members of the set, also called hyponyms) such that the extension of each E_i is a subset of the extension of L and the extensions of the E_i are pairwise disjoint.

Most common and interesting examples of contrast sets involve simple lexical covering terms and in many cases the union of the extensions of the members exhausts the extension of L. Examples:

```
day <=> sunday, monday, tuesday,...,saturday.
day <=> work-day,rest-day.
vegetable <=>  artichoke,..., zucchini.
parent([animate]) <=> mother([animate]), father([animate]).
color([thing]) <=> red, green, blue, yellow, orange, brown, purple,
black, white.
```

Here the predicate frame before the <=> denotes the covering term. The hyponym list may contain the symbol "..." to indicate non-exhaustiveness. A graphical representation of contrast sets is given in Fig. 4.9 and inspired by the NIAM approach. The unlabelled edge denotes a subtype relationship and the "x" marks the sister subtypes as excluding one another.

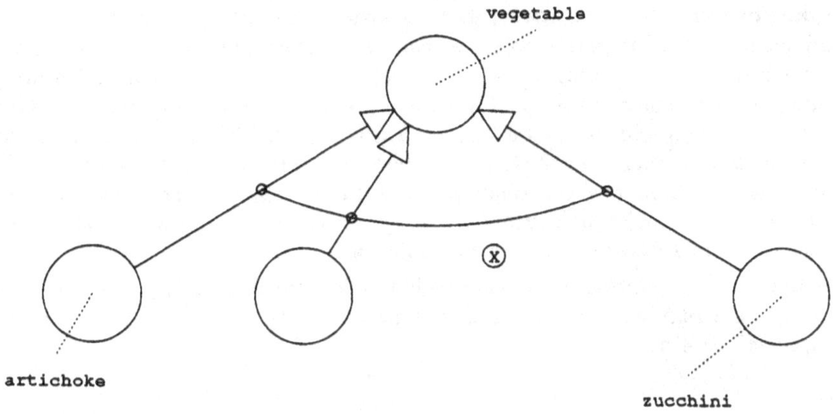

Fig. 4.9 Contrast set pictured with NIAM exclusion

Contrast sets are of three types. The first type is illustrated by the first three examples. Both the covering term and the hyponyms are simple T-frames. In the second type of contrast set, the covering term is a relator and the hyponyms are relators too (example: parent). In the third type, the hyponyms are qualifiers, such as colors.

Contrast sets of natural kinds are often non-exhaustive and somewhat open-ended, while those for artifacts are often closed and exhaustive. Note that contrast sets occur at different levels of generality. "Dog" will be a member of the contrast set specified by mammal but wil also cover a contrast set that includes poodle and dachshund. "Dog" may also be a member of another contrast set, say, of pets. In the examples above, the first three contrast sets were made up by terms whereas the fourth one contained qualifiers. In such a case, the covering term is usually an attribute, although occasionally it may be a qualifier as well:

```
red <=> scarlet,crimson,....
```

The use of contrast sets requires some discipline. The following rules are adapted from Grandy (1987):

(1) "layering": if contrast set S contains a proper subset covered by another term *t*, then this subset should be replaced by *t* and a new contrast set should be formed with covering term *t*;

(2) "completeness": each contrast set should be made as broad as possible (without changing the cover term of course). Ideally, the contrast set exhausts the extension of the covering term.

Contrast sets dealing with the same domain can be grouped together. A group of interdependent contrast sets is called a semantic field.

In the examples above, an isa-relation exists between the members of the contrast set and the covering term. However, there is also a class of contrast sets in which the relationship is one of part/whole. A car has a brake and wheels, the human body has a heart and a mouth, a room has walls and a ceiling and a real number has an integer part. The part-of relation must be distinguished from the "location" relationship. For example, a person can have a pencil in his hand, or a room can give room to some persons. In these cases, there is a relationship of "location" but not of part/whole. A part/whole relationship requires that the part is a *functional* part of the whole. There is, of course, an important connection between part/whole and location: if x is a part of y, then x is located in y.

Whereas the location relation is transitive - if x is located in y, and y in z, then x is located in z -, the part/whole relation is in general not. So in Fig. 4.10, "ring" is a part of "piston", but not of "car".

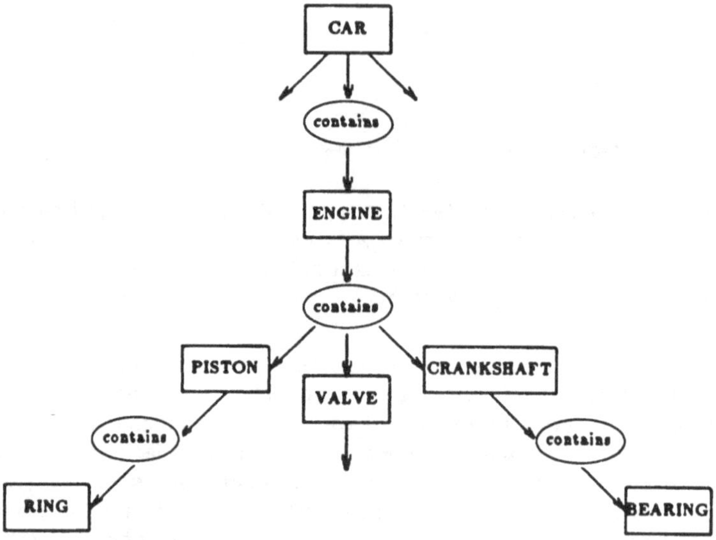

Fig 4.10 Part-of relationships (adapted from Cammarata & Melkanoff, 1984)

In our framework, `part([thing])` is an independent predicate frame. So we represent the information in a contrast set as:

```
part(engine)  <=> piston, valve, crankshaft, ....
```

and do not use a special semantic function "part_of", since this is neither necessary nor warranted by linguistic data.

4.3.3. Information system

Using the taxonomic ordering and the contrast sets, we can define an information system on the Fund (cf. 4.5).

Definition 4.6. An information system for the taxonomy (T, <) with a set of contrast sets Contrast is a structure (D,Δ,Con,⊢) with the usual axioms and where:

(i) dataset D = T;

(ii) $\{a\} \vdash b$ iff $a \prec b$

(iii) u is inconsistent iff $[u]$ contains a pair $\{a,b\}$ that is (a subset of) some contrast set $c \in$ Contrast.

Con is defined as the not inconsistent subsets of D.

end 4.6

The information system structure of the Fund makes the Fund a structure of types. This structure can be considered as a refinement of the type structure given in the previous chapter. At that place, we equated predicates with types. Now we can be more precise. A type cannot be identified with a predicate, although they are not independent. The first difference is in the step from predicate to predicate frame. If we have several predicate frames with the same predicate (such as the three frames distinguished for `government`), they nonetheless lead to different types. The second difference is in the step from predicate frame to deductive closure of the predicate frame. This makes it possible, in principle, to recognize synonyms: if two predicate frames entail each other, their deductive closure is the same. It is an open issue whether true synonyms exist.

4.4. COMPLEX FRAMES

The basic predicate frames given in the thesaurus make up the building blocks of our language. We first define a conceptual language consisting of complex frames. A complex frame is an extension of the predicate frame, in such a way that each complex frame is subsumed by some predicate frame.

4.4.1. Frame subsumption

The definition of frame subsumption is again derived from Ait-Kaci (1984). In contrast to the taxonomic structure, frame subsumption is purely syntactic. It is not a relationship on types but on forms (where the forms are f-structures).

Intuitively, one frame is subsumed by another if the former is more specified than the latter. This may mean that it contains more addresses (1), or that the symbols at each address are more specific (3) with respect to the ordering on the domain in question, or that the co-reference conditions are more restrictive (2).

Definition 4.7 An f-structure $\phi_1 = (A_1, \psi_1, \tau_1)$ is subsumed by an f-structure $\phi_2 = (A_2, \psi_2, \tau_2)$ (written $\phi_1 \leqq \phi_2$), if and only if

1. $A_2 \subseteq A_1$;
2. $\mathrm{Ker}(\tau_2) \subseteq \mathrm{Ker}(\tau_1)$;
3. $\psi_1(w) < \psi_2(w)$, $\forall\, w \in L^*$ (address space).

end 4.7

"Ker" stands for the kernel of the tag function, that is, the coreference relation defined by $\tau \circ \tau^{-1}$. In other words, addresses a and b are in the same equivalence class iff $\tau(b) = \tau(a)$.

The ordering "<" in (3.) stands for the ordering on the domain(s). This ordering may be defined differently from one domain to another. However, if some ordering is defined on each domain, then these orderings together can be used for defining a subsumption ordering on frames over these domains. In some sense, we can say that the frame subsumption ordering is inherited from the orderings on the domains.

Example. Let ϕ_0 be the predicate frame of *to bar (a place)*:

```
(pred => (stem => "bar"; cat => v);
 cat => p;
 sem => (ag => (type => [human]);
         go => (type => [place])))
```

Then the following frame ϕ_1 is a complex frame subsumed by ϕ_0:

```
(pred => (stem => "bar"; cat => v);
 cat => p;
 sem => (ag => (pred => (stem => "soldier"; cat => n);
                cat => t;
                type => [human]);
         go => (pred => (stem => "road"; cat => n);
                cat => t;
                type => [place])))
```

It is easily seen that all addresses in ϕ_1 are also in ϕ_0. The co-reference constraints are trivial.† The ψ-functions are equal on all addresses $w \in A_0$, and for all other $w \in \mathrm{L}$, $\psi_0(w) = \Delta$ (the top element).

Note that the set of predicate frames in the Fund is usually finite (although, in principle, the predicate formation rules may cause it to be infinite), but that the set of frames that are subsumed by some frame in the Fund is infinite, due to the recursiveness of the frames. For example, we have frames `father([animate])`, `father(father([animate]))` etc. In other words, the subsumption ordering defines a *language* of frames: a frame is part of the language iff it is is subsumed by a basic predicate frame. This idea of defining a language by means of subsumption is explored in the next section.

4.4.2. Complex predicate frame

We now go over to define the complex predicate frame. Complex predicate frames are necessary for the formal definition of predicate schemata.

Complex predicate frames are subsumed by basic predicate frames. In fact, the

† Non-trivial examples are difficult to give yet. In chapter 6, we will see that at the level of the predication, the address of the syntactic function Subject co-refers with the address of one the semantic functions. If in predication p, Subject co-refers with Agent, then it does so in all predications q such that $q \leq p$.

constraint must be even tighter. Not only the complex frame itself must be subsumed by a basic predicate frame, but the same must hold for each P-frame, T-frame, Q-frame that is a subframe of it. Putting this requirement on complex predicate frames, has the same purpose as the FG statement that nuclear predications are formed by *inserting* terms in predicate frames (or one-place open predications as restrictors in terms). The advantage of our treatment is that it does not refer to a *procedure* but to a mathematical *condition*.

In the following, we will assume that each complex predicate frame is not only subsumed by at least one basic predicate frame, but that there is also not more than one. Otherwise, the frame would be ambiguous. We assume that the supertypes specified for the frame and for its arguments are sufficient for distinguishing between several frames. This does not mean that sentences cannot be ambiguous; there may be several underlying clauses. But in the underlying clause, all predicate frames are uniquely identified. If p is a complex predicate frame, then $\hat{}p$ is the basic predicate frame such that p is subsumed by $\hat{}p$.

Complex predicate frames differ from basic predicate frames too by the fact that the address space L is extended. The extensions are fourfold (let L be the address space defined earlier for predicate frames):

(1) L ⋃ {sat, instr, ben, reason, frame, tmp, loc, ...}. That is, a complex frame may contain satellites for instrument, beneficiary etc, and frame satellites for time and location. Example:

```
(pred => (stem => "bar"; cat => v);
 cat => p;
 sem => (ag => (type => [human]);
        (go => (pred => (stem => "road"; cat => n);
                  type => [place]));
 sat => (instr => (pred => (stem => "truck"; cat => n);
                   cat => t;
                   type => [thing])))
```

"Barring roads with trucks"

(2) L ⋃ {var}. For frames like *to bar oneself in*, the agent and the goal are required to co-refer. This co-reference is semantic and should not be confused with the co-reference of addresses (for which we used tag-symbols). In the case of semantic co-reference, we have to do with two subframes with *different structures* (no structure sharing), but who are said to denote the *same object*. This is achieved by adding an address var. In general, two T-frames $A \backslash t_1$ and $A \backslash t_2$, where t_1 and t_2 are addresses in A, co-refer semantically iff $\psi(t_1.\text{var}) = \psi(t_2.\text{var})$. This is achieved also when $\tau(t_1.\text{var}) = \tau(t_2.\text{var})$, since then the two variables are even syntactically the same.

```
(pred => (stem => "bar"; cat => v; sepref => "in");
 cat => p;
 sem => (ag => (var => X; type => [human]);
         go => (var => X; type => [human])))
```

"Barring oneself in"

(3) L ⋃ {res, sit}.

In FG, terms may contain *restrictors* to restrict the reference set. Restrictors may be qualifiers (adjectives) or one-place open predications (relative clauses). The first are assembled in a set address res, the second at address sit

```
(pred => (stem => "dog"; cat => n);
 cat => t;
 var => X;
 res => (pred => (stem => "black"; cat => a);
          type => [thing];
          cat => q);
 sit => (pred => (stem => "bark"; cat => v);
          type => [animal];
          cat => p;
          sem => (ag => (var => X; type => [animal])))
```

"black dogs that bark"

The predication at address sit fulfils the same function as the lambda expression $\lambda x.bark(x)$ in Montague Grammar, or the *resource situation* in Situation Semantics (cf. 5.3.3).

(4) L $\cup$ {cond,pre, post, gen, in, purpose}.
The meaning of a predicate frame is described by means of meaning conditions that are put in the frame. Examples will be given in the next section.

Definition 4.8

(i) A *complex predicate frame* ϕ is a frame with address labels L' = L $\cup$ {res, sit, cond, pre, post, in, gen, purpose, sat, ben, instr, reason, frame, tmp, loc, var}, such that, if $\phi = (A,\psi,\tau)$,

$$\forall w \in A: \ \psi(w.\text{cat}) < \Delta_{cat'} \Rightarrow \exists! \, \phi' \in \text{Fund} \ \phi \backslash w \leqq \phi'$$

Let $\hat{\phi}$ be the subsuming predicate frame of ϕ, and $\check{\phi}$ the f-structure such that $\phi = \hat{\phi} \wedge \check{\phi}$.

The taxonomic structure of complex predicate frames is parasitic on the taxonomic structure of the Fund and the subsumption ordering on frames. We indicate it by the symbol "$\leq$". For ϕ and ψ being complex predicate frames this ordering is defined as:

(ii) $\phi \leq \psi$ iff $\check{\phi} \leqq \check{\psi}$ and $\hat{\phi} < \hat{\psi}$

end 4.8

The first definition guarantees that each T-frame (and Q-frame, P-frame) occurring in the frame is well-formed. In particular, it follows that each predicate frame is subsumed by some predicate frame from the Fund, indicated as $\hat{\phi}$. Therefore it can be written as a unification of $\hat{\phi}$ and $\check{\phi}$ (for the existence and uniqueness of $\check{\phi}$, see appendix A).

The second condition, on the taxonomic structure, connects the frames as syntactic structures with corresponding types. This condition is the basis for subsumptive reasoning. Given a frame ϕ, subsumptive reasoning can derive from ϕ:

- every superframe, that is, every frame ϕ' such that $\phi \leqq \phi'$ (syntactic subsumption - this can done for example by eliminating a subframe)
- every supertype, that is, every frame ϕ' such that $\phi \prec \phi'$ (taxonomic subsumption - for example, *dog* $\prec$ *animal*).

The following derivation illustrates both kind of subsumptive reasoning (the arrow designates derivation):

```
(pred => (stem => "dog"; cat => n);
 type => [animal];
 cat => t;
 res => (pred => (stem => "black"; cat => n); cat => q))) →

(pred => (stem => "dog"; cat => n);
 type => [animal];
 cat => t) →

(pred => (stem => "animal"; cat => n);
 type => [animal];
 cat => t)
```

A warning is due that these procedures only work in positive contexts, not in negative ones. At the schema level, we only work with positive contexts, but at the instantiation level, subsumptive reasoning becomes a bit more complicated.

4.4.3. Meaning conditions

If x is a condition of y, then the occurrence of y implies the occurrence of x. Depending on the dynamicity of the predicate frame, four subtypes of conditions can be distinguished:

(a) **preconditions**: y is a dynamic SoA and x holds at the start of y;
Notation: y <-- x.

(b) **postconditions**: y is a dynamic SoA and x holds (immediately) after y;
Notation: y --> x.

(c) **inconditions**: y is a dynamic or static SoA and x holds during y;
Notation: y :-- x.

If it is not known whether a condition is a precondition, postcondition or incondition, we call it a **general** condition. In that case, the condition x holds sometimes. Notation: y :- x.

Moreover, we also consider a special type of condition, that is not necessarily implied but holds by default:

(d) **purposes**: y is a controlled SoA and the agent wants x to hold (usually after y)
Notation: y ->> x.

Some examples:

```
sell(ag X human)(go Y thing)(rec Z human)
            <-- own(po X human)(go Y thing).
sell(ag X human)(go Y thing)(rec Z human)
            --> own(po Z human)(go Y thing).
```

```
sell(ag X human)(go Y thing)(rec Z human)
          :- pay(ag Z human)(go F thing))(rec X human).
kill(ag X animate)(go Y animate)
          <-- alive(Y).
kill(ag X animate)(go Y animate)
          --> dead(Y).
keep(po X human)(go Y thing)(loc Z place)
          :-- Y at(loc Z).
```

It must be noted that postconditions, such as those of `sell`, only hold after successful completion of the action. When the predication has a progressive aspect, as in *He was selling bananas*, the successful completion is not known and no conclusion can be drawn from such a proposition.

Conditions are inherited from supertypes to subtypes. This is expressed by the following addendum to definition 4.5 in which some extra requirements are expressed with respect to the taxonomic ordering.

Definition 4.5a Let T be the Fund with taxonomic ordering $\prec$.

(iii) For every $p \in$ T, ψ_p(cond.a), where $a \in$ {`pre`, `post`, `in`, `gen`} is a set of complex predicate frames;

(iv) If $p \prec q$, then

$$\psi_p(\text{cond.prec}) \leq \psi_q(\text{cond.prec})$$

Similarly for `post`, `in`, and `gen`. However, it is allowed that what is a general condition in q is a specific condition (e.g., precondition) in p.

end 4.5a

Part (iv) is the condition inheritance rule. The ordering assumed here on the domain of sets of predications is the one derived from the subsumption ordering on predications by using the set construction (Appendix A). Intuitively, one set of conditions is subsumed by another set of conditions if for each member of the latter some member of the former can be found that is subsumed by it. In other words, conditions get stronger for the subtypes.

Example. Let us suppose that the verb *transfer* is defined in a general way:

```
transfer(ag X human)(go Y thing)(rec Z human)
       <-- have(po X human)(go Y thing)
transfer(ag X human)(go Y thing)(rec Z human)
       --> have(po Z human)(go Y thing)
```

That is, *transfer* is defined so as to include sellings, borrowings, gifts etc.

To check that *sell* is a subtype of *transfer* we have to check that:

(1) for some $c \in$ Precond(`sell`), $c \leq$ `have(po X human)(go Y thing)`;

(2) for some $c \in$ Postcond(`sell`), $c \leq$ `have(po Z human)(go Y thing)`;

Both conditions are satisfied, at least if we assume that:

```
own(po X human)(go Y thing) < have(po X human)(go Y thing)
```

It is easy to check that the co-reference conditions are met too.

If we exploit the condition inheritance property, the specification of conditions is easier and more transparant. For example, suppose that we have already defined the conditions for predicate *to kill* and we want to specify the conditions for *to murder*. By stating the subtype-relation:

```
murder(ag X human)(go Y human) < kill(ag X animate)(go Y animate)
```

we are almost finished. The only thing that is to be added is the intentional character of the murdering. This can be represented by filling the purpose condition of *to murder* with a predication dead(Y). The selection restrictions on the frame of *murder* ensure that the arguments are persons. Conditions, such as the postcondition dead(y), are inherited and need not be specified.

Note the following properties of the condition relations:

- The interpretation of the conditions in a certain instantiated SoA is a topic that we postpone to chapter 6, but is supposed to be intuitively clear. The procedural interpretation of an incondition is very much the same as the interpretation of a Prolog clause. A preconditon is required to hold when a certain predication is inserted in the database, and the postcondition becomes true as a result of the insertion. There is one pecularity: we assume that every precondition that is not repeated as a postcondition, is false in the state immediately after the event. For example, if the precondition of *to sell* states that the agent owns the object, and this condition is not repeated in the postcondition, it is implied that the agent does not own the object afterwards.
- We have defined conditions here as complex predicate frames. In many cases, including all examples given in this chapter, this is sufficient. However, in general the condition may be any predication expressible in FG, including negative and modal ones. These will be defined in chapter 6.
- Frames of nominal frames do not have pre- and postconditions, but they may have inconditions (and perhaps purposes). For example, a judge, in a certain sense (Oxford Dictionary), is a person who decides in a contest:

```
judge   :--   person : decide(ag .)(co Y soa)([sit] X contest)
```

(the [sit] is a secondary semantic function, see 4.4.4)

A stock-room is a room in which stock is kept:

```
stock-room  :-- room : keep(po Z human)(go Y material)(loc in(.) )
```

In these examples, we use the restrictor operator ":" from FG and the special symbol "." at tag symbol position. Strictly speaking, we can not use the restrictor operator since it is not defined in this chapter. However, at the lexical level at which we are speaking now, the notation can be considered as a short-hand. Let the meaning condition be:

a :-- b : c

where b is the head and c is the set of restrictors. This is to be read as specifying the following:

(i) $a \leq b$ (a isa b), and

(ii) a :-- c (c is the incondition of a).

(iii) τ_a(var) = τ_b(var) = $\tau_c(w)$, where w is the address indicated by "." above.

Every T-frame is subsumed by some other T-frame or primitive type, so we always have a candidate for the head position. It is natural to assume that the meaning conditions always contain a reference to the variable of the definiens (otherwise it can't be a meaning condition). Therefore, it is not only the case that the "restrictor notation" can be rewritten to taxonomic links and inconditions, but also the inverse holds. For each term, the meaning conditions can be written as restrictors on the supertype (genus proximum).

- A special type of a condition occurs when the predication has a converse predicate frame. Examples of converse pairs are *buy/sell*, *more/less*, *precede/succeed* etc. Converses can be put in a separate relation, thus clearing up the specification of conditions. Examples:

```
converse(buy(ag X human)(go Y thing)([fro] Z human),
        sell(ag Z human)(go Y thing)(rec X human))
```

([fro] is again a secondary semantic function). The meaning of a converse relation is the same as that of an in-condition.

A notorious problem with meaning conditions or any other way of specifying the meaning of words, is the trap of circularity. If the meaning conditions of *to sell* refer to *owning* and *to own* is defined by means of *to sell*, then the meaning condition is not a definition, as Aristotle already warned us:

> First of all, see if he has failed to make the definition through terms that are prior and more intelligible. For the reasons why the definition is rendered is to make known the term stated, and we make things known by taking not any random term, but such as are prior and more intelligible ...; accordingly, it is clear that a man who does not define through terms of this kind has not defined at all" (Aristotle, Topics, 1968:141)

Dik (1978) has coined the principle of stepwise lexical decomposition that makes the following assumptions:

- the defining predicates in meaning definitions are lexical items of the object language, and the structure of the meaning definitions is of the same formal type as the structure of the linguistic expression.
- the defining predicates used in meaning definitions may themselves be defined in other meaning definitions; in fact, such a stepwise approach is to be preferred;
- the definiens of meaning definitions is not directly accessible to the operation of syntactic rules.
- in every language there is a set of simple lexical items the meanings of which cannot be defined by means of meaning definitions †

The first and third assumption deal with the form of the definitions and have been discussed before. The second assumption embodies the principle of lexical decomposition. It states that it is neither necessary nor preferable to define the meaning

† The classical example of a failure in handling indefinables is the French philosopher Père Noël (1647) who defined "light" as "a luminary movement of luminous bodies".

directly in terms of simple primitives, but that in-between predicates should be used whenever possible. The last assumption recognizes the fact that one cannot do without a small set of undefined primitive lexical items. Such a basic set could be the vocabulary of *BASIC English* (Ogden, 1930), which is a carefully selected set of about 900 words (particularly aiming at scientific and commercial discourse). Longman's *Dictionary of Comtemporary English* defines the meanings of 55,000 words using a vocabulary of only 2000 words. This dictionary is currently transformed to FG format in a project at the University of Amsterdam (see Voogt, 1987, and subsequent publications). Perhaps 2000 is still too much and a much smaller set is attainable (Wierzbicka, 1989:15).

For the knowledge base, the principle of lexical decomposition can be applied in several ways:

- it is not necessary that the data dictionary contains all definitions of common English words, but as soon as technical and relatively unfamiliar words are used, these must be defined in terms of familiar ones;
- the meaning ordering put on predicates can be used in developing the logical (internal) schema of the database. Since meaning conditions usually do not exhaust the meaning of the predicate, it seems best to *store* the most *complex* predicates, and to *derive* the more simple ones. Both the taxonomy structures (with its explicit ordering of complexity) and the meaning conditions introduced above can be used as *derivation rules* (Nicolas & Yazdanian, 1978).

4.4.4. Secondary semantic functions

Secondary semantic functions are semantic functions that are not part of the predicate frame but which can be added as satellite in an instantiation. Some satellites are general, such as `tmp`, and can be added to any predication. But there is also a class of satellites that is specific to the predicate frame in question. An example is the satellite for *price* (or return goods) in a sentence with *sell*:

The parts were sold for $4000.

The constituent *for $4000* has a specific meaning. This meaning can be found by examining the meaning conditions of *sell*. One of the general conditions says that the buyer pays a price. The specific meaning of the $4000 in the sentence is that it indicates this price.

Since the meaning of the secondary function makes an essential use of the meaning conditions, it is unlikely that we can define the set of secondary functions by means of some categorization, as we did with the primary semantic functions. Some secondary functions will have a "similar" meaning in different frames and then we can use the same symbol. Others are perhaps used in one frame only. A more practical approach could start with the expression of the function (the preposition or case-marking), and use this as a formal frame. This formal frame is attached to the predicate frame in the specification of its conditions.

```
sell(ag X human)(go Y thing)(rec Z human)([for] F thing)
```

The secondary semantic functions are satelllites that have to co-refer with a term occurring in one of the meaning conditions. To make this more precise, we put the conditions *in* the frame. For example (NB: the predicates are abbreviated to one symbol):

```
(pred => sell;
 cat => p;
 sem => (ag => (var => X; type => [human]);
         go => (var => Y; type => [thing]);
         rec => (var => Z; type => [human]));
 sat => ([for] => C:(var => F; type => [thing]));
 cond => (gen => { (pred => pay;
                    cat => p;
                    sem => (ag => (var => Z);
                            go => C;
                            rec => (var => X)))};
          pre => { (pred => own;
                    cat => p;
                    sem => (po => (var => X);
                            go => (var => Y))}})
```

The preconditions are now put in the set denoted by address `cond.pre`, and the inconditions are found at address `cond.in`. The "for" satellite co-refers with the goal of the incondition.

The following definition ensures that a secondary semantic function always co-refers with a term in one of the conditions.

Definition 4.9 Sf2 is a finite set of secondary semantic functions. The following holds for each occurrence of a secondary semantic function f in some (sub-)frame a

(i) f is a satellite, i.e., if $\exists\ w\ (w \equiv \alpha.f \wedge w \in \mathrm{A}(a))$, then $\alpha \equiv$ sat;

(ii) f co-refers, i.e., for some $\sigma \in$ {in,pre,post,gen,purp} and for some condition frame $c \in \psi_a(\text{cond}.\sigma)$, there is some semantic function σ' such that $\tau_c(\text{sem}.\sigma') = \tau_a(\text{sat}.f)$.

end 4.9

In the example, if $w \equiv$ `sat.[for]`, then $\tau(w) = \tau(w') = \mathrm{C}$, for $w' \equiv$ `cond.gen.sem.go`.

In the following, we will sometimes write the meaning conditions separately, to make them more easy to read. However, formally the meaning conditions are part of the predicate frame. Note that the condition inheritance rule (part (iv) of definition 4.5a) ensures that conditions are inherited between types. As being part of the frame, they are automatically inherited between frames standing in subsumption ordering (definition 4.7).

4.5. PREDICATE SCHEMATA

Tannen (1986) asks the question why it is that some constructions occur frequently in discourse, whereas others, though grammatically possible, do not. One possible explanation is that speech may have more to do with memory than with novel production. Bolinger (1961) talks about a "preestablished inventory" of sentences that are not produced by the speaker himself but transmitted to him in toto and with countless repetitions. Or elsewhere (Bolinger, 1976):

> "I want to take an idiomatic rather than an analytic view, and argue that analyzability always goes along with its opposite at whatever level, and that our language does not expect us to build everything starting with lumber, nails, and blueprint, but provides us with an incredibly large number of prefabs, which have the magical property of persisting even when we knock some of them apart and put them together in unpredictable ways"

For example, consider the numerous occurrences of the verb *to open*: "open a door", "open a bottle", "open a meeting", "open a shop", "open an account", "open one's heart", "open a file", "open one's hand" etc. Of course, *to open* has several predicate frames, but not as many as there are typical usages. I assume that there are different frames for "open a thing (window, bottle, door,...)", and for "open an event (meeting,debate,game...)", in the sense of starting it (see some conventional dictionary). There is no need for a predicate frame for *to open a door* since we could make such a construction already with our predicate frame combination rules, as it is a special case of opening a thing. Nevertheless, it may be useful to "can" this frame in the lexical knowledge base, with the instrument function *key* for example, and more specific meaning conditions.

Predicate schemata can be used for *prototypical* usages. An example is the verb *to bark*, which can be used for dogs, guns and persons. In the latter sense, it means "saying something in a sharp, commanding voice". For some reason or another, it is mostly used for officers: "the officer barked ...." It does not seem appropriate to take this as a selection restriction, since there is no reason why other persons could not "bark" occasionally. So the predicate frame contains only the selection restriction [human]. The barking officer is put in a predicate schema that is labelled as prototype (of bark).

A particular case of typical usage is the *idiomatic* expression, such as "black sheep", "pass the buck" etc. Whereas schemata normally do not affect the meaning conditions of the predicate frame, idiomatic expressions may change them drastically. The dictionary must contain the meaning conditions for these schemata.

Predicate schemata can be used also for *meaning definitions*. We already introduced meaning conditions. These are very important, but not sufficient for specifying the complete meaning of a predicate frame, especially in the case of T-frames. Meaning conditions for *cup* and *mug* will be very simple, and probably almost equal. To see where they differ, we need meaning *definitions*. Meaning definitions explicate, elucidate and explain the meaning of words. They do not deal with necessary conditions but with essential characteristics. They are not concerned with denotational structure but with *conceptual* structure (Wierzbicka, 1985:16). The concepts of cups and mugs are rather different, and this should be accounted for in the meaning definition.

So we see that predicate schemata do have several usages. Predicate schemata can be considered as a third level of the lexicon (after predicates and frames). The set of stored predicate schemata in a knowledge base is called the *Dictionary*. Let me briefly summarize the relationships and differences between basic predicate frames and schemata:

(a) Each frame of certain predicate has a different hyponym and/or different set of semantic functions. They make up the elementary frame types. Schemata are always derived from a predicate frame, either by subsumption or by a schema formation rule (see below).

(b) Predicate frames constitute the semantic level and predicate schemata the conceptual level. Predicate frame information (meaning conditions, contrast sets) is used in monotonic reasoning, predicate schema information (prototypes, meaning definitions) is used in non-monotonic reasoning, such as default reasoning.

(c) Over time, the set of predicate frames (thesaurus) is more stable than the set of predicate schemata (dictionary). Predicate schemata may also differ from one sublanguage to another. Scientific language, for example, makes often use of a controlled vocabulary.

By using the term "schema" I intentionally rejoin the traditional notion of "schema" as it is used in the philosophical and psychological tradition (see for instance Johnson-Laird, 1983:189vv, Sowa, 1984:42vv). Apparently, the term goes back to Kant who distinguished a schema from an image. The psychologist Bartlett gave the following definition (1932:201)

> ...an active organization of past reactions, or of past experiences, which must always be supposed to be operating in any well-adapted organic response. That is, whenever there is any order or regularity of behavior, a particular response is possible only because it is related to other similar responses which have been serially organized, yet which operate not simply as individual members coming one after another, but as a unitary mass"

The term "schema" is also close to the terms "script" and "frame" as it it used in de AI literature. In AI, scripts were introduced by Schank and Abelson (1977) and applied in several systems (Lehnert, 1978; DeJong, 1979). A script for a concept type, such as RESTAURANT, is a kind of large schema with conceptual relations that show the sequence of events that normally occur in a restaurant, such as selecting a menu, eating, tipping and paying. A script is very similar to a frame in the sense of Minsky (1975), but it is more concerned with stereotypical event sequences rather than stereotypical configurations. In my view, scripts are predicate schemata occurring at a certain level in the lexicon. What Schank and Abelson put into the the script for RESTAURANT is not principally different from what linguists would call the meaning definition of "restaurant".

4.5.1. Meaning definitions

The Dictionary is used for several purposes. Some of the schemata are idiomatic, some of them are prototypical of and/or take part in the meaning definition of some predicate frame, and some of them represent just stereotypical usages. This is expressed in the following assumption:

Definition 4.10 A *Dictionary* is a set of stored predicate schemata with the following substructures:

Thesaurus $\subseteq$ *Dictionary* is the set of stored predicate frames

IDIOM $\subseteq$ *Dictionary* is a set of idiomatic predicate frames whose meaning conditions do not adhere to the condition inheritance rule;

MEANING ⊆ *Dictionary* × *Dictionary* is a relation that assigns a set of predicate schemata to a predicate schema, in particular to each predicate frame in the Thesaurus. The meaning of a predicate frame consists of characteristic properties;

PROTOTYPE ⊆ *Dictionary* is a set of prototypical (generic) schemata.

end 4.10

Meaning definitions can become quite long. For example, for the definition of the word *cup*, Wierzbicka (1985) needs several pages. Note, however, that the more abstract predicate frames are much easier to define than those dealing with things of daily experience.

4.5.2. Predicate schema formation

We have argued that predicate schemata are usually transmitted in toto from one linguistic agent to another. This does not mean that no new schemata can be formed. New schemata are usually introduced by a metaphoric or metonymic process (cf. Jakobson, 1956). That is, they are derived from other schemata. Metaphoric schema formation takes a schema and applies it in a way that overtly violates the selection restrictions. The output frame has the same predicate, but the new schema can not be seen as a subtype of the old schema. Instead of an `isa` relationship, we will talk about an asa-relationship. For instance, when we talk about someone as a wolf, we make use of a special schema `wolf` that is categorized as a person, but is linked with an asa-relation to the standard schema of wolf as animal:

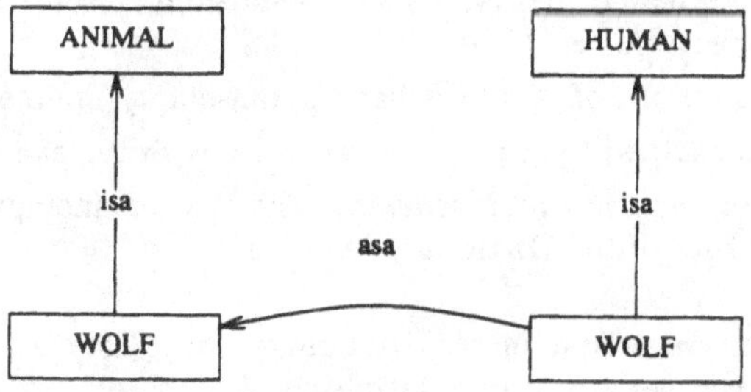

Fig. 4.11 Metaphoric schema

Metaphor is a process by which new schemata can be derived. We call it a predicate schema formation rule. Once a metaphoric schema has been derived and used, it can be stored. The above schema for "man as wolf" is a typical example of a stored metaphor (its use can be traced back at least to Plautus). Stored metaphors belong to the common knowledge of the linguistic community.

Metonymic schema formation takes a schema A and a related schema B and returns a new schema C with the predicate of B and subsumed by A. For example, let A = `book` and B = `cover(book)`, then C = `cover < book`. The relationship between A and B is often one of part/whole, but this is not necessary. Metonymy can be seen as a the process of introducing "short-hand" notations. It plays an enormous role in actual discourse (see e.g. Yamanashi, 1987).

Diachronically, schemata formed by schema formation rules may turn into genuine predicate frames with an equal status as the predicate frame from which they are derived. For example, we distinguish two predicate frames for `bark`, one for dogs and one for persons, where the latter is presumably derived from the former. However, diachronic derivations are not reflected in the FG lexicon.

It is very hard to have machines perform metaphoric and metonymic reasoning processes themselves. Because of its transcendental character, natural language resists full mechanization. But this is not necessary either. As far as the lexicon of the knowledge base describes the conceptual structure of the communication between the users, it should contain the metaphors and metonyms adopted by these users. This is no problem if these schemata are explicitly stored in the Dictionary. Each metaphorical schema must be linked by means of an `asa` link to the frame from which it has been derived. Both metaphoric and metonymic frames have their meaning conditions and definitions which may differ from the schemata from which they were derived.

Definition 4.11. The relationship `asa` $\subseteq$ Dictionary $\times$ Dictionary is defined as follows:
For two schemata A and B, we say that (A,B) $\in$ `asa` - A is like B - iff

(i) A and B have the same (head) predicate;

(ii) B is a "normal" schema, that is, a schema subsuming some predicate frame f with the same predicate (B $\leq f$);

(iii) the meaning definitions of A and B have a non-empty intersection;

(iv) A itself is not subsumed by a predicate frame g with the same predicate

We say that A is a *metaphorical schema*. The set of metaphorical schemata, METAPHOR is a subset of the Dictionary.
end 4.11

Metonymic schemata are stored in the Dictionary too. They are put in the taxonomic ordering and can get a meaning definition. Compare:

```
(pred => (stem => "cover";
          cat => n);
 cat => t;
 type => book;
 sem => -)
```

```
(pred => (stem => "cover";
          cat => n);
 cat => t;
 type => [thing];
 sem => (ref => (type => [book])))
```

The first one is derived from the second one. The first one is a subtype of "book", the second one of "thing".

4.5.3. Sublanguages

The Dictionary describes the "language" in the sense of a set of expression types shared by a linguistic community. In knowledge engineering we are often not concerned with a complete natural language but only with the language that is spoken in the given Universe of Discourse. Such a language can be called a *sublanguage*. In (Kittredge, 1982) several sublanguages are presented, such as the sublanguage of the hospital (cf. Lindberg & Humphreys, 1987) and of the stock exchange (Kittredge & Lehrberger, 1982). Besides specialist languages, we may also think of languages such as fairy tale language in which animals can speak. Not much research has been devoted yet to sublanguages, but they show at least the following characteristics:

- the vocabulary is restricted to the words that are relevant in the UoD;
- the grammatical structures are not different from the grammatical structures in the general language;
- the language often makes extensive use of schemata formed by metaphorical and metonymical schema formation, schemata that are not found in the Dictionary of the general language.

So the sublanguage does not differ from the normal language by means of a different structure, but simply by means of a different Dictionary. Therefore we can define a sublanguage as follows:

Definition 4.12 A *sublanguage* of language L with Thesaurus T and Dictionary D consists of a Thesaurus T' and a Dictionary D' such that:

(i) $T' \subseteq T$, and

(ii) for each $s_1 \in D'$, there is an $s_2 \in D$, such that either $s_1 \leq s_2$ or $\mathrm{asa}(s_1, s_2)_{D'}$.

end 4.12

In words: the thesaurus of the sublanguage is a subset of the thesaurus of the language and every metaphoric predicate schema is derived from some predicate schema of the language.

An interesting example of a sublanguage is the legal language, as studied in Gardner (1987). Legal discourse, such as cases, are usually a mixture of ordinary language and legal languages. Predicates like *to sleep*, *apples* etc are taken from ordinary language whereas words like *offer*, *acceptance*, and *consideration*, in contract law, are strictly technical. Their meaning must be stipulated by further rules. It is important to recognize that, in principle, each predicate may have an ordinary and a technical meaning. This much leaves room for both believed testimony that the defendant was observed to be sleeping in the railway station (in the ordinary-language sense) and for a conclusion that the defendant was not sleeping (in the relevant legal sense). However, as Gardner points out (p.44), the ordinary and technical uses of *sleeping* are not entirely distinct. "In choosing words in which to formulate a legal rule, one draws on their ordinary meanings". When cases arise after the rule has been formulated, the general lexicon suggests an answer to the question whether the rule applies. Other considerations may suggest a different answer. If these prevail, the technical usage begins to diverge from ordinary usage. But there are not pairs of words senses from the beginning. Gardner's observation is in accordance with the position defended here that sublanguages make use of predicate schemata derived from predicates in the general dictionary (by means of specialization).

The TAXMAN system (McCarty, 1977; McCarty & Sridharan, 1981) is a well-known continuing AI project aimed at giving a computational description of legal reasoning. Originally, this program worked with a set of of primitive semantic concepts. In the course of the project it was found that this approach was not always appropriate. For concepts like "business purposes" and "continuity of interest" (used in tax law), there is no once-for-all necessary and sufficient definition to give. To represent these so-called *amorphous* concepts, McCarty developed a *prototype-and-deformation* model. It is described as having three elements:

(1) There is an *invariant* component to provide necessary, but not sufficient conditions for the existence of the abstraction. Even this component would be optional, however.

(2) There is a set of *exemplars*, each of which matches some but not all of the instances of the concept. It is important, however, that this component be something more than an unordered, unstructured set, for this would give us only a disjunctive specification of the concept. Therefore:

(3) There is also a set of *transformations* in the definitional expansion which express the *relationships between the exemplars*, i.e. which state that one exemplar can be *mapped* into another exemplar in a certain way. (McCarty and Sridharan, 1982:7)

Although the details of this model may differ from ours, there is also much in common. The *invariant* component providing necessary conditions typically corresponds to the predicate frame (or perhaps a schema). The exemplars are different schemata subsumed by the frame. The schemata are not unordered, but structured by taxonomic links and metaphorical and metonymic predicate schema rules.

In contrast to TAXMAN, at least in its first version, Gardner prefers using English predicates without decomposing them in or identifying them as semantic primitives. She gives several considerations in support of this approach:

(a) levels of concreteness may differ from one problem to another and there is no level of detail that can always be regarded as ultimate;

(b) it is dangerous to identify coextensive predicates that seem to denote always the same event. For example, the same event in the world may often be describable as both a *receive* and a *deliver*. The troublesome situations, however, are likely to be the ones in which these predicates are not both applicable. A package can be delivered to you, by being placed on your doorstep, but can still be stolen before you receive it. If *receive, deliver* and *send* were all represented only as abstract concept TRANSFER, the necessary distinctions would be lost;

(c) with respect to physical objects (ordinary language), using English words as predicates may lead to less overlap rather than more. Wilks (1977:11) pointed out that no representation by a small set of primitives can be expected to distinguish among a hammer, a mallet and an axe. Still, someone who enters a contract to buy a hammer can justifiably complain if he gets a mallet or an axe instead.

4.6. APPLICATION

As an illustrative example of our theory to the practice of conceptual modelling, we present the sublanguage for the famous ISO car example (van Griethuysen, 1982; see Appendix B).

T-frames and schemata:

```
car ≺ vehicle
fuel ≺ liquid
fuel consumption(car) ≺ [quality]
fuel consumption(manufacturer) ≺ [quality]
garage ≺ company
manufacturer  ≺ company
maximum fuel consumption(year) ≺ [quality]
model(car) ≺ [quality]
person ≺ [human]
registration authority  ≺ company
registration number(car)  ≺ number
serial number(car)  ≺ number
number(thing) ≺ [quality]

fuel consumption(X car)
            :-- fuel : consume(fo X car)(go .)([per] [100] Z kilometer).
fuel consumption(M manufacturer)(tmp Y year)
            :-- AVG(fuel consumption(X car : produce(ag M)(go .)(tmp Y year))).
maximum fuel consumption(Y year)
            :-- fuel.
maximum fuel consumption(Y year)
            ->> MAX(fuel consumption(M manufacturer)(tmp Y year)) < Z.
registration number(Y car)
            :-- number : assign(ag X registration authority)(go .)(rec Y car).
serial number(C car)
            :-- number : assign(ag X manufacturer : produce(ag .)(go C car))
                                        (go N)(rec Y car).

model(car) <=> Citroen, Ford, VW, Daf, Honda, ....
```

P-schemata and conditions

```
assign(ag X [human])(go Z number)(rec Y car).
consume(fo X car)(go Y fuel).
destroy(ag X [human])(go Y car)
     <-- exist(Y).
establish(ag X registration authority)(go Z [soa])
     -->  Z.
operate(po X manufacturer).
own(po X [human])(go Y car).
produce(ag X manufacturer)(go Y car)
     --> exist(Y), own(po X)(go Y).
register(ag X registration authority)(go Y car)([id] Z number)
     :- assign(ag X)(go Z number)(rec Y car).
sell(ag X [human])(go Y car)(rec Z [human])
     <-- own(po X)(go Y).
sell(ag X [human])(go Y car)(rec Z [human])
     --> own(po Z)(go Y).
```

Remarks:

1. Most schemata are subtypes of lexical predicate frames. "Fuel consumption" is a composite frame derived by nominalization and composition, just as registration number.

2. The example shows one typical example of metonymy where "fuel consumption" is applied to manufacturers. The fuel consumption of a manufacturer is a short-hand for the average fuel consumption of the cars produced by the manufacturer.

3. The definition of maximum fuel consumption is a bit complicated. It is defined in the first place as an amount of fuel. For example "50 dollar" is not a good value. The maximum fuel consumption is further defined by its purpose: all fuel consumptions of manufacturers must remain below it (note that the "maximum fuel consumption" is not simply the maximal value of all fuel consumptions). Maximum fuel consumptions are established by the registration authority. *To establish* is a predicate frame which takes a SoA as goal argument with the intended meaning that the SoA holds afterwards. In this case, the registration authority can only establish that the maximum fuel consumption is such and such, but this restriction must be specified by deontic rules.

4. We have used MAX and AVG as abstract functions on terms (comparable to place functions), with the intended meaning of "maximum" and "average".

5. The lexicon defined in this way takes the functions of a conceptual model:

(a) it can be used to derive an *internal schema* for the database: the T-frames {`person, manufacturer, garage, registration authority, car, model, fuel, integer`} are treated as entity types. The P-frames are translated to relationship types, where we must add an attribute for time reference (see chapter 6). The attribute T-frames `serial number` and `registration number` can be treated as attributes or as relationships, depending on whether they are unique in the current UoD. To generate a relational database schema we can make use of techniques that work for Entity Relationship models as described in the literature (e.g., De Antonelli, 1984).

(b) it serves as a common reference point for different users. Since the schema is derived from the general linguistic knowledge of the users, it is easy to comprehend. The lexicon is stored in the knowledge base, so it can be easily accessed. It can also support help and explanation processes. For example, a user may ask:

U: *What is the fuel consumption of a manufacturer?*
A: *The fuel consumption of the cars produced by the manufacturer.*

U: What is the fuel consumption of a car?
A: *The fuel consumed by the car per 100 kilometers.*

(c) the conditions can be used as integrity constraints and transaction specifications, thus increasing the data integrity. Not all constraints are expressed in this way. For example, the rule that manufacturers can not sell cars to persons is not expressed yet. This is because the constraint is not analytic. It will be specified later as a deontic constraint (chapter 6).

(d) the grammatical information attached to the predicate can be used, together with the domain-independent expression rules, for setting up the natural language interface. Note that it is also possible, and in fact recommendable, to use a general lexicon/dictionary in combination with the sublexicon designed for this application. If the user uses words not contained in the sublexicon, they can be looked up in the general dictionary and probably translated to words known in the sublexicon. For instance, if the user asks, what cars have been *bought* by person X, the converse relation in the general lexicon can translate the buy-phrase to a sell-phrase so that the question can be answered.

(e) the information system defined on the predicate frames can be used in subsumptive reasoning. From the frame:

```
own(po X manufacturer)(go Y car)
```

we can deduce:

```
have(po X manufacturer)(go Y thing)
```

4.7. SUMMARY

In this chapter we have described the structure of the lexicon and how it can fulfill the objectives of a data dictionary. We have been able to formalize this structure as an information system with taxonomic subsumption relations. The dictionary has been described at several layers: the predicate level (vocabulary), the predicate frame level (Thesaurus/Fund) and the predicate schema level (Dictionary). To make the picture more concrete, we can imagine that the different parts of the lexicon are distributed over several tables:

- The VOCABULARY table is a table of lexemes indexed on predicate stem (phonological or graphological) and contains grammatical information;
- the THESAURUS table is a table of predicate frames indexed on

VOCABULARY identifiers and contains per entry the primitive supertype, the nearest supertype (genus proximum), the frame structure (with pointers to other entries in the THESAURUS table), and pointers to contrast sets, if any. The frames contain conditions.

- the DICTIONARY table is a table of predicate schemata indexed on THESAURUS identifiers and contains all schemata of the predicate frame in question. The schemata that have been defined already in the THESAURUS can be represented virtually by means of "symbolic links" or pointers. For each schema, the DICTIONARY contains a reference to the predicate frame by which it is subsumed.
- MEANING is a table indexed on DICTIONARY identifiers (the definiendum) and each entry consists of a set of schemata (definiens).

These data structures are supplemented by programs that derive new predicate frames by means of predicate formation or combination rules whenever necessary.

The lexicon formalized in this way has several theoretical and practical advantages over earlier proposals for data dictionaries and conceptual modeling:

ADVANTAGES

*1 the linguistic framework offers a rigid discipline which makes the process of defining semantic functions, entities and relationships less arbitrary, and hence a more scientific enterprise;

*2 the designer/knowledge engineer can make use of the general dictionary in setting up a DICTIONARY for the sublanguage he is describing;

*3 the taxonomic structure, combined with condition inheritance, gives a powerful mechanism for subsumptive reasoning.

*4 the conceptual structures (predicate frames and schemata) can be defined on an implementation-independent level (data independence). They are also to a great extent application-independent. Specific rules (deontic constraints) may differ from one application to another without affecting the lexicon.

*5 another advantage stemming from *1 is that establishing communication *between* different knowledge bases, with different Dictionaries, is not a hopeless task, as has been suggested sometimes in the data modelling literature. This is because the Dictionaries overlap in the portion imported from the general Dictionary. The general Dictionary can be used as "lingua franca", as it is already in practice.

*6 The discipline imposed by the constraint that predicate schemata must be linked to their subsuming predicate frame, and the bare presence of things like meaning definitions, has the potential of increasing the user-friendliness of the KBMS in orders of magnitude. It means that *all* terminology can be explained to the user in everyday language, in one or more steps.

5

Terms

5.1. INTRODUCTION: HOW TO DENOTE THINGS WITH WORDS

Any knowledge representation language must make a distinction between terms and propositions. Propositions (or parts thereof, the predications) are about something. Before we can determine the truth value of the propositions, we must have fixed the subject "something". Those parts of the proposition that are assumed to be known and identifiable (or reconstructable) for Speaker and Addressee, are called the *terms* (termini, "endpoints"). It is important to note that three functions of terms can be distinguished (cf. Mackenzie, 1987):

- a *referential* function (a term has a *referent*, usually called an entity);
- an *attributive* function (a term categorizes the entity, and provides properties);
- a *thematic* function (a term is what the discourse is about);

These three functions correspond with the three different aspects of the sign as spelled out by Peirce ("firstness", icon - the attributive function; "secondness", index - the referential function; "thirdness", symbol - the thematic function). All three aspects are contained in his definition of a sign as "something that stands for something in some respect or quality to an interpretant". There is also a correspondence with the three layers of the underlying clause.

In Functional Grammar, referring is regarded as a pragmatic, cooperative action of a Speaker within a pattern of verbal interaction between that Speaker and some Addressee. Leaving deictic reference aside, † the entities E referred to are mental representations, things that can be construed in the mind. Dik (1987) distinguishes two main usages:

(i) S may use a term T in order to help A construe a referent E for T, and thus introduce E into his mental model

(ii) S may use a term T in order to help A retrieve a referent E for T, where E was already present in his mental model

Entities are referred to by means of linguistic expressions. Terms, as part of the proposition, are not referents but referring expressions. In database theory, this distinction is contained in the concept of *value independence* (cf. 1.1.1): for example, even if keys are unique, there is a fundamental conceptual distinction between the key and the entity identified by the key.

† Such as demonstratives, *this, that* etc. Probably, deictic references are mental too. Note that deictic references do not necessarilly (and in fact often not) point to physical objects. Even if they do, it is disputable whether the referent is the object outside or the perceptual image of the object inside

It follows that there is also a distinction between introducing a new term into the knowledge base and introducing a new referent into the model although these two operations occur most often together. A typical case in which the introduction of a new term does *not* automatically introduce a new referent is the quantified term (universal quantification, term negation). A quantified term can be the antecedent of another term (such as an anaphor), but has no referent, or at least no unique referent:

(1) Every woman loves *her* father

(2) No one leaves *his* own child

We reserve the term operator *definite / indefinite* for terms: it is the term that is definite or indefinite, not the referent. When a term is definite, it has an antecedent, but not necessarily a (unique) referent.

Referents exist in a mental model shared by Speaker and Addressee. Therefore, the "ontology" of referents cannot be reduced to physical ontology. To use Frege's famous example, "Morning Star" and "Evening Star", have a different meaning, although they may be said to refer to the same physical object, the planet Venus. The latter form of physical reference is important as soon as knowledge is combined with action (contextualization), but plays a secondary role in the knowledge base itself. It is also possible to refer to fictional or non-existent things, such as "Sherlock Holmes" or "the golden mountain", or abstract things not measurable by means of laboratory equipment, such as "computability" or "capitalist economy". Because of this property of referents I will speak about the *intensionality* of terms. In AI, intensionality is addressed in KL-ONE (Brachman & Schmolze,1985) and SNePS (Shapiro and Rapaport, 1987). In fact, we have intensionality at two levels: (a) referents are supposed to be contained in a mental model rather than in the UoD itself; (b) terms as referring expressions are distinguished from the referents. Thus, one physical entity (the planet Venus) may have several referents in the mental model; and one referent in the model (say John) may be addressed by means of several terms ("he", "John", "the cop").

Referents are not necessarily singular. They may also represent sets of any cardinality. It is also possible that they are not countable at all, as in the case of mass terms ("some water", "much gold"). That there is no distinction in semantic *type* between singular and plural terms has been recognized also by Godehard Link (1983). In previous semantic theories it was often assumed that singular terms are interpreted as (concrete) individuals, while plurals are interpreted as (abstract) sets of such individuals. Link gives various arguments for the position that both are concrete individuals. One of his arguments is the following. Take sentence (1):

(1) Who made a mess of the living room?

This sentence can as easily be answered with a singular *John*, as with a plural *my kids*. It seems awkward to assume that (1) is ambiguous between (1a) and (1b):

(1a) Which individual made a mess of the living room?

(1b) Which set of individuals made a mess of the living room?

But if we assume that *my kids* denotes a concrete individual as much as *John* does, we do not have to postulate such an ambiguity. Link's formal treatment is in line with the conceptualization of terms in FG.

Formally, terms are instantiations of T-frames (4.4.2). From the T-frame, they inherit the nominal head, denoting the semantic category of the referent. The T-frame may be extended with cardinality, restrictors and satellites. The instantiation adds a reference marker used to indicate co-reference. In addition, the instantiated term can be specified for definiteness and situated with respect to a location or resource situation. Number and definiteness are called term operators.

Additional term operators include quantifiers. Some of these deal with the proportion of term domain and term (for instance, "many"). Other quantifiers specify the position of the term referents in the logical structure of the predication ("all"). The latter have been covered in chapter 3.

Just as T-frames, terms may be complex when they contain references to other terms (for example, *employer of immigrants*). These arguments may have a semantic function, as in the case of attribute T-frames and certain nominalizations, or satellites. Remember that a crucial difference between semantic functions and satellites is that semantic functions are used to ground the existence of the term, whereas satellites give additional information. This is independent of the fact that both can be used to identify a referent (in the sense of finding the referent in the knowledge base).

Before we discuss terms in some more detail, we first review how terms are treated in database languages.

5.2. TERMS IN DATABASE LANGUAGES

In the relational model (Codd, 1970), assertions are made in the form of *relations*. Relations are defined as Cartesian products over domains. Some examples are pictured in fig. 5.1:

SUPPLIER	CITY
S2	Meppel
S3	Ueno
S4	Avignon
...	...

MODEL	FRAMENR	OWNER
Honda Civic	H878349	Yamada
VW Golf	V123453	Vandenberg
Talbot	T784532	Montaigne

Fig. 5.1 Two sample relations

In the left table, the terms of the assertion are suppliers (represented by supplier number S2 and S3) and cities (Meppel, Ueno, Avignon). Supplier number is the key of the relation. In the right table, the key is composed of two attributes, MODEL and FRAMENR. Together they determine a term of type CAR. The other terms are persons identified by their name (Yamada etc). Note that terms are completely determined by their values (either a single or multiple attributes), thus disallowing a difference between intension and extension. When a relation is in *first normal form*, the term cannot be a set. That is, assertions over sets must be split up over several tuples. The identity of a term is dependent on its value (in the case of attributes) or its key (in the case of tuples). The key is unique only within a single relation.

In the extended relational model RM/T (Codd 1979; cf. Abrial, 1974) term identity is supported through *surrogates*. Surrogates are system-generated, globally unique identifiers, completely independent of any physical location or attribute value. "Two surrogates are equal in the [extended] relational model if and only if they denote the same entity in the perceived world of entities". The surrogate embodies the identity of the entity over time, just as reference markers in certain linguistic frameworks.

Entities are classified in *characteristic*, *associative* and *kernel* entities. Associative entities interrelate entities of other types and can be thought of as aggregations. Examples are second-order entities (SoA's), such as assignments. Kernel entities are defined independently of all other entity types. Examples are first-order entities, such as employees. Characteristic entities fill a subordinate role in describing entities of some other type. A characteristic entity cannot exist in the database unless the entity it describes most immediately is also in the database (characteristic integrity). It can play a role in representing multi-valued dependencies. For example, offerings are characteristic of courses; a given offering makes sense only as an offering of some particular course, it is meaningless by itself. Likewise, enrollees are characteristics of offerings (cf. Date,1986:440).

There are two kinds of relations (in the technical sense): E-relations and P-relations. The main purpose of an E-relation is to list all the surrogates of entities that have that type and are currently recorded in the database. P-relations define properties of entities. The (role of the) entity over which the property is predicated is called the K-role of the P-relation. So each P-relation has one K-role, although it may have more than one participant. Examples of P-relations are employee-name (where employee is the K-role) and assignment-employee-project (where assignment is the K-role, and employee and project are participants). A given property may serve to identify the entity in question, or to reference some related entity, or simply "stand for itself".

At first sight, it looks as if E-relations and P-relations cover all possible relations, but this is not the case. For example, if we want to represent a relation part-color, where parts may come in multiple colors, a relation is made with a composite key (part number, color), that is neither an E-relation nor a P-relation.

The extended model captures more meaning than the original relational model. One advantage is that it allows for composite terms. Roughly said, P-relations contain the predications and E-relations the terms. The K-role of the predication corresponds to the subject role of the predication. (Note that in the example assignment-employee-project, the subject of the predication is the second-order entity "assignment". It should be read as: "assignment x has employee y and project z"). Term identities are independent of the values of their properties, thus allowing in principle a distinction between term and referent. Characteristic entities can be used to represent complex terms, such as "offering Y *of* course X". As we see in the example of multiple colors, sets cannot be represented directly. Although the definition of entity is kept vague enough to include all kinds of terms, its use is in practice restricted to discrete singular terms. There is no provision for specifying the cardinality of the term, although it is possible to define a P-relation for that.

In the logic approach to databases, terms are either constants, variables or nested functional terms. Functional terms can be used to handle complex objects (Zaniolo,1985), but this approach has some undesirable limitations in supporting data abstraction and referential sharing. Bancilhon (1986) and Khoshafian and Copeland (1986) describe an approach in which complex terms can be built from atomic objects by applying to them recursively a tuple and a set construct. An example of such a complex term is:

```
course(no:231,
       title: db,
       instructor: prof(name:smith, sex:male, age:36),
       enrollees: students {student(name:john, age:17),
                            student(name:jane, age:18),
                            student(name:bill, age:20)})
```

$P\{O_1, O_2, ..., O_n\}$ represents a set and $(A_1:O_1, A_2:O_2, ..., A_n:O_n)$ is a tuple with attribute names A_i. One of the problems in the representation is that tuples and sets do not have an identifier of their own. Chen and Gardarin (1988) present a method by which complex terms are mapped to "flat" terms which starts by introducing these identifiers (thus coming closer to the FG representation of terms). A more serious deficiency of these approaches is that, if the term represents an attribute T-frame (characteristic entity, in Codd's terminology), no distinction is made between attributes of which the referred entity is existence-dependent and attributes that give additional information. For example, the "enrollees" field of the tuple above may be empty, and the same holds for the other fields. If a course happens to have no students, instructors, title and registration number, it can still be a course. However, in a tuple of the form:

```
father(person: john)
```

the person slot is essential. If someone is a father, he is the father of someone. If he is nobody's father, then he is no father.

Tuples are sometimes written as ordered tuples without field names. Compare (4a) and (4b):

(4a) `student(name: jan)(age: 18)`

(4b) `student(jan,18)`

As Aït-Kaci has argued (Aït-Kaci, 1986:116), this makes the definitions more inflexible. Firstly, the number of arguments is fixed and cannot be extended without redefining the whole tuple. Secondly, meaning is expressed by the *position*, so the original intended interpretation of the order of arguments must constantly be kept in mind. Thirdly, it is more difficult to define a subtype relation on tuples, since hyponym and hyperonym may have a different number of fields.

However, introducing field labels must be done with care in order to ensure that the field labels are used consistently throughout the database. The label "age" may be used in several tuple types, but it has a certain meaning of its own. It should be possible to speak about the age of x without having to know what x is (cf. Maier, Ullman, Vardi, 1984). Using an "age"-field in some complex term should not entail that "age" is fixed to that term (cf. the discussion of data independence in 1.1)

From our short overview of the status of terms in database languages we conclude the following:

1 the terms of a database language must be defined independently from implementation considerations (data structure, data value, data location). However, more often than not, languages leave the concept of "term" implicit or confuse it with term reference ("entity").

2 complex terms (with aggregation and set formation) are a desirable extension of languages in which terms can be atomic only.

The remainder of this chapter is devoted to the logical structure and semantics of FG terms. We first repeat the FG structure of terms, and show how terms can be defined as instantiations of T-frames. Special attention is given to numerals and the restrictors. Then we describe the semantics of terms extending the framework of chapter 3.

5.3. DEFINITION

The various elements of the term structure can be grouped over three levels.† We call these the lexeme level, the frame level and the instance level.

lexeme — The head of the term (CAT), typically a noun, specifies the stem, gender, discreteness, separable parts of the stem and other lexical information.

frame — The frame contains semantic functions (SEM), such as `ref` and `rel`, if any, is further specified for number (NUM) and can be extended by means of secondary semantic functions or satellites (SAT) and restrictors (RES)

instance — The information in the instance has the purpose of locating or identifying the intended referent of the term marked by the reference marker (REF). The term can be specified with respect to other operators (OP), in particular for definiteness. It can be further identified by means of localizers (LOC) or a predication (SIT).

In BNF form, the syntactic definition becomes then:

```
<lexeme>     ::= <CAT>
<frame>      ::= <NUM> <REF> <lexeme> <SEM> <SAT>* (":" <RES>)*
<instance>   ::= <OP>* <frame> (":" <LOC>)* (":" <SIT>)
<term>       ::= <instance>
```

Note that this syntactic definition applies to the "classical" FG notation, not to the f-structure format. In this chapter, we will use both notations but the formal definitions apply to the f-structure format.

† In (Dik, 1978), no levels were distinguished although the ordering of the operators suggested already a difference in scope. Rijkhoff (1988) has worked out a functional layering of term operators which I have gratefully incorporated in my present framework.

We will now consider the term structure in more detail.

5.3.1. T-frames

We recollect from chapter 4 that the predicate lexeme of the T-frame can be represented by means of an f-structure, for example:

```
(stem => "sheep";
 cat => n;
 forms => (plur => "sheep"))
```

The T-frame is an f-structure containing such a lexical predicate. Examples:

```
(pred => (stem => "sheep"; cat => n; forms => (plur => "sheep"));
 cat => t;
 type => [animate];
 sem => -)

(pred => (stem => "father"; cat => n);
 cat => t;
 type => [animate];
 sem => (ref => (type => [animate])))
```

In these f-structure, an extra address (or set of addresses) starting with SEM is inserted. This address must be continued with a semantic function such as `ref`. The semantic function may contain a selection restriction, such as `[animate]`, but at this place we can also expect an f-structure of an embedded term. Such an embedded term must comply to the selection restriction. Formally, this means that the embedded term is subsumed by the selection restriction frame. In the following example, the subframe corresponding to the term `child` is subsumed by the frame `(type => [animate])`.

```
(pred => (stem => "father"; cat => n);
 cat => t;
 type => [animate];
 sem => (ref => (pred => (stem => "child";
                          cat => n;
                          forms => (plur => "children"));
                 cat => t;
                 type => [animate])))
```

f-structure for `father(child)`

In the rest of this chapter, we will ignore the internal structure of the lexeme in order to concentrate on the higher levels. Thus we will write just `sheep` where we mean `(stem => "sheep"; cat => t; forms => (plur => "sheep"))`.

The T-frame can be *extended* by means of operators, satellites and restrictors:

T-frame operators - typically number and/or cardinality.

T-frame restrictors - qualifiers and restrictive relative clauses.

T-frame satellites - secondary semantic functions

Note that the possible extensions do not modify the T-frame. Hence every extended T-frame is still subsumed by a T-frame from the Thesaurus. If ϕ is the the extended T-frame, and $\hat{}\phi$ is the predicate frame from which ϕ is derived, then $\phi \leq \hat{}\phi$. In f-structure theory, this is equivalent to: $\phi = \hat{}\phi \wedge \psi$, for some ψ, where the $\wedge$ stands for unification. In most cases, this unification is simply the conjunction of the two f-structures, as in the following example:

```
(pred => sheep;
 cat => t;
 type => [animate])
∧
 (num => plur;
  count => 3)
=
(pred => sheep;
 cat => t;
 type => [animate]);
 num => plur;
 count => 3)
```

The second frame used in this unification can be defined formally as a frame whose address tree contains {ε,num,count}. The domains of these addresses are typed so that the ψ-value of num is restricted to {sing,plur} and the one of count to the domain of integers. In other languages, the number domain may be different (for example, including a dualis form, or not distinguishing singular and plural). Number and cardinality are treated further in 5.3.4. With respect to the representation of number, I admit that perhaps num, being a grammatical category, is better put *inside* the predicate, on the same level as the stem. This could be easily adapted in my framework.

What holds for the cardinality holds similarly for the other extensions of the T-frame, the satellites and restrictors. For these too, we can define subtrees. We will postpone the discussion till we have described the instantiation of T-frames.

5.3.2. Term instantiation

T-frames can be instantiated to terms. In chapter 4, we saw that T-frames can be embedded in term schemata. A term instance, or term for short, has the same format as a term schema:

```
(pred => T-frame;
 cat => t;
 var => )
```

Example:

```
(pred => (pred => father;
          cat => t;
          num => sing;
          sem => (ref => <john>));
 cat => t;
 var => X)
                    [s] x father(ref <john>)
```

(where <john> is an abbreviation of a term of its own). The tag symbol used at the var address marks *semantic* co-reference. If two var-addresses have the same tag symbol, the corresponding terms are said to co-refer. Note that we use capital letters for tag symbols, as usual, whereas the reference markers in FG are written in lower case. However, both stand for the same thing, namely, reference markers that are mapped to referents by a verifying function *f*. The process of *term instantiation* (or *interpretation*) consists in attaching the value of *f* to the var-address, for example:

```
(pred => (pred => father;
          cat => t;
          num => sing;
          sem => (ref => <john>));
 cat => t;
 var => X:x235)
                    [s] x/x235 father(ref <john>)
```

In general, when we write down the "deep structure" of a sentence, we are not interested in the actual denotation of the terms in it. We are only interested in the "logical form". The FG underlying clause represents the propositional (knowledge base) level. A term may have several denotations, depending on the database we are working with and the verification function.

It is at the instance level that the definiteness operator applies. Generally speaking, definiteness indicates for the Addressee whether or not (the Speaker assumes that) an intended referent can be identified. Another optional operator at schema level is prox (proximity, for demonstratives), a binary operator that in some languages can take an argument from the set {S,A}. The S stands for Speaker and the A for Addressee. In English *this/these* are +prox, and *that/those* are -prox. In Japanese, three operators are distinguished: +prox(S) (*kono*; "this"), +prox(A) (*sono*; "that"), and -prox({S,A}) (*ano*; "overthere").

If the frame is not an instance, but a predicate schema, this is indicated by the definiteness being Δ. Such frames are used when the term is generic.

5.3.3. Restrictors

In FG, the intended referent of the term is identified by an ordered list of "restrictors" which progressively narrow down the potential referents of the term. These restrictors are predications open in x_i, the referent marker of the term. These restrictors may be of several formal types:

qualifiers: a *big* order

terms: *John's* desk, the city hall *in New York*

predications: the terminals *that have been assembled in Chicago*

Note that in the case of term restrictors, the restrictor is not the term as such, but a term with a function, for example *loc* or *poss*, used predicatively.

Exploring the formal differences between restrictors, Rijkhoff (1988) has made a distinction between "adjectives" (qualifiers) and "embedded domains" (locative terms, predications). "As opposed to adjectives embedded domains do not characterize an intended referent with respect to its inherent, more or less (literally) typical properties. Embedded domains locate the intended referent set as a whole in time and/or space, in relation with one or more other referent sets. In other words, whereas adjectives (and nominals) specify *set membership* of each individual member with respect to their typical properties, embedded domains can be seen as *set localizers*, specifying some non-typical, external property or relation of the intended referent" (p.12). Rijkhoff proposes then a distinction between three layers of the restrictors: the head (what we call the predicate), the adjectival restrictors (the "simple predication" - what we call qualifiers) and the embedded domain (the predication above). These layers correspond to the layers of the term we described in 5.3 above with respect to the scope of the term operators.

For this reason, we will not, as in traditional FG, consider *one* function "restrictor", but consider several kinds of restrictors, besides the head predicate: *qualifiers, localizers,* and *resource situations*. Being different kinds of restrictors, they don't need to be of the same format. Qualifiers are typically adjectives and are part of the T-frame. Localizers are restrictors at the instance level. The resource situation is also a part of the instance frame. In our linear notation, we write first the qualifiers, then the localizers and finally the resource situation.

Let us give a representative example:

```
(pred => (pred => dog;
          cat => t;
          type => [animate];
          num => sing;
          res => { (pred => mean; cat => q),
                   (pred => little; cat => q) });
 var =>  X3;
 def => d;
 res => (loc => (pred => UNDER;
                 cat => q;
                 type => [place];
                 sem => (ref => (pred => (pred => table;
                                          cat => t;
                                          num => sing);
                                 def => d;
                                 var => X2)));
         sit => PAST(pred => bite;
                     cat => p;
                     type => [action];
                     var => E7;
                     sem => (ag => (var => X3);
                             (go => P1)))
```

which is in FG format:

```
d[s] x3 dog mean: little:
          (loc under(d[s] x2 table)):
          (sit PAST e7 bite(ag x3)(go P1))
```

The mean little dog under the table that bit me

Remarks:

- The term is definite singular and derived from the T-frame for "dog". What is added is a set of qualifiers (Q-frames), instantiations of the adjectives "mean" and "little". The instance frame contains a `loc` function referring to another entity "table". The `sit` function points to a P-frame of "to bite" such that one of the arguments (the agent) co-refers semantically with the term referent, x3. This is in fact a slight simplification, since the `sit` function actually contains a *proposition*. The structure of the proposition will be explained in chapter 6. The structure of the qualifiers is a bit simplified too; cf. 5.4.4.

- Note that we have two adjectival restrictors, written together as a set. Formally, this must be read as saying that the symbol function ψ maps address `pred.res` to a domain consisting of sets of f-structures. As we said earlier, restrictors in FG are stacked. Our use of the set construct for adjectives deviates from this. However, it occurs to me that by distinguishing between head, qualifiers, localizers and resource situations I already capture most of the information that standard FG expresses in the ordering of the restrictors. Besides, pragmatic functions (in particular, Focus) can be attached to restrictors. Finally, expression rules may decide which adjective to take first on the basis of general semantic criteria, such as the the degree of "intrinsicity" of the adjective (this has to be encoded in the meaning definitions).

- The representation of "under the table" as a restrictor containing a frame with head UNDER is motivated by the syntactic structure of prepositional phrases. Prepositional phrases can be used as restrictor ("the book on the shelf") or as a predicate ("John is in London"). This suggests that the interpretation must be an f-structure, more accurately, a Q-frame.

```
(pred => ON;                          (pred => IN;
 cat => q;                             cat => q;
 type => [place];                      type => [place];
 sem => (pred => shelf;                sem => (pred => London;
         var => X))                            var => Y))
```

It must be noted that this format is not generally accepted. In AI, it is customary to define a binary relationship ON:

`ON(x,y)` or in LISP: `(ON X Y)`

This structure may be easy to work with, but it is not transparant with respect to linguistic syntax (cf. Jackendoff, 1984).

Note that the heads of these locative qualifiers are written in upper case. This is because we assume that we can define a universal set of basic place functions, such as ON, IN, UNDER, ABOVE, BEFORE etc. These functions are expressed in English as "on", "in", "under" and "before". It may be possible that one basic place function has several expressions in a certain language.

The formalization proposed here has several advantages. First, it does justice to the scope differences of operators as described by Rijkhoff. Apparently, definiteness has scope over the whole phrase, including the embedded domain (resource situation), whereas number has only scope over the qualifiers. Secondly, it can help in formulating expression rules. In particular, it may help in explaining why relative clauses in many (all?) languages are never more proximate to the head than adjectives.

I have imported the term *resource situation* from the Situation Semantics of Barwise and Perry (*o.c.*, p.36,146). A resource situation is "a situation that is exploited to identify an object". Resource situations can become available for exploitation in a variety of ways, including the following:

(i) by being perceived by the Speaker

(ii) by being the object of some common knowledge about some part of the world

(iii) by being the way the world is

(iv) by being built up by previous discourse

Resource situations contribute to the efficiency of language. For example, if we wanted to describe Jackie's biting Molly but did not know Jackie's name, we might say something like "The dog that just ran past the window is biting Molly". By means of a resource situation we can identify discourse referents without having to come up with a unique identifier.

Barwise and Perry don't make a distinction between different types of restrictors as I do. For them, a qualifier does exploit a resource situation just as well as a relative clause, so my use of the term "resource situation" is more restrictive. On the other hand, it occurs to me that, even for Barwise and Perry, relative clauses differ from adjectives in that the former exploit a resource situation typically *different* from the situation described by the main predication, whereas the latter specify properties of the term referents *in* the situation described by the main predication.

Although the layering of the term - lexeme, frame, instance -, is in accordance with Rijkhoff's analysis, I have some problems with his equating identifiability with the possibility of locating the referent in a particular ST region. For me, identifiability is a property of terms in discourse. A term is identifiable (and hence definite) if it is retrievable (uniquely) by direct recall or by inference. But this does not necessarily include that the term referent exists in some known space-time region, although the reverse is true (all entities the the mental model have been introduced linguistically).

5.3.4. Number and cardinality

In the f-structure, num is used for number (sing, plur) and count for cardinality in the case of count terms, and for measure, used for both mass terms and count terms.† In English, count terms are derived from count nouns, such as *employee*, *part*, *father*, whereas mass terms are derived from mass nouns, such as *snow*, *money*, *unemployment*. Masses have parts and can be measured, but they do not have members, whereas count nouns refer to sets of entities that have members (and parts). Dik (1987) has proposed the following typology of entities:

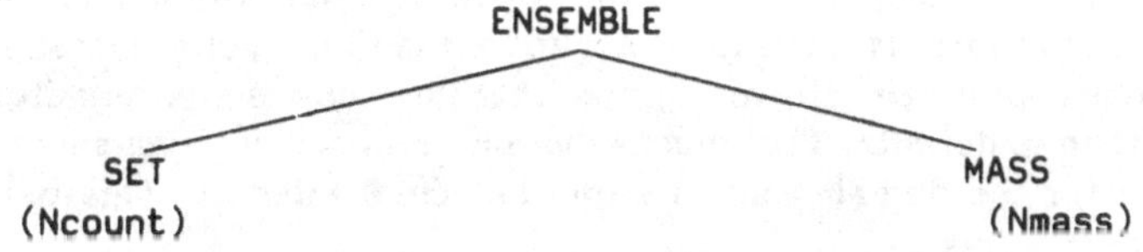

This typology says that all entities are "ensembles", and can be further classified as either sets or masses. Individuals are treated as singleton sets. Sets can contain ensembles (for example, the set "*bacon and eggs*", which contains a count term and a mass term). For the notion of ensemble, the user is referred to the mereology of Lesniewski (Lesniewski, 1929) and the work of Bunt. (Bunt,1985) contains an axiomatic foundation of ensemble theory that encompasses set theory but starts from the subset relation (instead of the membership relation). A formalization of mass terms using lambda calculus is given in (Krifka,1987).

In the case of count terms, the numerator function assigns a cardinal number to the

† Evidently, number and cardinality are closely related, but they do not always coincide. For example, mass nouns are usually singular but that does not mean that their cardinality is "one" (see below). Perhaps number is what in FG is called a *secondary operator*, that is fully determined by the noun type and cardinality. In that case, it need not be specified independently (cf. Rijkhoff, 1988).

term. Cardinal numbers are taken from the set of natural numbers. These cardinal numbers are terms themselves. Just as we have complex terms, built by term formation rules, we may have complex cardinals, such as *more than five*, *between ten and twenty*. It is also possible to question the cardinality (*how many ...?*). Some examples of complex cardinals are:

```
[5,.] X child
```
more than five children

```
[10,20] X guilder
```
between ten and twenty guilders

In the case of mass terms, the numerator function cannot assign a number to the term, but it may assign a measure to the term. Measures are terms themselves, typically count terms that are specified with respect to cardinality. Examples are *two slices of bread*, *three litres of wine*:

```
i[[3] litre] Y wine
```
three litres of wine

Note that it would be mistaken to take *litre* as the head of the term. If three litres of wine are spoiled, the wine is spoiled. If someone drinks a cup of coffee, he drinks coffee, not a cup. See also Dik, 1987.

Brown (1985) makes a distinction between numerators and proportions. Numerators specify the quantity of the referent set. However, we have also terms in which the referent is pictured as a subset of another set (called the *domain set* by Brown), for instance:

(1) one of the thousand wifes of Salomon

(2) some of the seven samurai

In these terms, the cardinality of both the referent set and the domain set is specified. The operator *some* is interpreted as "more than one", and treated in the same way as the other numerals. However, note that this construction is only possible if the domain term is definite. That means that the term actually contains two referent markers, one for the domain and one for the actual referent. This is reflected in the notation:

```
i[1] X in [1000] Y wife(ref [s] Z Salomon)
i[+] X in [7] Y samurai
```

We treat these terms as complex terms formally defined as frames subsumed by the following proportion frame.

```
(pred => X;
 cat => t;
 def => i;
 frame => (sub => (pred => X; cat => t; def => d)))
```

Given a term *x*, such as *the seven samurai*, a new term *y* (*some of the seven sumarai*) is created that is a part of *x* as indicated by the feature SUB (for subset). Subsequently, the new term can be unified with an instance frame specifying the number. The frame requires that the predicate of *x* and *y* co-refer. The same holds for the restrictors.

```
(pred => X;
 cat => t;
 def => i;
 num => plur;
 frame => (sub => (pred => X:samurai;
                   cat => t; def => d; num => 7)))
```

5.4. INTERPRETATION

In chapter 3, a term X has been interpreted by means of a referent xi. This referent participated in the mapping TYPE, which maps referents to elements of the lexicon. For example, the tuple {x7} TYPE {prince} contains the partial information that the TYPE of x7 is prince. Since the mapping TYPE induces a function, we can also write TYPE([x7]) = [prince].

Following definition 3.27, the interpretation of a term in a Tarskian model comes down to finding an *embedding* function f that "verifies" the term. I quote the word "verifies" because the term is a referring expression which does not have a truth-value, so strictly speaking, the word "verification" or "falsification" is not applicable. What I mean is that f maps the referent marker of the term to some referent such that the predicative part of the term, as well as other information specified in the operators, satellites and restrictors, is verified with respect to this referent. In other words, the term is *embeddable* iff the informational part of the term is verifiable. In this chapter I will describe in successive stages the conditions under which a term is embeddable. These conditions are cumulative (this is a consequence of the compositionality principle we adhere to throughout this work). The first definition considers a rudimentary term, consisting of a reference marker and a head, only:

Definition 5.1 Let $t \equiv x$ *HEAD* be a term with referent marker x and head *HEAD*. In f-structure format, t =

```
(pred => (pred => HEAD;
          cat => t);
 var => X)
```

Then t is *embeddable* with respect to a Tarskian model T, with referent set R(T), by an embedding f iff

(i) $f(x) = x_i$, for some $x_i \in$ R(T);

(ii) TYPE($[x_i]$) $\vdash$ HEAD

A term is embeddable iff it is embeddable by some embedding.

end 5.1

This definition is the basis for the interpretation of more complex terms. For the restrictor part, we have to work out the function QUAL whose target domain consists of adjectives. An important function is also the function COUNT. The COUNT of a referent is a type [integer]. This is not a referent, but a type, for example "two". We assume a precedence ordering $\leq$ on integers.

We also consider a function LOC for location. The LOC of a referent is another referent of type [location]. We assume a "contained-in" ordering on location referents.

The functions TYPE, COUNT and QUAL were already introduced in chapter 3. In this chapter, they are described in more detail.

5.4.1. The information structure of entity referents

Complex terms such as *two of the seven samurai* posit a subset relationship between referents. We interpret the subset relationship as an entailment between instances.

In chapter 4, we introduced an information system of entity *types*. An entity type entails another if it is subsumed by it. Two entity types are mutually inconsistent if they have contrasting features. In this chapter, we introduce an information system of entity *instances*. An entity instance entails another if it is a subensemble of it. Two entity instances are mutually inconsistent if their intersection is empty. The subensemble relationship satisfies properties such as transitivity, and reflexivity.

Before we define an information system structure on entity instances, we must ensure that the approximable mappings on them are well-defined. These mappings must be monotonic with respect to the entailment. There are three approximable mappings to consider:

- TYPE: from entity instances to entity types. If x1 is a subensemble of x2, then TYPE(x1) must be subsumed by TYPE(x2).

- COUNT: from entity instances to integers. If x1 is a subensemble of x2, then COUNT(x1) must precede COUNT(x2).

- LOC: from entity instances to locations. If x1 is a subensemble of x2, then LOC(x1) must be contained in LOC(x2).

All these requirements seem quite natural. Consider the term *some of the seven samurai*, represented as `i[+] X in [7] samurai`. Obviously, f(X) must be of type `samurai`. It is also clear that COUNT(f(X)) is smaller than 7. And it is equally clear that if the seven samurai are in Kyushu, then the samurai denoted by "some of them" are in Kyushu too.

Since we define TYPE, COUNT and LOC as approximable mappings, the requirements are met by definition, and we don't need additional axioms. This is a happy consequence of our data algebra approach.

Note that we make a distinction between the subensemble relationship between entity referents and the containment relationship between locations. If x1 $\vdash$ x2, then LOC(x1) $\vdash$ LOC(x2), but not the other way round. That is to say, if my chair is in my room, this does not mean that it is a subensemble of the room. In fact, it can't be since the typing is wrong. This example shows that we must be careful not to confuse the subensemble relationship with extensional containment.

The above considerations motivate the following definition, which can be regarded as a more specific statement of the assumption expressed in 3.10:

Definition 5.2 Let Ref_x be the domain of entity instances including Δ_x and ∇_x. Then we define an information system (Ref_x, Δ_x, Con, $\vdash$) where $\vdash$ is read as the *subensemble relation*, and inconsistency is defined by entailment. If $\{x,y\} \vdash \nabla$, then x and y are said to *exclude* each other.

end 5.2

We also write x **in** y when $\{x\} \vdash y$. The subensemble relation has the following properties:

Proposition 5.3

(i) x **in** x for all $x \in A_x$ (*reflexivity*)

(ii) if x **in** y and y **in** z, then x **in** z (*transitivity*)

(iii) if x **in** y, then COUNT(x) $\vdash$ COUNT(y) (*monotonicity*)

(iv) if x **in** y, then TYPE(x) $\vdash$ TYPE(y) (*monotonicity*)

(v) if x **in** y, then LOC(x) $\vdash$ LOC(y) (*monotonicity*)

Proof Immediate. For example, (ii) says that if $\{x\} \vdash y$ and $\{y\} \vdash z$, then $\{x\} \vdash z$. This follows from the sixth axiom of information systems. □

end 5.3

The subensemble relationship allows an extension of the definition 5.1 for the interpretation of terms:

Definition 5.4 Let $t \equiv$

x in y *HEAD*

be a term. Then t is embeddable (by embedding f) in Tarskian model T iff

(i) $f(x) = x_i$, $f(y) = x_j$, for $x_i, x_j \in$ R(T)

(ii) x **in** y

(iii) TYPE($[x_j]$) $\vdash_T$ *HEAD*

end 5.4

This much for the internal structure of the referent domain. We now turn to the count operator.

5.4.2. Masses and measures

In the formal definitions of chapter 3 we assumed that entities could be counted. However, mass terms cannot be counted directly. They take either one of the following forms:

(A) indefinite proportional: *some water, much research, a lot of work*
Example: *John drank some wine*

(B) measured: *three litres of wine, a cup of coffee, 200 gallons of oil*
Example: *John drank a litre of wine*

(C) generic: *wine*
Example: *John abhors wine*

In the first case, no absolute measure is given. The word *some* has little semantic content, but it is a referring expression, in contrast to (C). Thus, the sentence in (A) introduces a new referent categorized as "wine", without further measure. Whether sentence (C) introduces a referent for "wine" is open for discussion. It introduces at least a referent for "John" and predicates the verb phrase *abhor wine* over this referent. Finally, sentence (B) introduces a new referent categorized as "wine" and measured by a measure term *litre* . This term *litre* in turn is counted by an integer referent of type "3". Note that the term expression *three litres of* in itself has no referent, it just a count of the wine referred to.

The reason that sentence (C) perhaps does not introduce a referent is that in the case of (A) and (B), but less easily in (C), the new referent can become the antecedent of a definite term or anaphor, as in:

(D) definite: *Unfortunately, it was poisoned*

However, an definite reference is not totally impossible:

(E) *This is because it is always served at official parties*

I will not go into details about generic terms. See (Heyer,1985) for a number of relevant suggestions.

The operator *much* under (A) will not be treated in this thesis, just like *a lot of, many, most* etc (cf. Barwise & Cooper, 1981). All those cases presuppose a norm or prototypical quantity of the term category. In our framework, we could put this in the prototype information stored in the Fund of the lexicon. The operator *much* can be interpreted then as a comparison between the term referent and the prototype measure.

The incorporation of mass terms in our framework urges us to enlarge the domain of numbers. In chapter 4. the approximable mapping COUNT mapped entity referents to integers (the latter being lexical predicates). The extension we propose here involves the introduction of a new domain of *measures*, such as "litre". The range of COUNT is not just the set of integers, but a set of functions. That is, if x is an entity, then COUNT(x) is a function from measures to integers. So if m is a measure, then COUNT(x)(m) is an integer. The new treatment if fully compatible with the old one as far as discrete entities are concerned.

The domain of measures is a domain of types. When you hear that your tank contains five litres of gas, it is useless to ask *which* litres (but it is possible to ask which gas). What are the measure types? We assume that the lexicon contains a finite set of measure predicates, such as *litre, meter, gallon, cup* etc. Some languages also have a system of sortal classifiers, such as Japanese *hon* for small long things, *nin* for people etc. By stipulation, each language has an abstract classifier DISC, for discrete things. Measure predicates, classifiers and DISC are put together in a set of measure types (MSRTYPE). A measure *frame* is of the following form:

```
(pred => msrtype;
 cat => m;
 car => integertype)
```

where the "m" symbol is a new category besides {p,t,q}, because a measure frame (M-frame) is neither a term nor a predication nor a qualifier. Some examples of M-frames:

```
(pred => litre;        (pred => DISC;       (pred => hon;
 cat => m;              cat => m;             cat => m;
 car => 3)              car => 5)             car => san)
```

where the third one is Japanese (*sambon*). As before, the predicates should be read as lexemes, not as atomic symbols.

We now turn to the interpretation of M-frames. If we call the entity domain E, the measure domain M and the integer domain C, the domain COUNT is a function domain E → M → C. This domain is isomorphic to the domain E × M → C (Scott, 1982). Therefore, we can easily represent the function COUNT in tabular form as a ternary table with a binary key composed of the entity referent and the measure type. The new situation can be illustrated with the following example. Suppose we have the terms:

```
[2] x1 prince
[7] x2 dwarf
[1] x3 in d[7] x2 dwarf
[[3] litre] x4 wine
[+] x5 poison
```

These terms are interpreted as follows:

TYPE	
ent	type
x1	prince
x2	dwarf
x3	dwarf
x4	wine
x5	poison

COUNT		
ent	msr	int
x1	DISC	2
x2	DISC	7
x3	DISC	1
x4	litre	3
x5	Δ	Δ

SUB	
ent	ent
x3	x2

In this way, we can represent count expressions for both mass terms and discrete terms. We also added the table SUB that is used for representing the SUBensemble relationship. Note that the referents occurring in SUB can be both mass terms and count terms. An example of the former is contained in the term *some of the wine*.

It must be kept in mind that the type "prince" in the example is in fact a T-frame. The precise representation of the tuple <x1,prince> ∈ TYPE is, therefore:

<x1,*t1> ∈ TYPE
<*t1,prince> ∈ PRED

where "prince" now stands for a *lexeme*.

The following definition of the interpretation of terms accounts for measures. We allow single count values (such as in *7 dwarfs*) as well as interval values (such as *10 to 20 books*). Such an interval is represented as [10,20]. The count operators *more than* and *less than* can be specified in an interval by leaving one of the two values open.

Definition 5.5 Let t be a term with part "[C] x" or "[[C] UNIT] x". Then t is embeddable by an f iff t is embeddable according 5.1 and 5.2 *and*

(i) $f(x) = x_i$, for some $x_i \in$ R(T);

(ii) [COUNT([x_i])([UNIT])] = [C], if UNIT ∈ MSRTYPE, or
[COUNT([x_i])([DISC])] = [C], if UNIT is not specified

If the count operator is of the form [C_1, C_2], then condition (ii) should be replaced by:

(ii)' COUNT([x_i])([*UNIT*]) ⊢ C_2
$\{C_1\}$ ⊢ COUNT([x_i])([*UNIT*])

end 5.5

Notice that condition (ii)' is a genuine extension of (ii). We can define [C] to be equivalent to [C,C]. Then (ii)' says that COUNT(...)(...) $\vdash$ C $\wedge$ {C} $\vdash$ COUNT(...)(...). That means that [CAR(*m)] = [C].

The entailment relationship defined on the integer types is to be interpreted as the $\leq$ precedence ordering. So [7] = $\{7,8,9,\ldots,\Delta\}$, etc. In general, we have the axiom:

$\{i\} \vdash succ(i)$

where *succ* is the successor function as used in the Peano axioms. Condition (ii)' can be written also as:

$\mathrm{COUNT}([x_i])([UNIT]) \leq C_2$
$\{C_1\} \leq \mathrm{COUNT}([x_i])([UNIT])$

5.4.3. Grouping

Although our term logic does allow singular and plural terms, it cannot handle conjoined terms yet. Examples are:

(1) *Pat and her husband own an estate*

(2) *The committees of the CIA and the committees of the State Department watch each other*

(3) *Jimmy, Ron and George are married to Rosalynn, Nancy and Barbara, respectively*

(4) *Peter and Mary are students*

We do not have an interpretation of the *and* (nor *or*) yet. A possible solution is the following extension of the grammar. First, change <REF> in the definition of <TERM> to <REF'>. <REF'> is defined as:

<REF'> ::= <REF>
<REF'> ::= <REF> "=" <TERM> ("&" <TERM>)*
<REF'> ::= <REF> "=" <TERM> ("or" <TERM>)*

Sentence (1) can now be rendered as:

(a) `e own(po [p] x = [s] y Pat & [s] z husband(ref y))(go i[s] u estate)`

Note that the first term contains three reference markers: one for Pat, one for her husband and one for their conjunction. All three can be used as antecedent of an anaphor (*he, she, they*). Each one has its own operators. For example, the conjoined term may be quantified, as in *Pat and her husband each own an estate*.

In linguistics, it is customary to make a distinction between collective (sometimes called corporate) and distributive readings. Some sentences can be read in only one way, and some are ambiguous. For example, (4) has a distributive reading only: from (4), we can deduce that Peter is a student and that Mary is a student. Sentence (1), however, is ambiguous. It can mean that Pat and her husband each own an estate, but it can also mean that they are co-owners, that they own the estate together. Furthermore, we have sentences like (2) and (3) that exclude the distributive reading, but cannot be called collective either. I will confine myself to collective and distributive terms, leaving sentences like (2) and (3) for further research (see Sowa, 1984:118,119 and Landman, 1987 for some inspiring ideas). Terms like *a committee*, *a group* are not treated differently from other terms. So in contrast to, for instance Link (1983) and Landman (1987), I will not interpret it as a set or group, just as I don't interpret the term *body* as a set of organs. The *member-of* relation between committees and persons is a lexical predicate with its own meaning definition (which may or may not refer to the subset relationship).

In some cases, the collective or distributive reading is enforced by the predicate. For example, a property like *being a couple* can not be predicated over singular individuals, thus excluding a distributive reading of (5):

(5) *John and Joni are a fine couple*

On the other hand, a property like *being a student* can hardly be predicated over groups, thus enforcing a distributive reading in (4). † Similarly, a verb like *to grasp* enforces a distributive reading of the agent, but a verb like *to lift* (*to lift a piano*) is still ambiguous. The collective or distributive reading interferes also with the term operators, as Scha noted (1981). A term with term operator *each* can only be read distributively. Scha also states that plural definite terms always get a collective reading, but this is not correct (see Roberts, 1987).

To account for phenomena of collectivity, Brown (1985) introduces a term operator "corp" (corporate). Let us abbreviate it to "C". The "C" is put at the operator position before the number. So if sentence (1) has two readings, then there are two underlying clauses:

(b) `e own(po C[2] x = [s] y Pat & [s] z husband(ref y))(go i[s] u estate)`

(c) `e own(po [2] x = [s] y Pat & [s] z husband(ref y))(go i[s] u estate)`

Let us now turn to the interpretation. It is natural to use the subensemble relationship between entity referents. That is, the interpretation of propositions (b) will include (f is the embedding):

f(z) **in** f(x),
f(y) **in** f(x)

For the rest, the interpretation is as usual:

COUNT(f(z) (DISC)= 1
COUNT(f(y))(DISC) = 1
COUNT(f(x))(DISC) = 2
{ f(e)} po { f(x)}
TYPE(f(e)) ⊢ own
...

Note that the predication is applied to the group term x. This holds for the

† In FG, we can use the selection restrictions of the predicate. In 4.3.1 we introduced a basic taxonomy of entities. This taxonomy can be juxtaposed to the individual/collection dichotomy. For example, a family is of type [human], but also a collection, whereas father is of type [human] and an individual. Hence the type of family becomes [human,c] and the type of father [human,i]. A "collective" predicate requires that it is applied to a collection, and this usually enforces a collective reading but not necessarily so. For example, if we say that *John and Joni and Peter and Mary are fine couples*, then the second *and* should be read distributively.

collective reading. However, in the case that the term is not marked for collectivity, the proposition must be applied to each of the conjuncts. The following definition defines embeddability for collective terms and then specifies how to interpret distributive conjuncts and disjuncts.

Definition 5.6 (Collective and distributive terms). Let t be a collective term of the form $x = t_1 \ \& \ t_2 \ \& \ \ldots \ \& \ t_n$. The reference marker of t is x and the reference markers of t_i are y_i. Then t is embeddable (in model T) if t is embeddable according to 5.1 and 5.4, each t_i is embeddable *and* embedding f embeds x and each y_i such that

$f(y_i)$ **in** $f(x)$, for i=1...n

If $p[x]$ is a proposition containing a distributive conjunct x, of the form $x = t_1 \ \& \ t_2 \ \& \ \ldots \ \& \ t_n$, then $T \models p[x]$ iff

$T \models p[t_i/x]$, for $i = 1,\ldots,n$.

If $p[x]$ is a proposition containing a distributive *disjunct* x, where $x = t_1$ or t_2 or ... or t_n, then $T \models p[x]$ iff

$T \models p[t_i/x]$, for some $i \leq$ n

end 5.6

The interpretation of collective terms is such that "static" predicates are inherited, but SoAs are not. This is because the functions PRED, COUNT and LOC are monotonic with respect to the subensemble relationship. However, the semantic functions ag etc, are not defined on entities, but on SoAs. The entity domain is the range of these functions. Therefore it does not follow that, if $ag(e)=x$, and x is a collective term *John and Jony*, then $ag(e)=f(John)$, $ag(e)=f(Jony)$.

As far as distributive terms are concerned, definition 5.6 urges us to interpret proposition (c) by intepreting the two propositions:

(c1) `own(po [s] y Pat)(go i[s] u estate)`

(c2) `own(po [s] z husband(ref y))(go i[s] u estate)`

Apart from the complication that the verifying embedding must obey the coreference restrictions, so that the reference marker `y` in C2 co-refers with the one in C1, the two propositions can be interpreted in the normal way. We don't introduce a referent for `x`. The reader may be tempted to suggest that in that case, the variable `x` is superfluous. However, it can be used as an antecedent on the knowledge base level. *Pat and her husband* (distributive reading) is a genuine term, although it lacks a referent.

5.4.4. Qualifiers

A term does not only contain a head and operators, but also a range of restrictors. In this section, we give the interpretation for the qualifiers. For the resource situation, the interpretation has to await another chapter. Moreover, we only give the interpretation of adjectival qualifiers. Derived qualifiers, such as the *-ing*-form of verbs, are not treated.

For the interpretation of qualifiers we make use of the function QUAL ranging from instances to qualifier types, represented as q_1 etc. For example, if x is a little prince (`x prince: little`), then QUAL([x]) $\vdash$ q_i, for some q_i, such that

PRED($[q_1]$) = [little] and TYPE($[x]$) $\vdash$ prince.

There is an old philosophical discussion going back at least to Aristotle about the question whether individual qualities exist. One side maintains that we only have the predicate (type) little which is predicated over the term referent. According to the other side, "littleness" may be instantiated in the same way as "dog". The "littleness" of prince A may be another "littleness" than the one of prince B.

Sticking to the approach advocated in this thesis, I will not go into philosophical quarrels about the ontology of qualities. The following linguistic observations suggest at least that qualities are complex objects:

1 Qualities can be measured just as entities and SoAs. The prince may be 10 years old and 5 feet long. These measures can be compared and one quality can be said to be greater than another (A is taller than B).

2 Qualities can be qualified themselves, just as entities and SoAs. Snowwhite may be *remarkably* pale, and the prince may be *extremely* small. John's paper may be *stylistically* bad, but *scientifically* good. At least in Dutch, it is possible to use a localizer "the in Holland triangular but in Germany square traffic sign".

3 Consider sentences like *Peter was surprised when he saw how beautiful she was.* What did Peter see? Not *that* she was beautiful, but the beauty she showed.

On the other hand, qualities have no identity conditions. Even a deictic expression such as *that green* refers to a type (I want a coat that is *that* green...). Therefore we treat qualities as types, but these types may be complex. The function QUAL maps entities to quality types.

Definition 5.7 Let t be a term with term referent x_i and qualifier Q with head A. Then t is embeddable by f in T iff, in addition to the other conditions:

(i) $QUAL([x_i]) \vdash q$, for some qualifier type q

(ii) $PRED([q]) \vdash$ A

end 5.7

The qualifier qualifiers and measures are not discussed here. The interpretation is essentially the same as with entity referents. For the interpretation of comparatives (*younger, taller*) we draw upon the precedence ordering on measures. In the same line, it is possible to interpret sentences like *John is stronger than Mary is intelligent* as saying that count(q_2) < count(q_1), where q_1 is John's strength and q_2 is Mary's intelligence.

The definition QUAL is such that, if the seven samurai are happy, then each one of the seven samurai is happy too. In some cases, this seemingly leads to odd results. For example, if the seven samurai are strong together, it is not implied that each one of them is strong. However, it can be maintained that each one of them is strong together. Apparently, "strong together" is a different property than "strong". This can be accounted for easily in our framework by adding the feature [c(ollective)] to the *type* of the Q-frame.

```
(pred => strong;
 cat => q;
 type => [animate,c])
```

This Q-frame represents a schema different from the individual "strength", although both are presumably subsumed by the same predicate frame (with type [animate]; other senses of "strong", for example for alcoholics, correspond to other frames). It must be assumed that some Q-frames are marked in the lexicon as collective (for example, *numerous*), some as individual (*red*), and some as unspecified (*strong, heavy*). The latter Q-frames can be applied both collectively and individually, which is effectuated by means of an operator.

Anticipating on the next chapter, we also recall that qualities are not only assigned to first-order entities, but also to second-order entities (SoAs). In that case, they are expressed as adverbs ("quickly, tenderly"). The semantic interpretation is the same (mutatis mutandis).

5.4.5. Locations

The interpretation of a term "the book on the shelf" makes use of a semantic function LOC on entity referents, and a place function ON (cf. 4.2.5). There is much to say about locations, locative expressions and primitive place functions, and I admit that the following rudimentary treatment does not do justice to all problems in this field.

Our approach is based on the fact that places are always referred to by means of a first-order or second-order entity (a thing or a SoA). This suggests that no new referents should be introduced. In fact, the situation is similar to the one of measure types. These too exist as predicate schemata. They are linked to the instances by means of the function MSR, but they are not instances (referents) themselves. In the same vein, we define a function LOC to place types. Just as *two litres* and *happy* are types, so is *under the desk*:

```
(pred => litre;          (pred => happy;            (pred => UNDER;
 cat => t;                cat => q;                  cat => q;
 type => [quantity];      type => [animate])         type => [place]
 car => 2)                                           sem => (ref => <desk>)
```

The first frame may be the function value of MSR([x1]), where [x1] is an amount of wine. The second frame may be the function value of TYPE([x2]), where [x2] is a person. The third frame may be the function value of LOC([x3]), where [x3] is some mouse.†

The representation of the term: "the books in the library" becomes then:

† Perhaps these three functions capture what Aristotle had in mind in his discussion of movement (in the sense of change): "movement ... pertains exclusively to quality, quantity, and locality, each of which embraces contrasts" (Physics, V. II) (cf. Rijksbaron, 1988 cited in Rijkhoff, 1988). In my framework, entities also have the function TYPE, which is equally vulnerable to change, although usually with lower frequency.

TYPE([x10]) ⊢ book
TYPE([x5]) ⊢ library
LOC([x10]) ⊢ IN([x5])

This is formally contained in the following definition:

Definition 5.8 Let t be a term with referent x_i and containing the locative restrictor *loc* $L(t_2)$, where L is a place function and t_2 is a term with referent x_j. Then t is embeddable iff, if (in addition to what is specified in the previous definitions),

(i) LOC(x_i) ⊢ L(x_j)

end 5.8

5.4.6. The predicative use of terms and restrictors

Terms can also be used predicatively, as in the predication *John is a painter*. The f-structure of this predication becomes

```
(pred => (pred => (pred => painter;
                   num => sing);
          var => Y;
          def => i;
          cat => t);
 cat => p;
 syn => (subj => (pred => (pred => john;
                           num => sing);
                  var => X;
                  def => d;
                  cat => t)))
```

This structure consists of a P-frame containing two different terms. One is the head (predicator) and the other is the subject (more about the structure of P-frames is in the next chapter). The referent markers indicate antecedent relations and need not be the same. The (predicate part of this) predication is verified by f iff f(X) ⊢ f(Y).

It is also possible that *a painter* in the sentence *John is a painter* is to be read as a *type*. For the difference between these two readings, see Mackenzie (1988) (in Dutch, the two readings may get different expressions). If so, the term is marked as "generic", by `def` being undefined.

```
(pred => (pred => pred => painter;
                  num => sing);
          def => Δ;
          cat => t);
 cat => p;
 syn => (subj => (pred => (pred => john;
                           num => sing);
                  var => X;
                  def => d;
                  cat => t)))
```

Now the (predicative part of the) predication is verified iff TYPE(f(X)) $\vdash$ painter.

The predicator can also be a qualifier or localizer:

```
(pred => (pred => intelligent;
          cat => q);
 cat => p;
 syn => (subj => (pred => (pred => john;
                           num => sing);
                  var => X;
                  def => d;
                  cat => t)))
```

John is intelligent

This predication is verified iff QUAL(f(X)) $\vdash$ intelligent. An example of a localizer:

```
(pred => (pred => IN;
          cat => q;
          type => [place];
          sem => (ref => <library>));
 cat => p;
 syn => (subj => (pred => (pred => john;
                           num => sing);
                  var => X;
                  def => d;
                  cat => t)))
```

John is in the library

This predication is verified iff LOC(f(X)) $\vdash$ IN(y), where TYPE(y) $\vdash$ library.

5.5. CONCLUSION

In this chapter we have focused our attention on terms. The representation of complex terms in knowledge bases is an unresolved problem. Most current approaches are too restrictive. Moreover, there exists some conceptual confusion on the meaning of terms. We have tried to solve this confusion by making a distinction between the referent of the term in some model and the term itself (as a referring expression) and by assuming that the knowledge base contains terms rather than referents, whereas the database contains term referents.

We have outlined how terms are instantiated from T-frames, and have considered several term operators. We have given an interpretation for the measure operator that applies both to count terms and mass terms. The domain of entity instances was formalized as an information system where the entailment is interpreted as subensemble relationship. This relationship is necessary for the interpretation of proportional and conjoined terms.

The subensemble relationship can be used for other purposes as well. In some cases, we need to distinguish between different *roles* of an entity. For example, if John is both a judge and a hangman (Landman, 1987), we can encounter propositions such as: "As a judge, John earns $300 and as a hangman he earns $15". Or: "The judges are on strike" (so John strikes as a judge, but not as hangman). To model these propositions, we introduce *three* referents: one for John, one for "John as a judge" and one for "John as a hangman". The latter two are subsumed by the former, but otherwise unrelated.

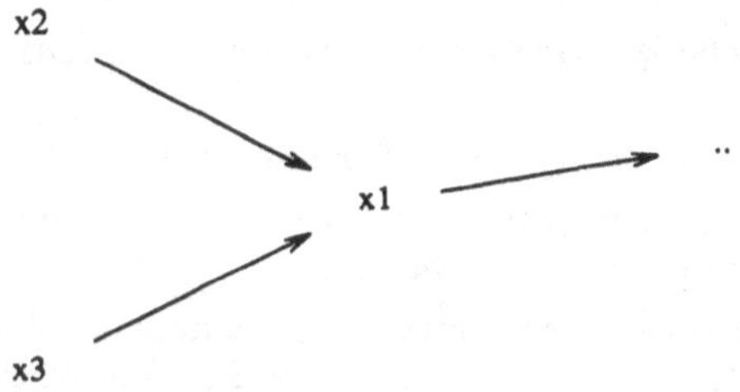

It follows that everything said about "John" (x1) also holds for "John as a judge" (x2) and "John as a hangman" (x3), but not the other way round. Of course, the count of each of them is one, but that does not necessarily imply that they are equal (this is an advantage of the subensemble relationship over the subset relationship in set theory). The embedding conditions of "John as judge" are simply a referent that has both type "John" and type "judge".

6

Propositions

6.1. INTRODUCTION

The central level of the FG underlying clause is the proposition. A proposition represents a *judgement* that is true or not with respect to facts. It is a piece of information that can be shared by linguistic agents and stored in their knowledge bases. In the functional perspective, a language is conceived of in the first place as an instrument of social interaction between human beings, used with the primary aim of establishing communicative relations between linguistic agents. In view of this, the proposition, as being the message content, has several functions:

(a) it presents or represents some State of Affairs, by means of the predication(s) it contains

(b) it characterizes an Intentional state of the Speaker

(c) it provides the Addressee with clues for building or updating a mental model (which in turn may prompt some action).

Ad (a). A proposition conveys information. This is what Barwise and Perry call the *external significance* of language (*o.c.*,pp.28-31). For example, Jonny takes his dog Jackie to the vet because she is limping badly. The doctor takes an X-ray, examines it, and tells Jonny "She has a broken leg". His utterance contains information about Jackie, that she has a broken leg. This is a certain State of Affairs that Barwise and Perry call the *interpretation* of the statement. Thus the reference of the statement (proposition) is not a truth-value, but a situation.

Although I agree with Barwise and Perry that language has external significance, I have my doubts about their reduction of language to information flow. They run into trouble when they identify linguistic meaning with a constraint to which the linguistic agents would be attuned, as Pratt points out (Pratt, 1987). These problems have to do with the assumed language-independence of information and with the required sincerity and well-informedness of the Speaker. In the framework I am building in this thesis, an atomic proposition may represent a State of Affairs in reality, but not necessarily so (as in the case of fiction, proposals, counterfactuals etc). Even if it does, it does so only indirectly (a) by mediation of a *model* in the mind that already *abstracts* from the reality, and (b) by mediation of a certain natural *language* and certain meaning conventions shared by the Speaker with a linguistic community to which he belongs, and (c) through an *act* of judgement or agreement by the Speaker.

Ad (b). I use the phrase "Intentional state" in the sense of Searle (1983). Intentional states are beliefs, desires, hopes, fears, doubts etc. There are several connections between Intentional states and speech acts. One connection is that, "in the performance of a speech act with a propositional content, we express a certain Intentional state with that propositional content, and that Intentional state is the sincerity condition of that type of speech act." (*ibid*, p. 9). Thus, for example, if I make the statement that *p*, I express a belief that *p*. If I make a promise to do *A*, I express an intention to do *A*. If I give an order to you to do *A*, I express a wish or desire that you should do *A*. If I apologize for doing something, I express sorrow for doing that thing etc. This does not rule out the possibility of lying. A lie or other insincere speech act consists in performing a speech act, and thereby expressing an Intentional state, where one does not have the Intentional state that one expresses. If the speech act would not express an Intentional state, there could be no insincerity either.

Ad (c). The characteristics (a) and (b) of propositions were both "Speaker-oriented". But if a proposition is to fulfil its function of communicative content, it should do something to the Addressee too. This can be understood in two ways. First, the Addressee must be able to make sense of the proposition. One necessary requirement in this regard is that the discourse is coherent, that terms can be identified and that he is able to build a mental model that *is similar* to the one of the Speaker. If his interpretation would be incomparable with the original Intentional state of the Speaker, there would not be communication. Perhaps this goal is not met in all communications, but at least it is the case in the communication of thought. I recall Michael Dummett's statement (cf. 1.6), that "it is the essence of thought that I can convey to you the very thought I have, as opposed to being able to tell you merely something about what my thought is like".

Second, the proposition does something to the Speaker in the sense that the Speaker intends a certain effect. For example, if a supplier informs a client that he sells parts A for so much, his intention is that the client believes this proposition, and he hopes to bring about that the client orders some parts. In this chapter, the first aspect will be covered in the sense that we provide an *operational* semantics to propositions compatible with the truth-theoretic semantics. The second aspect will be treated in the next chapter when we are talking about speech acts and communication.

This chapter builds on chapter 3 about algebraic semantics and chapter 4 about the lexicon. The frames that make up our propositional language are described as *instantiations* of predicate schemata. The frames will be formalized as f-structures. In chapter 3, we already gave the semantics of atomic propositions without predicational or modal operators. In this chapter, it is our task to extend the semantic framework so as to include:

- *tense and aspect*. The facts stored in the knowledge base are bound to a given time. Traditional databases only stored "snap-shots" of the databasee. A *temporal* database (Gadia,1988; Clifford, 1983) provides an extra level of data independence by associating time values to the data items. This extension poses some interesting problems, not only on the side of efficient implementation but also in the semantics. Logical problems with temporalized data have been addressed before in tense logic (Reichenbach, 1947; Van Benthem, 1983; Burgess, 1984). Tense logic has been used also for the formulation of temporal integrity constraints (Kung, 1984; Lipeck and Saake, 1987). Reasoning about time in the context of predicating, planning and heuristic reasoning, is a topic in AI studied by McDermott (1982) and Shoham (1987). For the use of tense and aspect in narratives, see Almeida (1987) and (Lo Cascio & Vet, 1988), among others. In this thesis, I will limit myself to the presentation of a temporal framework of a rather classical nature in the context of a data algebra.

- *modality*. An adult knowledge base must be able to deal with possibility and necessity. The possibility operator adds considerably to the expressive power of the language, but as far as I know it has been not been explored in databases yet. The necessity operator is useful for the expression of integrity constraints that embody a necessary truth. Our use of partial models requires some modifications to the classical treatment for which we make profitable use of Veltman's work on data logic.
- *deontic operators*. Many integrity constraints in databases take the form of a deontic proposition, as in: ***Books must be returned in three weeks***.

Since modal and deontic operators are used in the specification of integrity constraints in knowledge bases, I will start by a short discussion of these.

6.2. INTEGRITY CONSTRAINTS IN KNOWLEDGE BASES

According to the ISO report on conceptual schemata (van Griethuysen, 1982), a *constraint* (or rule) is a "prescription or prohibition of the behaviour of the Universe of Discourse or parts thereof". A rule or constraint may be asserted by sentences, where a sentence is defined as "a linguistic object which contains a predicate and one or more terms and refers to a proposition of which it can be said that it is true or false in the Universe of Discourse". Under this definition, a constraint is always explicit (cf. Brodie, 1978, where constraints are classified as being inherent or explicit; briefly, an inherent constraint is one that is an integral part of the implementation model, for example that integers are smaller than 32,000). I will follow the ISO report definition and consider explicit constraints dealing with the Universe of Discourse only. These integrity constraints are sometimes called *user-defined* integrity constraints.

In (Meijer et al., 1988), we classified integrity constraints into static and dynamic constraints, and into analytical, empirical and deontic constraints (see Fig. 6.1).

	STATIC	DYNAMIC
analytical	age $\in \mathcal{N}$	An employee must be hired before he can be fired
empirical	age < 150	The combustion of methane produces water
deontic	The balance of a bank account should not be less than n	A library user should return a borrowed book after at most 3 weeks

Fig. 6.1 Typology of constraints

A constraint is static if it is true of each possible state of the UoD and it is dynamic if at least two states are needed to verify its truth. The difference between analytical, empirical and deontic constraints is motivated by the following observation. Under the "standard" model-theoretic view of an integrity constraint (cf. Kung, 1984; Nicolas & Gallaire, 1978; Reiter, 1984), an integrity constraint (IC) of a knowledge base (KB) M is a sentence ϕ such that $M \models \phi$. What is not commonly realized in the literature is that this view implies that an IC is a *necessary truth* in the model named by M. In modal logic a necessary truth is defined as truth in all possible worlds. This seems to be at odds with the status of a constraint like $age < 150$, which is not necessarily true in the UoD at all. The same holds for constraints like "the user should return the book in three weeks". These puzzles can be solved by the following classification of IC's.

The constraint $age \in \mathcal{N}$ is an *analytical* statement, i.e. one which follows from the meaning of the predicates occurring in it, and is therefore a necessary truth. This has two important consequences concerning IC change and constraint violation.

1. A *change* of an analytical constraint is a change of the meaning of some of the predicates occurring in it. For example, we may decide to measure temperature in degrees Kelvin instead of degrees centigrade. The constraint $temp \in \mathcal{R}$ then becomes $temp \in \mathcal{R} \wedge temp \geqq 0$ (by definition, degrees Kelvin start at 0).
2. An analytical constraint can be used to *check* if the current state of the knowledge base implements a possible world. If in the implementation a record has a negative value in its age field, the knowledge base does not represent a possible world. A proposition which does not conform to analytical constraints is semantically incoherent.

The constraint $age < 150$ is an *empirical* statement, i.e. one which depends on contingent factors like the state of our general health, physical constants of our universe etc.

1. A *change* of empirical constraints is a change in the behavior of the UoD.
2. If some proposition violates an empirical constraint, the proposition or the constraint may be in error. What usually happens in practice and in the literature is that we use only empirical constraints which during the life of the KB we can reasonably treat *as if* they were necessary truths.

A *deontic* constraint is a rule instituted by agents in the UoD to constrain the possible states of the UoD. Like empirical constraints, deontic constraints can be violated by the UoD. But where in the case of empirical constraints this is a novel way for the UoD to behave which is logically possible and ethically neutral, in the case of deontic constraints it is a case of behavior which is logically and physically possible but inadmissible to certain agents.

1. A *change* of a deontic constraint is a change in the norms pertaining to the UoD. For example, we may decide to allow a library user to keep a borrowed book at most six weeks.
2. A deontic constraint can be used to *check* if the agents in the UoD behave in a permissible way. With the constraint in hand, proper action can be taken if a user returns a book too late. Deontic constraints do not constrain the implementation, but the UoD. The implementation must be able to implement a KB which violates deontic constraints.

Note however that it is still possible to define integrity constraints as necessary truths. For empirical constraints, this can be done by choosing only weak ones, that are never violated during the life of the KB. As far as deontic constraints are concerned, we must make a distinction between the extensional content of the proposition and the proposition itself. That is, although it may happen that a user returns a book *after* 3 weeks, the rule itself remains valid. The statement "books are returned within 3 weeks is not necessarily true, but the modal statement "books should be returned within 3 weeks" is. Deontic statements cannot be falsified by data.

Lee (1988) has argued that deontic rules play an essential role in organizations. He goes as far as characterizing a bureaucratic organization as a deontic system. The word "bureaucracy" stems from Max Weber and is a management form based on explicit *rules* and *procedures*, rather than interests and personalities of specific individuals. These rules are identified with *roles* in the organization rather than individual people. For Weber, this is a positive development leading to a greater effectiveness and efficiency, and less favorism. Bureaucracy is a technology of social equity, holding officials accountable to explicit responsibilities and standards of performance. In so far as organizations are bureaucratic, they are not merely information processing systems. They are systems of organizational and social control. They convey more than data; they convey orders, commands, obligations, contracts, permissions, licenses, vouchers, receipts, prohibitions, waivers, verifications and so forth. These are performative transactions in that, by their communication, they change the nature of social relationships within the organization.

These general considerations about integrity constraints can be easily accounted for in our FG framework. Analytical constraints are of course the constraints formulated in the lexicon: the taxonomic links, the pre- and postconditions etc. Recall that a lexicon is not monolithic but may vary from one sublanguage to another (within certain boundaries). Deontic constraints are not in the lexicon but in the knowledge base. They are distinguished from extensional propositions by the deontic operator they contain. Deontic propositions are entered into the knowledge base by means of messages. They can be formulated in the design process or added during use. If the rules change, the deontic message can be revoked.

Empirical constraints correspond to what Hengeveld calls the "knowledge of possible situations obtaining in Speaker's conception of reality or of a hypothesized universe" (Hengeveld, 1988:13). This knowledge is used in the evaluation of modal statements. Note that empirical constraints are considered to be necessary with respect to a chosen UoD (they are true in every state), but in a different UoD (e.g, in science fiction), different empirical constraints may hold. In our framework this is reflected by the fact that the knowledge base may contain several theories, each dealing with one intended UoD, and usually linked with one particular discourse in the message base. Empirical (and deontic) constraints may vary from one theory to another. As we noted before, it is possible that an empirical constraint gets falsified.† In that case, the knowledge base becomes inconsistent and the constraint must be revoked or adapted.

† We coin the name *Popperean* for a theory that consists of falsified empirical constraints only.

Integrity constraints serve several purposes:

1 Usually, when a deontic constraint is violated, some action is triggered (a reminder, warning, punishment) against the tresspasser. That is to say, deontic constraints are essential for the behavioral specification of the knowledge base.

2 Propositions that violate analytical constraints must be rejected. In certain cases (not always), propositions violating deontic constraints can be rejected as well. For example, consider a library information system, and suppose someone can borrow no more than five books. If the library information system only registrates, then the proposition that some client borrows six books cannot be rejected, although a warning can be given. However, if the library is organized in such a way that someone can only borrow a book after having passed the information system, then it is possible to *reject* the proposition, because, in that case, the borrowing itself can be blocked. In short, constraints can be used for preserving data integrity.

3 Constraints can be profitably used in help functions as well. Queries containing a subquery violating some constraint should be answered by pointing out the rule, rather than returning an empty set (cf. chapter 7). It must also be possible to ask queries about the constraints themselves ("What should a library user not do?" "Is Peter permitted to hire a new employee?" etc).

4 Finally, constraints can be used for tuning the implementation. For example, the empirical constraint that the age of a person is lower than 150 justifies the use of "short integer" for the type of the age field. Of course, it must be possible to change the constraints during use, in which case the implementation may need restructuring.

6.3. DEFINITION

We now consider the syntax of propositions. A distinction is made between the proposition and the predication. We present the FG syntax and the formalization by means of f-structures.

6.3.1. Predication versus proposition

Predications consist of predicate frames where the slots have been filled with terms. A predication as a whole designates a State of Affairs (SoA), something which can be the case in some world. FG makes a distinction between propositions and predications (cf. Davidson, 1967). Propositions are the bearers of truth-values, that is, a proposition is the sort of thing which may be true or false. Propositions can be the objects of verbs such as *know* and *believe*. SoAs, on the other hand, are spatio-temporal entities much like ordinary physical objects. They occupy intervals of time and space. They can be the objects of perceptual verbs such as *see* and *hear*, and they can be said to "occur".

In simple cases, a proposition can formally coincide with the predication it contains, but, in general, the two diverge for the following reasons;

1. A proposition can contain more than one predication:

(a) *John saw Jackie biting Molly*

(b) *Clients living in European countries are asked to fill in form B*

Proposition (a) contains two predications, one being embedded. Proposition (b) contains one main and two embedded predications, one functioning as object of *ask* (*to fill in form B*) and one functioning as restrictor of *clients* (*living in European countries*).

2. A proposition may contain modal operators:

   (c) *John must have left*

3. A proposition may have satellites not available to the predication, such as *condition*:

   (d) *If the parts have been shipped last week, client will receive them before June, 1st*

The following table gives a schematic overview of the levels to be distinguished with their intended meaning and some suggestive examples.

PREDICATE FRAME	type	open(ag animate)(go thing)
PREDICATE SCHEMA	concept	open(ag human)(go window)
PREDICATION	SoA	e1 open(ag john)(go window)
EXTENDED PREDICATION	fact	(PERF e1 open(ag john)(go window))
ATOMIC PROPOSITION	factual judgement	p1 (PERF e1 open(ag john)(go window))
COMPLEX PROPOSITION	judgement	p1 (e1 open(ag john)(go window)) (cond warm(e))

Note the transition from extended predication to atomic proposition. The same structure can perform two functions. On the one hand, it denotes a fact (that is, a situated SoA). But it can also be regarded as a proposition, that is, as a judgement. This situation has a counterpart in formal logic in the Herbrand construction where *ground atoms* such as *employee(john)* in the Herbrand base (syntactic objects) are conveniently identified with their interpretation (semantic objects).

6.3.2. From P-frame to proposition

Predications are derived from P-frames. We recall from chapter 4 that a P-frame is an f-structure of the following form:

```
(pred => [predicate];
 cat =>  p
 type => [soa]
 sem => ()
)
```

Where the `[predicate]` is another f-structure containing the phonological representation of the predicate, lexical features, separable prefixes etc. The semantic type of the p-frame is a subtype of [soa], for example, [action], [state], or [transformation]. The P-frame can also include semantic functions.

The *Fund* is a set of predicate frames, defined by a given finite set of basic frames plus a number of predicate formation rules (chapter 4). The *frame language L* (for some natural language) can be defined as the set of all frames that are subtypes of the frames in the Fund. The *Dictionary* is defined as a subset of L whose members are called predicate schemata. Actual predications are typically subsumed by one of the predicate schemata in the Dictionary.

An example of a basic P-frame is:

```
(pred => (pred => "give";
        cat => v;
        forms => (past => "gave"; pap => "given"))
 cat => p
 type => [transfer]
 sem => (ag => [animate]; go => [object]; rec => [object]))
```

In FG, a predication which results from the insertion of term structures into the argument slots of some predicate frame is called a *nuclear predication*. A nuclear predication corresponds to a SoA type. The nuclear predication may be extended with additional slots called secondary semantic functions (also called *level 1 satellites*), such as instr (instrument), and with restrictors. The result is called a *core predication* which has the following form:

$$P\ (\alpha)\ (\sigma_1)$$

where P is the head of the frame (typically a verb), α is a set of arguments, and σ_1 a set of the secondary semantic functions, also called level 1 satellites. The secondary semantic functions are optional.

Example:

```
touch(ag x person)(go i[s] y person)(instr d[p] z lips)
```

Here, the Head is the verb *touch*, with two semantic functions "agent" and "goal" and a secondary semantic function "instrument".

In the general overview of chapter 2, we ignored the predicate operators working on P-frames. Typical examples are the perfective/imperfective operators. The distinction between perfective and imperfective is expressed in many languages. For instance, in French *parlait* is imperfective and *parla* is perfective. The former pictures the event as a "process" during for some time and the latter pictures the event as an indivisible whole. One way of dealing with perfectivity is to include it as an extra feature in the P-frame, for example, as part of the type function. There is some analogy with the count/mass distinction in terms. In some languages, the perfectivity is inherited from the lexical P-frame (some predicate frames are intrinsically perfective, and others imperfective), and in others it is filled in by means of an operator. It is also possible to combine these two approaches, when the perfectivity is specified for a part of the lexicon and not for others.

We now return to the definition of nuclear and core predication. Our treatment deviates slightly from Dik's approach although the net result is the same. Our notion of predicate schema includes both the nuclear and core predication: the predicate schema is a subtype of the basic predicate frame. This implies that the frame may contain additional functions or that the arguments are subtyped. The following P-frames are both subtypes of the P-frame above:

```
(pred => (pred => "give";
       cat => v;
       forms => (past => "gave"; pap => "given"));
 cat => p;
 type => [transfer];
 sem => (ag => (pred => man; var => x3; cat => t;
                type => [human]; num => sing) ;
        go => (pred => flower; cat => t; type => [inanimate]; num => plur);
        rec => (pred => wife; cat => t; type => [human]; num => sing;
                 sem => (ref => (var => x3)))))
```

(1) give(ag d[s] x3 man)(go i[p] flower)(rec d[s] wife(x3))

```
(pred => (pred => "give";
          cat => v;
          forms => (past => "gave"; pap => "given"));
 cat => p;
 type => [transfer];
 sem => (ag => [human]; go => present; rec => [human]));
 sat => (reason => birthday; sem => (ref => (var => x)))))
```

(2) give(ag [human])(go present)(rec [human])(reason birthday)

We have abbreviated the T-frames, in the sense that "man", "flower" etc actually stand for a T-frame with lexical head "man" etc.. In the first sentence, the terms have been instantiated, and in the second sentence, a satellite has been added. However, both are subtypes of the basic P-frame of *to give*. This is sufficient for the characterization of the Fund, and so the distinction between nuclear predication and core characterization plays no fundamental role.

The predicate schema may contain satellites and it seems that these are all T-frames. The examples mentioned sofar, Beneficiary, Instrument, Reason (the kind of reason in phrases like *for birthday*) certainly meet this restriction.

A core predication can be *instantiated* to represent a particular SoA so that we get structures of the form:

$[n]\ e\ \Phi\ (loc\ l)(tmp\ t)$

where e is the SoA variable, l the location, t the event time, n the quantity and Φ the core predication. The result is called an *embedded* predication, since the predication is embedded under the SoA variable. The event time can be further specified as to its type, its duration or its relationship with other time variables. Location and event time are sometimes called *implicit* arguments, because SoA instances necessarily exist in space and time. If they are not expressed (in the sentence, in the predication), this means that their value is unspecified rather than absent. Quantification is only possible if the event is discrete (telic). In the majority of cases, there is no quantification at all. The quantification is an operator that may be omitted.

Using f-structures, the embedded predication is derived from the core predication by adding a variable slot, and slots for time, location and number (in a frame called "frame"). For example:

```
(pred => give;
 cat => p;
 type => [transfer];
 var => e0;
 num => Δ;
 sem => (ag => A)(go => B)(rec => C);
 frame => (loc => (var => l2); tmp => (var => t0)))
```

Again, just as with term instantiations, we note that an instantiation can be written as a unification of a core predication and an instance frame:

```
(pred => give; cat => p; type => [transfer]; var => e0; num => Δ;
 sem => (ag => A)(go => B)(rec => C);
 frame => (loc => (var => l2); tmp => (var => t0)))    =

(pred => give; cat => p; type => [transfer];
 sem => (ag => A)(go => B)(rec => C))
 ∧
(var => e0; num => Δ;
  frame => (loc => (var => l2); tmp => (var => t0)))
```

In other words, an embedded predication has a dual nature, being both a subtype of a predicate schema and a subtype of the instance frame.

Embedded (instantiated) predications can be extended by means of predication operators, restrictors and satellites. Predication operators represent grammatical means by which the SoA can be located with respect to a reference frame, notably a reference time. Predication satellites such as *yesterday* represent lexical means for specifying the reference time. The final result is an *extended predication*, or *predication* for short, which takes the form:

$\pi_2\ [t]\ E\ (\sigma_2) : \phi_2(e)$

where π_2 stands for the predication operators, E is the embedded predication, t is the reference time, and σ_2 and ϕ_2 are the (level 2, i.e. predication) satellites and restrictors, respectively.

An extended predication denotes what we call a *fact* or situated SoA. The difference between a fact and a SoA proper is that the latter is not located in time yet. A fact is basically a SoA plus a reference time. The time reference occurring in the fact is called the *fact time* (later on, we will also consider another time reference at propositional level that must be distinguished from fact time, the reference time). We represent extended predications in f-structure format by a frame in which the embedded predication is embedded (sounds tautological):

```
(pred => (pred => give;
          cat => p;
          sem => ..;
          frame => (tmp => ET))
 frame => (tmp => FT))
```

where ET and FT stand for structures denoting Event Time and Fact Time to be explained later. For the moment, it suffices to say that ET is the time of duration of the event, while FT is the time at which the event is conceived. FT may be in ET, as in the Progressive, or ET may be in FT, as in the Perfective.

The frame is a substructure pointing to the reference time and perhaps other coordinates (cf. section 6.3.3) of cognitive and spatial dimensions. The head of the extended predication is the embedded predication.

According to Dik (1989), it is at the level of the (extended) predication that syntactic (or "presentative") functions can be assigned. Syntactic functions are Subject and Object. They specify the perspective from which that State of Affairs is presented in the linguistic expression (Dik, 1978:13). An example of a predication with Subject function assigned is:

```
([t1] e2 kiss(subj ag d[7] z dwarf)(go d[s] y snowwhite) : tender)
```

"*the seven dwarfs kiss snowwhite tenderly*"

In f-structure format, this is represented as:

```
(pred => (pred => kiss; cat => p; var => e2;
          sem => X:(ag => (pred => dwarf; car => 7; var => z);
                    go => (pred => snowwhite; num => s; var => y));
          frame => (tmp => ET:(var => t0));
          res => { tender });
 syn => (subj => X);
 frame => (tmp => FT:(var => t1)));
```

Note that we make use here of structure sharing. The subject of the predication co-refers with the agent of the embedded predication.

As we saw in chapter 2, the predication can include predication operators. The *phasal* aspect operators can be represented in f-structures in the head of the frame. The operators PROG, INGR and EGR (progressive, ingressive, egressive) are put in the head of the embedded frame, and PERF and PROSP (perfect and prospective) are put in the head of the outer frame. For example:

```
PERF(pred => PROG(pred => kiss; cat => p; var => e2;
                  sem => X:(ag => (pred => dwarf;
                                   car => 7; var => z);
                            go => (pred => snowwhite;
                                   num => s; var => y))
                  frame => (tmp => ET:(var => t0);
                  res => { tender });
     syn => (subj => X))
     frame => (tmp => FT:(var => t1)));
```

```
PERF [t1] PROG e2 kiss(subj ag d[7] z dwarf)
                      (go d[s] y snowwhite) : tender)
```

The seven dwarfs have been kissing Snowwhite tenderly

Satellites occurring at the predication level situate the SoA with respect to another SoA. The most important types are Circumstance, Purpose, Result, and Cause.

"Cause" is to be understood here in the sense of "causa fiendi" rather than "causa cognosciendi" (cf. 1.1.3). "Result" must be distinguished from "Purpose" which refers to the intentions of the agent, while Result refers to the consequences of a factual State of Affairs.

Having described the syntax of the predication, the step to the atomic proposition is easy. A propositional frame is a frame whose predicator is a fact. It also has a slot for time, which now indicates the *reference time* of the proposition (RT). RT may be before or after the Speech Time, or be contained in it, leading to different tenses. Basically, the propositional frame looks as follows:

```
(pred => FACT;
 var => p;
 frame => (tmp => RT))
```

This is the atomic proposition that can be extended with other operators, satellites and functions. By means of the operators, the Speaker can express his personal evaluation towards the propositional content, or the source through which he has obtained the information. We will consider these so called epistemological operators in the next chapter.

As we will see shortly, the formal interpretation of the PERF operator is that FT is before RT By a slight abuse of syntax, I will write down this inequation in f-structure format as:

```
frame => (tmp => FT < RT)
```

(this is the subframe `pred.frame` of the proposition). This notation should be read formally as:

```
frame => (tmp => FT:(var => t0; prec => RT:(var => t1)))
```

In other words, `prec` is a label in the predicate frame of the time reference that points to another time reference frame. The label `succ` is used for the inverse relation ">".

Functions at the propositional level typically include `cond` (condition) and `src`. (epistemological source). We also find it useful to consider *informational* functions at the propositional level, in particular the *clause topic*. In FG, (Given/New) Topic is a pragmatic function defined at the illocutionary level. Against this view, it has been argued that subclauses may have topics too (van der Auwera,1987). Let me use the term "clause topic" for the "topic" of a proposition. We have used this "clause topic" already in our truth-definition of structured propositions in section 3.4. Under this definition, the two propositions:

(1) In every class room, a student broke one of the windows

(2) A student broke one of the windows in every class room

may get different truth-conditions: sentence (2) requires that there was one student that broke all the windows. We have accounted for that by supposing that the prepositional clause "in every class room" is "clause topic" in sentence (1). This might also explain the differences in the linear ordering of the constituents. In this case, it could be objected that the prepositional clause is pragmatic (given) topic as well, and it is this function that is responsible for the scope differences and linear ordering. However, the sentences (1) and (2) can also be embedded, for example in the proposition *Yesterday, John saw that*, and similar propositions can be used as restrictors on terms. In such cases, an appeal to the (pragmatic) Topic or Focus function seems no longer possible.

I see no other way of handling the scope phenomena than by positing a clause topic. This is not to invalidate the FG treatment of topics at the illocutionary level. I only want to distinguish an *additional* topic function at clause level, as it is also used in systemic grammar (Halliday,1985). The pragmatic topic function at illocutionary level has to do with what the sentence is about. New topics can be introduced, rejected, accepted and continued. The informational topic function at the propositional level, in my view, stands for the primary perspective from a cognitive point of view, in terms of information processing.

With respect to the two propositions (1) and (2) it must be remarked that the scope analysis I presented is not without problems. Probably a better treatment is the "flexible" approach of Hendriks (1987) who is able to derive both scope readings from both propositions. The problem is that the topicalization may indeed favour one reading for another, but does not exclude others. I do not go into that. Note that FG, using a non-linear format for the deep structure, can adopt such a flexible approach quite naturally.

6.4. INTERPRETATION

A proper interpretation of propositions calls for an extension of the algebraic framework built up in chapter 3. This chapter ended with the notion of a *Tarskian model* consisting of supported and rejected situations. The extension we will consider here bears some similarity to the Kripke extension of first-order models. Intuitively, a Kripke structure K consists of a *collection* of first-order models which are called the worlds or states of K. Between the states of K, an accessibility relation is defined. One state may be different from another one. The states can be interpreted in various ways, for example as different states of the history (in the succession of time), or as epistemic alternatives of the cognitive agent. Kripke structures have been used extensively for all kinds of modal logics. The structure I will introduce here is not a Kripke structure proper but it also takes a set of Tarskian models.

6.4.1. Chronicles

Facts hold at certain times. It is possible that Ronald is a president at time index t1 and not a president at time index t2. Alternatively, we can say that at a certain time, a number of facts hold. That is, we have a set of time indices and to each time index, we attach a Tarskian model stating what is true and false at that time.

Note that this step is really necessary and that the *tmp* satellite we have attached to SoAs is not sufficient yet for handling all temporal information. This satellite specifies the event time of the SoA. But the terms in the predication are translated to entailments and TYPE mappings, for example the term *the prince* is interpreted as the equation:

```
{x7} TYPE {prince}
```

But if at some time t2, the referent x7 is not a prince but a frog,

```
{x7} TYPE {frog}
```

this causes an inconsistency. One remedy would be to consider referent/time index pairs instead of referents. Then the two terms would become:

```
{<x7,t1>} type {prince}
{<x7,t2>} type {frog}
```

However, this does not only lead to an enormous overspecification in most cases, but introduces also an undesirable gap between syntactic and semantic form, since the time index is not found in the term frame. Admittedly, we could inherit it there from the predication in which the term is embedded, but we have no linguistic basis for doing so. Linguistically, the time is always attached to the predication, or some higher level of the predication. Therefore the introduction of a time-indexed set of models is a better solution in view of the grammaticality constraint.

Time-indexed sets of models have been used in temporal logic. The general picture of a temporal model structure is a tree:

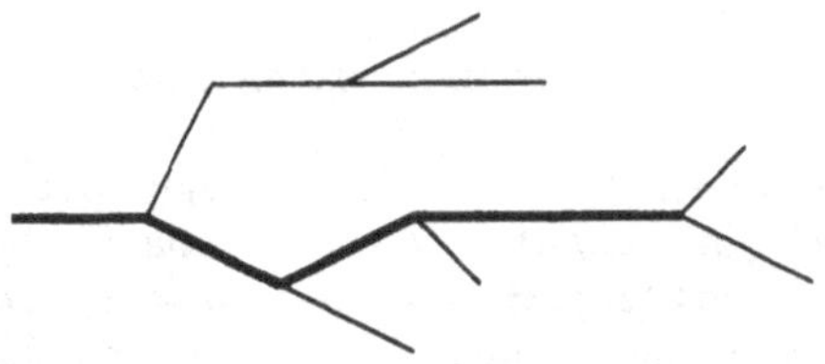

Fig. 6.2 A tree of chronicles

In the traditional terminology (cf. Prior, 1967; Burgess, 1984; McDermott, 1982), each node of the tree is called a *state* and each branch of the tree a *chronicle* or *course of events*. The domain of time referents (T,<) is called a *frame* with a total ordering. This allows us to define a chronicle as a function on a frame that attaches a set of propositions to each time referent. The fact that the nodes are organized as a tree reflects the partial ordering on states that is presupposed. The structure is also backwards linear. This reflects the asymmetry of our knowledge of the past and the future (Mays, 1986). Although we could imagine several possible futures from the past, each possible future traces a path backwards into now. The past is determined.

Dynamic logic (Harel, 1984) adds to the Kripke structure a reachability relationship between states. The reachability relationship is labeled with actions. Using the picture above, we could say that the actions correspond to edges between the worlds. Actions are interpreted then as state transformers, in the sense that given a state s in the chronicle, we associate with each atomic action α a set $W_{\alpha,s}$ of reachable states. The set of reachable states is thus the set of states which can be reached by performing one step involving the execution of α (and possibly more actions in parallel). A simplistic but suggestive picture is sketched below:

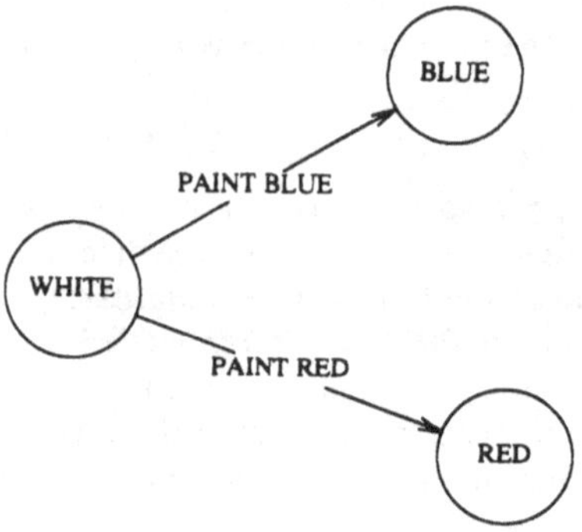

Fig. 6.3 A dynamic chronicle tree

Our formalization is based essentially on dynamic logic, but it uses some concepts of temporal logic as well. In contrast to standard dynamic logic, we will consider both the states and the actions (edges) as Tarskian models. The first will be called Static and the second Dynamic. Linguistically, the first correspond with static SoA's, and imperfectives, and the second with dynamic SoAs, and perfectives. The following definition introduces the necessary concepts. We assume a given domain of time referents. This domain will be described in the next section.

Definition 6.1. A *frame* F over time domain T is a tuple (Stat,Dyn,I,O), with Stat $\cup$ Dyn $\subseteq$ T, I $\subseteq$ Stat$\times$Dyn, O $\subseteq$ Dyn$\times$Stat. The elements of Stat are called Static states, the elements of Dyn are called Dynamic states. I is read as "input" and O as "output".

A *trace* in F is an ordered n-tuple $(s_1,...,s_n)$, with n>1, where for all $i<n$, $(s_i,s_{i+1}) \in$ I or $(s_i,s_{i+1}) \in$ O. A trace contains a cycle iff some state occurs twice. A frame is acyclic iff no trace contains a cycle. In an aclycic frame, $s<t$ (s precedes t) iff there is a trace from s to t. A frame is *historic* iff there is an index $s_0 \in$ Stat such that there is (exactly) one trace $(s_0, ..., s_k)$ for every $s_k \in$ Stat $\cup$ Dyn. This s_0 is called the *source*.

A *chronicle* on an acyclic historic frame F over T is a function C that attaches to each element $t \in$ T a Tarskian model M. A *coe* (course of events) in a chronicle C is the restriction of C to a totally ordered subset of F (where the ordering is the precedence ordering).

end 6.1

Remarks

- The chronicle function C must be monotonic on the time domain. This is explained in the next section.
- If we denote the set of Tarskian models by $\mathfrak{M}$, then a chronicle on frame F is

defined as function $F \rightarrow \mathfrak{M}$.

- A course of events is a branch of the chronicle, but it is not necessarily a complete branch lasting from here to eternity. It may also contain "gaps". Intuitively, a course of events is a partial trace.
- The difference between dynamic and static states will be shown to be relevant when we introduce the dynamic and deontic logic part.
- The relationships I and O are to be taken as products over information systems, as spelled out in 3.2.4.
- Not every element of the time domain must be in the frame. The frame is only an index on states.

6.4.2. Time domain

Definition 6.1 does not say yet anything about the internal structure of the time domain T. In the present framework T can be modeled successfully by means of a Scott information system, just as the entity domain. We have an instance level and a lexical level. The lexical level is part of the lexicon and contains predicates such as names of months and days. The instance level is made up by T whose elements are called time referents t_i. To be more precise, the domain consists of a dataset of time referents t_i, and an entailment and consistency relationship. The entailment relationship is interpreted as time inclusion. This works in the same way as the subset relationship between term referents. Informally $[t_1] \vdash [t_2]$, when $[t_1]$, conceived as an interval on the time axis, is contained in the interval $[t_2]$. On the domain T, a measure function COUNT can be defined, just as with entities. This function is to be interpreted as duration. Chronicles are monotonic with respect to inclusion, in the following sense:

Proposition 6.2 (monotonicity of chronicles)
Let T be a time domain, C a chronicle function on frame F over T:

$$\text{if } [t_i] \vdash [t_j], \text{ then } C([t_i]) \models C([t_j])$$

Proof

If C is defined by means of an approximable mapping, this assumption is met immediately, since monotonicity is a property of approximable mappings on Scott domains (3.2.3). □

end 6.2

There has been a long discussion in AI and philosophy about the question whether we should take time points or time intervals as basic. We prefer a relativistic viewpoint. If we want certain time indices to be points we should specify somehow that no time index is properly contained in them. In practice, the use of time points raises some problems since we can only approximate them to a certain degree. Hence it seems better to take time indices as basic without requiring these to be points. It is always possible to consider the maximal elements (in a certain information state) as "points". It is also possible to consider a special discrete measure unit "moment". When a certain time index is said to endure for one moment, any time index included in it must be either zero or one moment too. In the first case, it is not consistent, in the second case the two time points must be equal. Time indices of duration "one moment" are called momentaneous.

Definition 6.3 The time domain T (Ref_t, Δ_t, Con, $\vdash$) is defined by:

- a dataset Ref_t of time referents, including Δ_t and ∇
- a set of entailments between time referents, inclusion relationships

A set is inconsistent iff it entails ∇. A set is consistent iff it is not inconsistent.

Furthermore, we assume:
- an approximable mapping TYPE from T to Lex
- an approximable mapping COUNT for time duration, with an accompanying domain of time measure units

end 6.3

The frame ordering given in definition 6.1 is monotonic with respect to the domain in the following sense: if $[t_1] \vdash [t_2]$, and $[t_2] < [t_3]$, then $[t_1] < [t_3]$. This follows from the fact that the chronicle is an approximable mapping, and the relationships I and O are defined as product systems on information systems.

6.4.3. Temporal logic

In chapter 3, we defined truth for simple predications. For temporalized predications we need a more elaborated definition. This definition is built up in several steps. We first give an informal description, then an example and then the formal definition.

RT, FT and ET are tag symbols, but we use them also as abbrevations for the time references at these addresses. That is, RT = $\psi(\tau^{-1}$(RT)`.var`) etc. If p is some proposition, then the address `frame.tmp` is tagged with RT, the address `pred.frame.tmp` is tagged with FT and the address `pred.pred.frame.tmp` is tagged with ET. RT is the syntactic structure that denotes the reference time, the time at which the proposition is evaluated. FT denotes the fact time, the time before or after the reference time at which the reported fact holds. ET denotes the time at which the event takes place. ET can either contain or be contained in FT. For the use of embedding functions in truth-definitions, see chapter 3.4.

- We say that a predication p_1 (ignoring fact time) is true with respect to an index t_i iff $C([t_i]) \models p_1$. This definition draws on definition 3.12, where truth was defined for propositions with respect to Tarskian models. $C([t_i])$ is a Tarskian model. The proposition is true iff there is a verifying embedding. The phrase "ignoring fact time" must be understood in the sense that the subframe at the address `frame.tmp` is removed from the address tree.
- We say that a predication p_2 (with fact time FT, related to a reference time RT) is verified by an embedding f that embeds RT to some index $f(\text{RT}) = t_i$ iff p_2 (ignoring FT) is true with respect to the index $f'(\text{FT})$, $f'(\text{FT}) \models p_2$, for some verifying embedding $f' \supseteq f$ that embeds FT such that $f(\text{FT})$ op $f(\text{RT})$ when FT op RT (op being some comparison operator).
- We specify that a *contingent* atomic proposition p_3 is true (verified by some embedding f) with respect to a *chronicle C* iff p_3`\pred` (the predication contained in proposition p) is true with respect to some index $f(\text{RT})$, where f is a verifying embedding of the reference time.
- Finally, a *universal* atomic proposition p_3 is true with respect to a chronicle C iff p_3`\pred` is true with respect to index $f(\text{RT})$ for *every* embedding f of RT.

The syntactic difference between a contingent and a universal proposition is that

RT is indefinite in the first case and universally quantified in the second. Semantically, a contingent proposition is true iff it is true in some state, whereas a universal proposition must be true in every state (falling under the reference time).

Note the difference with Kripke semantics, where it is stated that $K \models \phi$ iff $\sigma \models \phi$ for all $\sigma \in K$. We get a Kripke-like semantics only when all propositions are universal.

Before giving the formal definitions, we give a small example. Let p be the proposition:

```
(pred => PERF(pred => (pred => walk;
                       sem => (ag => X:john);
                       frame => ET:(tmp => (var => t0 in t1)))
              subj => X;
              frame => (tmp => FT:(var => t1)))
 frame => (tmp => RT:(var => t2)))
```

We use subsumption rules to rewrite this structure to another structure in which the PERF operator is explicated. The subsumption rule is:

```
(pred => PERF(frame => FT)) ≤ (pred=> (frame => FT < RT))
```

Applied to the example, we get:

```
(pred => (pred => (pred => walk;
                   sem => (ag => X:john);
                   frame => (tmp => ET:(var => t0 in t1)));
          subj => X;
          frame => (tmp => FT:(var => t1 < t2)));
 frame => (tmp => RT:(var => t2)))
```

Note that p is contingent (RT is not quantified). It does not say that John has walked in every state, but only in some state. Let C be a chronicle. Then p is true with respect to this chronicle iff p is true for some embedding f of reference time t2. Since the reference time is not further specified, we may choose any index. Let this index be t. Then p\pred is true with respect to t iff *"John has walked"* is true at t. To evaluate this predication, we must find a verifying embedding f' for the fact time t1, such that $f \subseteq f'$, so $f'(\text{t2}) = t$. According to the equation (t1 < t2), the index $f'(\text{t1})$ must be before $f'(\text{t2})$, that is, before t. Suppose we have found such an index, say, t'. Then we must find a verifying embedding f'' such that $C(t') \models_{f''} p$\pred holds. In plain English, "John walks" is actual at t'. See Fig. 6.4.

The equations for the aspectual operators are given in the next section. Let us now first formalize our definition of truth.

Definition 6.4 Let p be an atomic proposition. Let C be a chronicle for frame F into $\mathfrak{M}$. We say that p is universal when RT is universally quantified, otherwise it is contingent.

I Truth of proposition:

(a) if p is contingent, then p is *true* (*false*) with respect to C iff there is a verifying (falsifying) embedding f for p.

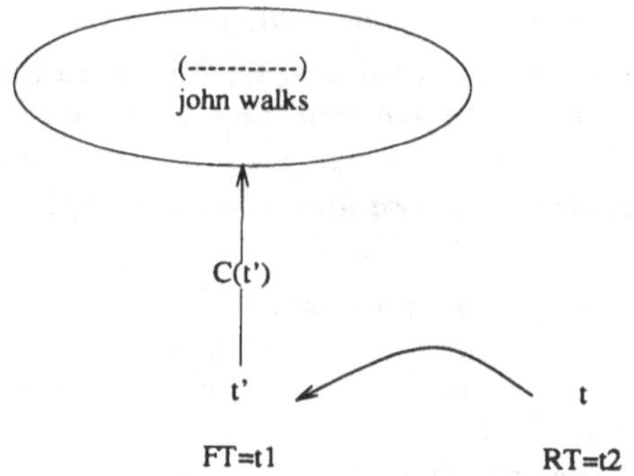

Fig. 6.4 $C \models$ *John has walked*

(b) if p is universal, then p is ***true*** with respect to C iff for every verifying embedding f of RT, there is a verifying embedding $g \supseteq f$ for p with respect to f(RT). The proposition p is false iff there is some falsifying embedding.

II Verification of proposition with respect to chronicle:

(c) p is verified (falsified) by f such that $f(\mathrm{RT}) = t$ with respect to C iff $C(t) =_f p$ (or $=\!\!|$, respectively).

III Verification of predication with respect to a Tarskian model:

(d) $\mathrm{M} \models_f p$, where the subframe at FT is empty (`frame.tmp` is a leaf) when M $=_f p$ according to the definition of Tarskian models. Similarly for falsification and $=\!\!|$.

(e) $\mathrm{M} \models_f p$, where FT < RT (FT > RT, FT = RT, respectively) when for some embedding $f' \supseteq f$, such that $f'(\mathrm{FT}) < f'(\mathrm{RT})$ (> and =, respectively) it holds that $f'(\mathrm{FT}) \models_f p'$, where p' is the predication obtained by pruning the subframe at FT from p.

end 6.4

Remarks

- Note that an atomic proposition may contain non-atomic predications, such as $p \wedge q$. The truth-definition of these was already given in 3.11 and is supposed here in part (d) of the definition. The definition of complex propositions, in particular propositions containing conditional clauses, is postponed to sections 6.4.5. and 6.4.6

- As the example above showed already, aspectual operators are interpreted by means of equations on the RT, FT and ET. This will be explained in the next section. By a slight abuse of syntax, we write FT < RT where we actually mean: $\psi(\tau^{-1}(\mathrm{FT}).\mathtt{var}) < \psi(\tau^{-1}(\mathrm{FT}).\mathtt{var})$. FT, RT and ET are tag symbols but we mean the symbols attached to these addresses.

6.4.4. Aspectual logic

The presence of aspectual operators puts restrictions on FT and ET. Some operators define FT with respect to RT and some define ET with respect to FT. An example of the first is the Perfect tense which requires that FT < RT. A example of the second group is the Progressive. This operator requires that FT $\subseteq$ ET: the event is "in process" at FT. PERF and PROG can be combined, at least in English. In that case, FT $\subseteq$ ET and FT < RT. Note that PERF PROG α does not warrant the conclusion PERF α: if John has been winning, it does not follow that he has won. This is traditionally called the "imperfective paradox" (cf. Almeida, 1986). In our framework, the imperfective paradox offers no special problems, if at least we assume that in the phrase *John has won* (without Progressive marking) the predication has not only Perfect aspect, but is perfective as well. Then the phrase is translated to a predication with FT < RT and ET $\subseteq$ FT. This predication cannot be verified in a chronicle where we only have that at some fact time, *John was winning* (ET $\supseteq$ FT).

The following combinations of aspectual operators can be interpreted now:

PROG	FT $\subseteq$ ET	progressive
INGR	FT < ET	ingressive
EGR	ET < FT	egressive
PERF	FT < RT	perfect
PROSP	FT > RT	prospective

And combinations thereof such as:

{PERF,PROG}	FT < RT and FT $\subseteq$ ET
{PERF,INGR}	FT < RT and FT < ET

By means of ET, FT and RT, we can represent quite a range of aspectual distinctions found in natural language. Using the semantics defined above, the aspectual operators are given a rigorous interpretation. To be honest, I must say that I have only given a representation. I have not broached the question of how to determine this representation from the surface sentence, for a certain language with certain verbal inflections and auxiliaries. This topic has raised a lot of interest over the last decade. See for example (Lo Cascio & Vet, 1988) and its review by Erhard Hinrichs (Hinrichs, 1989).

I already remarked that the imperfective paradox does not occur in my formalization. On the positive side, we observe that several valid deductions can be made. Let the PAST tense operator be interpreted as RT < ST (reference time before speech time). Then, for example, PERF α $\Rightarrow$ PAST α: If John has walked, then he walked (at some time). Or, if Peter had seen Mary yesterday, then Peter has seen Mary: PAST PERF α $\Rightarrow$ PERF α.

6.4.5. Data logic

We understand data logic as the logic concerning *may* and *must*. Traditionally, these operators are called modal operators but since there are so many of them, we need some more precision. Our treatment of these operators differs from the classical treatment of necessity and possibility, although the latter can be defined in terms of the former. It is based essentially on work by Veltman (1985), and is known as "data logic". Akama and Kawamori (1988) have extended this theory at some points and have applied it to problems with linguistic presuppositions.

Data logic differs from traditional truth-functional logic in the sense that truth is not defined in terms of what holds in absoluto, but as what can be known on the basis of incomplete knowledge of the world. The underlying semantics is a collection of *information states*, and for each information state, an evaluation function V on atomic formulas (facts). V is a partial function with range $\{0,1\}$. Since V is partial, some formulas are neither 0 nor 1.

As our knowledge grows, we move from one information state into another, in such a way that the new information state is an extension of the old one. An important concept in this regard is the notion of T-stable sets (and its companion notion F-stable). A proposition p is T-stable if it remains true from one information state to another. Not every proposition is T-stable although of course atomic propositions are. In particular, a proposition of the form *may* ϕ will turn out to be not T-stable: if in information state 1, ϕ is possible, it may turn out that, because of more knowledge, it is no longer a possiblity in information state 2.

The semantics of data logic consist of an information model defined as follows:

Definition 6.5 (Veltman, 1985:157) An *information model* (for language L) is a triple $(S, \leqq, V)$ with the following properties

(i) $S \neq \emptyset$

(ii) $\leqq$ is a partial ordering of S

(iii) V is a partial function with domain S; for each $s \in S$, V_s is a partial function assigning at most one of the values 1 or 0 to the atomic sentences of L. If $s \leqq s'$, $V_s \subseteqq V_{s'}$.

An information model is *closed* iff in addition to (i), (ii) and (ii) it has the following property.

(iv) Each maximal chain in $(S, \leqq)$ contains a maximal element. If s is a maximal element, V_s is total.

end 6.5

Now let us consider a set of Tarskian models with respect to a data algebra M. In theorem 3.11 we proved that situations form a Scott information system. In section 3.4, we defined an evaluation function V on (structured) propositions with respect to Tarskian models. Hence we have the following lemma:

Lemma 6.6. The set of Tarskian models $\mathfrak{M}$ with respect to a non-empty data algebra M with evaluation function V is a closed information model.

Proof The entailment between Tarskian models is derived from the entailment on situations (definition 3.12). Since situations are ordered in an information system, so are Tarskian models. The entailment relationship is a partial ordering.
The function V defined in definition 3.15 is monotonic, as required in (iii). Finally, since $\mathfrak{M}$ is a Scott information system, every chain has a limit (Prop. 3.1), so the information model is closed as well. $\square$.

end 6.6

We now present the extension of the definitions presented in 3.9 that involve *must* and *may*. These correspond with the FG operators NEC and POS defined on predications. These operators are specified at the predication level. For example:

```
NEC PERF leave(ag d[s] x john)
```

John must have left

This is in f-structure format:

```
{NEC,PERF}(pred => (pred => leave;
                    cat => p;
                    sem => X:(ag => (pred => john; num => s; var => x));
                    frame => (tmp => ET in FT));
           syn => (subj => X);
           frame => (tmp => FT < RT))
```

We also consider conditional clauses attached to the proposition, as in:

```
p present(x1) (cond available(i[s] x1 book)
```

If a book is available, it is present

which is in f-structure format:

```
(pred => (pred => (pred => present)
                   cat => q;
                   var => q2);
          frame => (tmp => FT);
          syn  => (subj => (var => x1));
 frame => (tmp => RT);
 inf => (top => Y);
 sat => Y:(cond => (pred => (pred => available;
                              cat => q;
                              var => q3);
                     frame => (tmp => FT);
                     syn => (subj => (pred => book; num => s; var => x1)))
))
```

Note that we have assigned the informational topic function to the conditional satellite.

The truth-conditions for modal and conditional propositions are as follows. We write $p \rightarrow q$ for the proposition with head q and hypothetical part p.

Definition 6.7 Let T be a Tarskian model and let p and q be predications.

- $T \models p \rightarrow q$ if for no $T' \supseteq T$, $T' \models p$ and $T' \mathrel{=\!\!|} q$
  $T \mathrel{=\!\!|} p \rightarrow q$ iff for some $T' \supseteq T$, $T' \models p$ and $T' \mathrel{=\!\!|} q$
- $T \models$ NEC p if for no $T' \supseteq T$, $T' \mathrel{=\!\!|} p$
  $T \mathrel{=\!\!|}$ NEC p if for some $T' \supseteq T$, $T' \mathrel{=\!\!|} p$
- $T \models$ POS p iff for some $T' \supseteq T$, $T' \models p$
  $T \mathrel{=\!\!|}$ POS p iff for no $T' \supseteq T$, $T' \models p$

The truth-conditions for propositions with respect to chronicles is built on top of this definition in the line of definition 6.4.

end 6.7

Some properties of these operators are:

D1. NEC $\phi \Leftrightarrow \neg$ POS $\neg \phi$

D2. POS $\phi \Leftrightarrow \neg$ NEC $\neg \phi$

D3. NEC $(\phi \wedge \psi) \Leftrightarrow$ NEC $\phi \wedge$ NEC ψ

D4. NEC $\phi \Rightarrow$ POS ϕ

However, we do not have:

* NEC $\phi \Rightarrow \phi$

On the contrary, we do have for non-modal predications:

D5. $\phi \Rightarrow$ NEC ϕ

That is, the NEC behaves rather differently from necessity in modal logic. It is better thought of as expressing information based on indirect evidence. This fits in neatly with the analysis of Karttunen (1972) of sentence pairs like:

(a) *John must have left*

(b) *John has left*

> "Intuitively, (a) makes a weaker claim than (b). In general, one would use (a), the epistemic *must*, only in circumstances where it is not yet an established fact that John has left. In (a), the Speaker indicates that he has no first hand evidence about John's departure, and neither has it been reported to him by trustworthy sources. Instead (a) seems to say that the truth of *John has left* in some way logically follows from other facts the Speaker knows and some reasonable assumptions that he is willing to entertain"

The kind of *must* described here is close to *inferential* mood (cf. Palmer, 1986). In Hengeveld (1988), the inferential mood is classified as an epistemological operator. As in (Weigand, 1989), I will identify the inferential with the necessity operator. Note that the "lack of direct evidence" to which the characterization alludes, does not imply that the sentence is only heuristally true. The deduction can be quite rigid, as in:

(c) *If x-1 is greater than three, x must be greater than four*

The interpretation of NEC in data logic urges us to classify it as a predication operator rather than a proposition (epistemological) operator. This classification is in accordance with FG as far as necessity is concerned.

The data logic NEC is quite useful for knowledge bases. For example, consider the meaning definitions in the lexicon and other necessary integrity constraints. As integrity constraints on the database we would like them to have the following features:

(i) they must hold in every state of the model

(ii) since the model maintained in the knowledge base (the database) is finite, we do not require that every derivable fact is also present in the database. It suffices that the fact is present in every maximal extension of the database

These requirements are met if we interpret integrity constraints as both *universal* (holding at each reference time) and *necessary* (NEC). For example:

```
[*t] p NEC have(po x1)(go i[s] x2 employer)
        (cond employee(i[s] x1 human))
```

If someone is an employee, he always must have an employer

The interpretation of this proposition is that in each state of the chronicle, if someone is an employee, then in every maximal extension of that state, he has an employer. The constraint is falsified when in some state, an employee is said to have no manager.

This example also shows that a more classical definition of necessity can be attained in our framework also by exploring the quantification of the reference time.

6.4.6. Dynamic logic

In (Wieringa, Meijer, Weigand, 1988), a deontic logic is presented that is a simple extension of dynamic logic. This deontic logic has several advantages over other proposals such as the one of Anderson (1967) which has been shown by McArthur (1981) to contain a number of paradoxes. The deontic variant of dynamic logic, first developed by Meijer (1987) does not suffer from these paradoxes.

Dynamic logic (Harel, 1984) is not only useful for deontic logic, but has also several merits of its own for knowledge representation. For example, consider conditional propositions such as:

(1) If x=283 and we double it, its value is more than 500

(2) If someone returns a book, the library assistant must update the database

In both sentences, the predication in the if-clause denotes a dynamic event. The intended meaning is that the main clause predication holds in the state *after* the event. It would be totally inappropriate to interpret sentence (1) in a Kripke model as saying:

(1') (for all states s), if $s \models x=283 \wedge x = 2*x$, then $s \models x>500$

or

(1'') (for all states s), if $s \models [x=283 \wedge x = 2*x] \Rightarrow x>500$

The statement would even be inconsisent. It is of no help to use data logic. The problem is that the proposition makes reference to two states, one before the doubling of x and one afterwards. The same holds for sentence (2). The obligation to update the database becomes effective when the book is returned (after the action).

Whether such sentences are "real" conditionals or not is not relevant. The problem is that we cannot represent the intended meaning in a static structure. A solution is offered by dynamic logic. In dynamic logic, we have the following formula construct added to standard first-order logic:

$$[\alpha]\ \phi$$

where α is an *action* and ϕ is a wff. Some examples of formulas containing an action are:

D1 [kill(x)] dead(x)

D2 $x=283 \Rightarrow [x := 2*x]\ x>500$

D3 **[x:=1] ([x:=x+1]** x=2)

In 6.4.1 we already sketched an intuitive interpretation of dynamic logic. Originally, the semantics are described in a Kripke structure but the results carry over smoothly to our our partial models. Actions are state transformers that link static states of the chronicle to other static states reachable by the action. The "edges" between static states are formed by the dynamic states (cf. def. 6.1).

Definition 6.8 Let p be a proposition of the form $[\alpha]\ \phi$, where ϕ is the main proposition and α is a conditional predication such that α is perfective. Proposition p can be either universal or contingent.

The predication α takes one of the following forms;

$$a \mid \alpha_1 \vee \alpha_2 \mid \alpha \wedge \alpha_2 \mid \text{NEG}\alpha \mid \textbf{any} \mid \textbf{fail}$$

where a is an atomic predication, $\alpha_1 \vee \alpha_2$ is a non-deterministic choice of the actions α_1 and α_2; $\alpha_1 \wedge \alpha_2$ is the parallel execution/performance of the actions α_1 and α_2; NEGα is the non-performance of the action α; "**any**" denotes the unspecified action; "**fail**" denotes the failing (empty) action.

The actions "**any**" and "**fail**" have the following truth-conditions:

$C(s) \models$ **any**, for every $s \in$ Dyn
$C(s) \mathrel{=\!\!|}$ **any**, for no $s \in$ Dyn

$C(s) \models$ **fail**, for no $s \in$ Dyn
$C(s) \mathrel{=\!\!|}$ **fail**, for every $s \in$ Dyn

Let t be (the index of) a static state in chronicle C. Then

$W_{\alpha,t}$ is the set of state indices s such that $(t,r) \in$ I and $(r,s) \in$ O, for some index r such that $C(r) \models \alpha$.

Now suppose p is universal (contingent, respectively). Then

C $\models [\alpha]\ \phi$ iff for every (some, respectively) embedding of RT such that f(RT) $\in$ Stat:

$$C(s) \models_f \phi, \text{ for every } s \in W_{\alpha,f(RT)}$$

end 6.8

- The definitions for falsification are straightforward adaptations and are omitted.

- The actions "**any**" and "**fail**" are introduced for technical reasons. The set of states reachable by the action "**any**" is the set of all states reachable in one step. The action "**fail**" is never verified. They correspond to the top element Δ_e and the bottom element ∇_e of the SoA instance domain.

- The set of states reachable by the action $\alpha_1 \vee \alpha_2$ is equal to the set-theoretic union of the sets reachable by α_1 and those reachable by α_2.

- The set of states reachable by the action $\alpha_1 \wedge \alpha_2$ is equal to the set-theoretic intersection of the sets reachable by α_1 and those reachable by α_2.

- The negated action NEGα is interpreted as the the set of states reachable by the explicit non-performance of α. In dynamic logic, either α is performed or NEGα is performed. Tertium non datur. Our approach is deviant because it is also possible that neither α nor NEGα are verified in the dynamic state M. However, if we assume that all dynamic states are maximal, then our definition is equivalent to the standard one. NEGα is verified iff α is falsified.

Dynamic logic can be used profitably for the interpretation of postconditions. Recall that the meaning definition of dynamic predicate frames (in the lexicon) contained, among others, a postcondition as in:

```
kill(ag X animate)(go Y animate)
        --> dead(Y).
```

Using dynamic logic, we can interpret this as a universal proposition of the form:

```
[kill(ag X animate)(go Y animate)] dead(Y)
```

saying that for each state in the chronicle, Y is dead in the state reached by the action "kill". Similarly, a precondition

```
kill(ag X animate)(go Y animate)
        <-- alive(Y).
```

can be rendered as follows:

```
NEG alive(Y) ⇒ [kill(ag X animate)(go Y animate)] ∇
```

which says that the action of killing a not living person leads to an inconsistent state (in other words, is impossible).

It occurs to me that the "dynamic conditional" of dynamic logic is indispensable in a general knowledge base system. The use of preconditions and postconditions has a long tradition, but in most cases, no precise semantics is offered. Exceptions are for instance (Khosla, Maibaum & Sadler, 1986), who also use dynamic logic, and various temporal logics (Lipeck & Saake, 1987; Sernadas, 1980).

That the logical implication alone is insufficient for the interpretation of natural language conditionals, has been recognized long before. The "dynamic conditional" does not solve all the problems, but at least some of them. Data logic solves some other ones.

6.4.7. Deontic logic

Deontic statements (obligation, permission, prohibition) can be reduced to the concept of prohibition. That is, if α is obliged this is equivalent to saying that NEGα is prohibited, and α is permitted is equivalent to the statement that α is not prohibited. Prohibition in turn can be reduced to the concept of an action leading to a *violation* of a rule. Instead of expressing the rules explicitly, we thus state when they are violated. We do this by defining, for each action α, one or more *violate predicates*, one for each of the reasons why the execution of α is forbidden. If a violation frame is verified in some state, this means something like "liability to punishment", "trouble with conscience", etc (Meijer, 1987). In FG, I represent a violation frame by means of a head symbol *fail* assigned to the predicate:

```
(pred => (pred => fail(pred => "return"; cat => v);
          sem => (ag => X:john)(go => book));
 syn => (subj => X))
```

Violation frame *"John has not returned the book (although he should have)"*

A violation predication is verified in the same way as ordinary predications.

Using violation frames, the different deontic propositions are interpreted as follows:

Definition 6.9 Let M be a Tarskian model.

$M \models F\alpha$ iff $[\alpha]$ V:α
$M \models P\alpha$ iff $M \dashv F\alpha$
$M \models OBL\alpha$ iff $M \models F\ NEG\alpha$

"Fα" is to be read as "forbidden α", "Pα" as "permitted α", and "OBLα" as "obliged α".

end 6.9

Note that we have formalized deontic statements for actions (perfective SoAs) only. For imperfective deontic statements, we have no semantics yet. However, it is always possible to convert a static description into a dynamic one (as in Meijer et al, p.29,30).

6.4.8. Example

Let us now give some examples. The example is about a library information system.

```
p1 P borrow(ag i[s] x member)(go i[s] y book)
   (cond p10 (available(y) or PERF reserve(ag x)(go y)) &
             NEG dispose(po x)(co [>3] z book)))
```

This proposition says that a member is permitted to borrow a book if (a) it is either available or reserved by him, and (b) he does not dispose of more than three books. The intended meaning is that he is permitted to borrow a book *only* if the conditions hold (conditions are necessary). Therefore a translation to

$\phi \rightarrow$ P borrow

where ϕ stands for the condition, is not appropriate. Rather we should have:

P borrow $\rightarrow \phi$

which makes ϕ a *necessary* condition. This means that the condition argument has restrictive Focus.

```
p2 OBL return(ag x )(go y)(tmp t2 < t1 + [3] week)
   (cond PERF borrow(ag x member)(go y book)(tmp t1))

p3 OBL pay(ag x)(go [2] dollar)(tmp t)
   (cond PERF borrow(ag x member)(go y a book)(tmp t1) &
         NEG PERF return(ag x)(go y)(tmp t > t1 + [3] week))
```

The second proposition says that if a member has borrowed a book, he must return it within three weeks. The third one specifies that a member must pay $2 if he has borrowed a book and has not returned it after three weeks. We may be tempted to use the "violation frame" to abbreviate the condition. Proposition p3 would then become:

```
p3 OBL pay(ag x)(go [2] dollar)
   (cond FAIL:return(ag x member)(go y book))
```

The problem with this notation, however, is that it violates the grammaticality constraint, i.e. the violation frame has no direct translation in English. Therefore we prefer the first form.

6.4.9. Counterhistoricals

A counterhistorical (cf. Mays, 1984) may be thought of as a special case of a counterfactual. An example of a counterfactual is: "If kangaroos did not have tails, would they topple over?". A counterhistorical is: "Could I have taken CSE 110 last semester?". Counterfactuals suppose that the present state of affairs is slightly different and then question the consequence. Counterhistoricals, on the other hand, question how a course of events might have proceeded otherwise. If we recall the temporal structure of our model, we see that although there are no branches into the past, there may be more than one branche from the past into the future. These are alternative histories to the one we are actually in. Counterhistoricals explore these alternate histories. Whereas counterfactual propositions are very tough to handle in logic (because there are usually many ways in which a state of affairs can be slightly different from the current one), the treatment of counterhistoricals is feasible in the present framework.

Intuitively, a counterhistorical may be evaluated by "rolling back" to some previous state and then reasoning forward, disregarding any events that actually took place after that state, to determine whether the specified condition might arise. For the question, "Could I have registered for CSE 110 last semester?", we access the state specified by last semester, and from that state description, we reason forward regarding the possibility of registering for CSE 110. More constrained questions might be: "Could I have taken Phil 6 when I was a sophomore?", or "Could I have taken CSE 220 and then CSE 110?".

Before illustrating the treatment of counterhistoricals in our framework, we introduce the following extension of the data logical POS. In data logic, POS ϕ can be evaluated when ϕ is some imperfective predication that applies to a state. The interpretation of such a proposition is that in some information state extending the actual one, ϕ holds. However, if the predication is perfective, the intended meaning is not that ϕ holds in the state in question, but in some dynamic state accessible from this state. Hence we must adapt our definition of POS for perfective predications as follows:

Definition 6.10 Let α be a perfective predication, of the form α = Pf ϕ. Then

$$T \models \text{POS } \alpha \text{ iff } T \dashv [\alpha] \nabla$$

end 6.10

In words, a proposition of the form POS α, where α is some action, is true w.r.t a state iff the performance of α does not lead to an inconsistent state.

Using this definition, we can interpret the counterhistorical "Could I have taken course CSE 110 last semester?"

```
PAST p POS [t semester: last] Pf take(ag P1)
                                     (go d[s] x course: CSE110)
```

where Pf stands for the Perfective, as:

$C(t') \models$ POS [take()()]

for some embedding f of fact time t to time index t' such that FT < RT < ST (ST denotes speech time). The proposition in the question "Could I take CSE 220 and then CS110?" is true when

$C(t') \models$ POS Pf take()(go CS220) & Pf take()(go CS110)

which is true when the following two expressions are true (remember that & is simple conjunction):

$C(t') \models$ POS Pf take()(go CS220)
$C(t') \models$ POS Pf take()(go CS220); take()(go CS110)

where the second expression is translated as:

$C(t') \models$ NEG [take()(go CS220)] [take()(go CS110)]∇

The "dynamic conditional" $[\alpha]\phi$ turns out to be a useful construct for the interpretation of counterhistoricals. More detailed research is needed on the exact linguistic form of these expressions. The question is not only whether counterhistoricals can be evaluated in the model, but also whether this evaluation is contained in the linguistic form.

6.5. CONCLUSION

In this chapter, we have given truth-conditional semantics of all kinds of propositions, including modal and deontic ones. We have defended the relevance of such propositions in a KBMS. The introduction of modal operators called for a generalization of our model concept by means of possible-world semantics with chronicles and dynamic logic.

In the extended model, we can interpret integrity constraints of several kinds, including analytic, empirical and deontic ones. Constraints can be static or dynamic.

We have omitted a discussion of the constructive meaning of propositions. The constructive meaning of a proposition with respect to a database (standing for a model) is not the truth-value, but its *effect* on the database: how the database must be updated to make the statement true. We need this constructive meaning all over the life of the knowledge base. Atomic propositions, without quantifiers, can be translated directly to a situation (the normal form can be used as intermediary), and this situation can be unified with the current state. If the predication is perfective, a new time index has to be introduced, pointing to a new dynamic state in which the predication obtains, if at least the preconditions are met. If so, the postconditions obtain in the output state.

We stress again that database and knowledge base both have their own function. The database is a "flat" structure in which facts can be accessed and processed fast. In cognitive terms, the database provides a "mental model". Although each proposition in the KB must be true with respect to the database, this does not mean that the KB is redundant. In particular, propositions of the form NEC ϕ require only that ϕ is true in every maximal extension of the database. Therefore, it says more about what the database can *not* contain than about what it actually contains at some time. This allows us to use *finite* databases as models even when all "classical" models of KB are infinite.

This chapter concludes the logical part in the traditional sense of the word. In the next chapter, we will investigate messages. Messages contain propositions, but, in general, they cannot be assigned truth-values. For example, a question or an imperative has no truth-value. It is possible to talk about logic on this level (illocutionary logic), but this logic differs from truth-conditional logic.

7

Messages

7.1. INTRODUCTION: HOW TO DO THINGS WITH WORDS

In the chapters 3-6 we have been dealing with various levels of the proposition and their logical interpretation. A knowledge base, in a narrow sense, can be defined as a set of propositions (a theory). However, it would be presumptuous to stop there. Propositions have little value on their own. They are used in a certain communicative context. A typical context is the "office", or some organizational framework. In an office, knowledge bases are part of the *information system* which has a communicative purpose. In the language/action perspective taken by (Lehtinen & Lyytinen, 1986) an information system "consists of speech acts that create, set up, control, and maintain an organization's transacting contracts, and report on their status" (see als Flores et al, 1988, Hirschheim, 1986). By organizational transacting they mean — following (Ouchi, 1980) — an organized exchange of goods and services between at least two social agents. A contract governs a transacting process by defining conditions that all contracting parties must fulfil. They typically contain promises, obligations, permissions etc. Information systems can sustain the mutual adjustment of the social agents, hence reducing the uncertainty and increasing the efficiency (Cyert & March, 1963). The information system may deal with communication within one organization or communication including external agents or communication between autonomous organizations.

From a functional point of view, one important goal of knowledge bases is the *coordination of activities*. Other functions include *tutoring* and *decision support* (for instance, in the form of an expert system). In all these cases, the knowledge base, and the theory contained in it, is not only a "representation" of some Universe of Discourse, but at the same time an instrument in the communication in some Environment of Discourse, between teacher and pupil, between medical specialist and general practicioner, etc. †

Just as we must have conceptual models for the abstraction of the UoD, we must have informational models for the abstraction of the EoD. The informational model specifies the social agents involved, the communication links between them, interaction patterns and the relationship between information and action. The UoD and the EoD may have some overlap but their logical functions with respect to the

† The most widely understood goal of artificial intelligence is to understand and build autonomous, intelligent, thinking machines. Recently, however, there have been a number of suggestions for other goals in this field that give more attention to the communicative aspect. Mark Stefik, for example, suggested the goal of building an "interactive knowledge medium" (Stefik, 1986). See also the work of Terry Winograd (below).

knowledge base must be distinguished sharply.

7.1.1. Example

The idea of an EoD can be illustrated by means of the ISO car example. In chapter 4, we defined the lexicon for this sublanguage (the conceptual model) and in chapter 6 we showed how additional deontic integrity constraints can be formulated. However, this does not specify yet the EoD. In the verbal description it is said that the UoD is described from the perspective of the registration authority (van Griethuysen, 1982):

> "The universe of discourse to be described has to do with the registration of cars and is limited to the scope of interest of the registration authority. The registration authority exists for the purpose of:
>
> 1. Knowing who is or was the registered owner of a car at any time from construction to destruction of the car.
> 2. To monitor certain laws, for example regarding fuel consumption of cars and their transfer of ownership".

The agents in the EoD are in particular:

- the registration authority
- manufacturers
- the government

The communication between manufacturers and registration authority consists of several speech acts, such as:

- asking permission to operate
- reporting the introduction of a model
- reporting the production of a car

The registration authority's responses are, among others,

- granting permission to operate
- confirming the acceptability of a model
- expressing a warning about excessive fuel consumption
- declaring a car to be registered

The government is not explicitly present in the model description, but plays an important role too. It is the source of various laws that the registration authority is held to monitor. The communication with the government includes:

- the government declares a law
- each year, the government declares what is the maximum fuel consumption
- the registration authority informs the government about violations of the law

Note that the communicative acts are interrelated in several ways. In the first place, there is the connection between statement and answer. For example, the manufacturer asks permission to operate and the registration authority grants permission. In the second place, one message can contain instructions for dealing with other messages. For example, the government sends a message to the registration authority specifying the conditions under which a new manufacturer can be registered.

According to the example, the registration authority is also bound to certain rules on what should be recorded. For example, the year of production of a car must be recorded. The history of a car must be kept until the end of the second calendar year following its destruction. These are "meta-rules", not about the cars themselves but about recorded facts about cars. In my opinion, these rules are therefore not part of the UoD, but of the EoD. They should be made explicit, but stored in a separate part of the knowledge base, the message base.

7.1.2. Information system modeling

In conceptual modeling, a distinction can be made between *formal* approaches and *linguistic* approaches. In the first kind of models, predicates, syntax and the like are purely formal, whereas in the latter kind of approaches, predicates are supposed to be taken from natural language and the logical syntax (the structure of the proposition) is supposed to be a linguistically motivated "deep structure". A similar distinction between formal and linguistic approaches is found in informational system modeling. Formal methods are for example ISAC (Lundeberg, Goldkuhl,Nilsson, 1979) and SA/SD (Structured Analysis / Structured Design) that is based on DFD's (Data Flow Diagrams) (Gane & Sarson, 1977; Yourdon, Constantine, 1979; DeMarco,1978). The representations are usually graphical in nature.

In linguistic approaches to informational modeling, communication is more than data flow and intrinsically related to the linguistic dispositions of the social agents. The best representative is SAMPO (Lehtinen & Lyytinen, 1986; Auramäki et al, 1987). Two central components in SAMPO are:

(1) The use of *speech act theory* that allows a more detailed analysis of the communication patterns;

(2) The use of *discourse analysis* as an information system specification method.

7.1.3. Speech acts

Speech act theory has its origin in Anglosaxon analytical philosophy (Austin, 1962; Searle, 1969; Searle & Vanderveken, 1985). Speech acts are constituted by rules that are shared by Speaker and Hearer. Speech acts have four aspects:

(1) *utterance act*: the act the Speaker performs by uttering an expression

(2) *illocutionary act*: the basic unit of human communication, such as a promise, an apology, a question etc. An illocutionary act is performed with a certain intention.

(3) *propositional act*: a speech act contains a proposition, and therefore includes an act of referring, of predicating etc.

(4) *perlocutionary act*: the act seen by its effects on the feelings, attitudes and subsequent behaviour of the hearers. Perlocutionary acts are "making someone upset", "selling a house" etc.

When a utterance act is made with certain intentions, we call it an *illocutionary act*. The illocutionary act has a *propositional content*, an *illocutionary force*, and a *context*.

The illocutionary force functions as an operator on the proposition. Its main component is the *illocutionary point*, being either *assertive*, *commissive*, *directive*, *declarative* or *expressive*. Some examples, taken from (Lehtinen & Lyytinen, 1985) and the ISO car model:

assertive:	the price of the product x is y. car XY10103 has been produced in September, 1988.
commissive:	we shall fulfil your order in two weeks. the car will be paid within 15 days.
directive:	we order product x in quantity y. please registrate us as car manufacturer under the name ..
declarative:	we classify you as a credit customer. the maximum fuel consumption is 120.
expressive:	we express you our gratitude on the occasion that your orders have increased 20 % this year. we express you our concerns about the fuel consumption of your company which already exceeds the maximum value.

The key in distinguishing these illocutionary points is the *direction of fit*: a *word-to-world direction of fit* means that the propositional content fits an independently existing state of affairs (SoA) in the world. A *world-to-word direction of fit* means that the world is altered to fit the propositional content. The former states how the world *is*, the latter how the world *should be*. According to Searle, the assertive corresponds to word-to-world fit, the commissive and directive correspond both to world-to-word fit (diverging on the responsibility assignment, either S or H), the declarative to the conjunction of the two fits, and the expressive to the absence of any fit direction.

The *context* in the illocutionary act specifies the Speaker, Hearer, Speech time, Location, and some "possible world" in which the speech act has to be interpreted. This may include for example the presupposed authority of the speaker over the hearer. Other components of the context are the discourse topic and focus (see next section).†

The illocutionary force is more than the illocutionary point. In Searle & Vanderveken (1986), the illocutionary force consists of seven components one of which is the illocutionary point. Other components are particularly the *preparatory conditions* and the *conditions of satisfaction*. A preparatory condition for a request is that the Hearer is able to perform the intended action. The conditions of satisfaction specify when the illocutionary act is successful. A assertion is succesful when the world is as described (the conditions of satisfaction of an assertion are the truth-conditions of its propositional content), and a directive is succesful when the Hearer performs the intended action.

7.1.4. Discourse analysis

In the methodology of SAMPO, the communication in an organization is regarded as a set of *discourses*, i.e, sequences of speech acts. These discourses exhibit systematic regularities that can be studied and analyzed. An example of a discourse is

† In man-machine dialogues, elements of the context are represented as "shell variables" or "desktops". These specify, for example, the current directory, the system name, the user name, and the command history. See (Caruso & Sciore, 1988) for the usability of "context" in the specification of database queries.

order processing or a software development process.

Discourse analysis is a step in information system development (see Fig. 7.1). The first phase is *change analysis* which investigates what are the current problems and how to cure them. Next, in information system *specification* the purposes and structures of the discourses are specified as well as the content and structure of elementary parts thereof. The third step is information system *design*. During this phase, the architecture of the IS is designed and implemented.

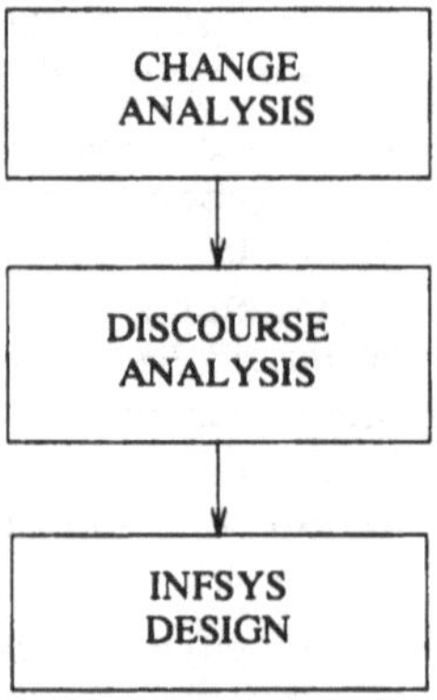

Fig. 7.1 Phase structure of IS Development in SAMPO

Discourse analysis deals with the following tasks:

(1) discourse types

(2) speech act patterns

(3) discourse segments

(4) moves

(5) topicalization

The *discourse type* is the largest unit of communication to be taken into account. Examples are teaching, entertainment or selling.

Speech act patterns are ordered sequences of speech acts that form a logical whole. An example is order processing. This process may consist of several elements: asking for information, proposals, promises, the actual order, confirmations, invoices etc. In the Coordinator system of Flores and Winograd (Flores et al, 1988), these are called conversation types and modelled by means of finite state diagrams.

Discourse segments (Reichman-Adar,1984; Grosz, 1978) are groups of speech acts that can be distinguished in the speech act pattern. Segments share a common topicalization and have a subgoal that is relevant to achieving the purpose of the discourse type. *Moves* are the individual speech acts. Under this heading, we can also study the *turn-taking* mechanisms.

Topicalization deals with what the utterance is "about". At the base level, topicalization deals with the discourse topics (terms). Topics may be proposed, accepted or rejected, continued etc. In a discourse, topics are interrelated in a relevance structure: one topic can be a subtopic of another one (Yule 1984; Hannay, 1985).
At the illocutionary level, the utterance is "about" a commitment. Commitments may be proposed, accepted or rejected, and confirmed too. The commitment may concern a desire or a belief.

For more details on SAMPO, the reader is referred to the original publications. From the vast literature on discourse analysis, I mention (Labov & Fanshel, 1977; Sacks, Schegloff & Jefferson, 1974; Brown & Yule, 1983; Tannen, 1982).

7.1.5. Message systems

The Discourse Analysis, as part of the Information System Development, tries to analyze the communication. However, it must be kept in mind that it takes only part of it into account. The first restriction is that it only looks at *recurrent* patterns of the communication, whereas a significant part of the communication is unique and not foreseen. The second restriction, which is inherent to the use of databases, is that it considers *structured* information only. But many messages are not structured, or only semi-structured. Present-day databases don't offer any support for such messages. Computational tools for this purpose include electronic mail systems, bulletin boards and electronic conference systems. However, the boundary between a message system and the database is fluent. For example, an "intelligent" mail system must be able to process requests for appointments by inspecting the user's agenda (a calendar system, some structured database) and updating it under certain conditions. In an *office automation system* the mail and database systems are fully integrated, thus contributing to. a greater functionality of the knowledge base system.

The system LENS (Malone et al, 1987; Lai, Malone, Yu, 1988) is an advanced message system for information sharing in organizations. Its basic idea is using semistructured message templates. A semistructured message is "a message of identifiable type, with each type containing a known set of fields, but with some fields containing unstructured text or other information". For example, seminar announcements can be structured as templates that include fields for "time", "place", "speaker" and "title", along with the usual header fields of messages (such as "to", "from", "cc", "subject"), and any additional text describing the content of the talk.

The message templates are arranged in a frame inheritance network so that specific message templates can inherit properties from more general types. Fields that are inherited by all message types are *topic* and *message type*. The *topic* field, together with the From and To field, is very handy for filtering incoming messages. It corresponds to the discourse topic mentioned above. The designers conceive the possibility that the topic field is filled in automatically by a natural language parse of the text. The *message type* field specifies the purpose of the message. The highest level classification of messages is based on speech act theory (p.128), and includes types like "action request", "notice", "question" etc. More specific message types in a given setting may be a "bug fix request".

The processing of messages in LENS is knowledge-based. That is, it makes use of a set of IF-THEN rules, where the conditional part may refer to any field in the message frame. The action specified in the THEN part may be a "move" (to file), "delete", "show" etc. Some examples:

```
IF     message type: action request
       action deadline: today, tomorrow
THEN   move_to: urgent

IF     message type: meeting proposal
       sender: not Axsom
THEN   resend: Axsom
```

According to the authors, semistructured messages are surprisingly useful for computer-supported communication. It seems to me that they also offer good prospects for the integration of knowledge bases and mail systems. An advantage of such an integration is for instance that the *topic* field can be handled with greater accuracy by using the lexicon and the UoD knowledge. For example, we can exploit the taxonomy of lexical types and T-frames. Moreover, the message type taxonomy can be simplified if UoD knowledge is taken into account. Consider again the example of the seminar announcement. This message type consists in essence of a basic type "announcement" and a topic "seminar". By using the conceptual knowledge about seminars, additional fields such as "speaker", "title", "place" can be provided automatically. In other words, if the topic structure gets more flesh, we can reduce the number of basic message types. The set of all message types is then the cross-product of these basic message types and all possible topics.

From the example of LENS we make the following observations:

(a) the two most important new fields in a semi-structured message, *message type* and *topic* correspond with the linguistic notions of speech act type and (discourse) topic. The "old" fields such as "From" and "To" correspond with Speaker, Addressee, and other parts of the illocutionary context.

(b) mail systems are profitably integrated with knowledge base systems;

(c) the specification of the rules for message handling can be knowledge-based.

7.1.6. Interface design

Information System Development describes (structured) message types and dialogues. A knowledge base session is an instance of such a dialogue type. This part of the knowledge base is usually studied under the heading of human-computer interface management. The specification of the interface still requires a large amount of application programs. Issues that must be handled here are among others:

- input specification
- how input symbols are echoed
- interpretation of function or cursor keys

- screen format
- menu or form specifications
- error messages
- feedback
- help and explanation facilities
- control structure
- command parsing
- etc

Interfaces are very hard to specify and to maintain. A keystone concept is *dialogue independence* (Ehrich & Hartson, 1981; Hartson & Hix, 1989). Dialogue independence is a characteristic that separates design of an interface from design of the computational component of an application system so that modifications in either tend not to cause changes in the other. Such independence allows easy modification of dialogues to meet the changing needs of end-users. The design of the interface involves decisions such as the choice between a command language and form filling, and the error messages to be given on illegal keystrokes. The design of the application includes for example semantic checks on the input and error messages to be given on semantically ill-formed commands.

In the Command Language Grammar of Moran (1981), a dialogue is represented at four levels: task level, semantic level, syntactic level and keystroke (or interaction) level. The first two make up the conceptual component and the other two the communication component (in addition, a physical component describes all physical features, but this component can be ignored here). The task level describes the task domain addressed by the system and the semantic level describes the concepts represented by the system. This includes not only entity types, but also methods for achieving tasks. The syntactic level describes the grammar of the command language. The operational meaning of the commands can be given in terms of the semantic level. The keystroke level specifies the "tokens" of the command language.

The distinction between the conceptual component and de communication component reflects the dialogue independence principle. It is possible to change the command language (communication component) without affecting the functionality of the system as defined by the conceptual conmponent.

Dialogue independence is a powerful idea, but it does not tell us yet how to represent dialogues at each level. Techniques for the representation of sequential dialogues are for instance BNF grammar rules (and extensions thereof, such as Shneiderman, 1982) and state transition diagrams (Wasserman & Shewmake, 1985). These techniques turn out to be useful in the communication component, but are insufficient for the conceptual component, since they have only a rudimentary logic.

In natural language interfaces, dialogue independence is reflected in the separation of the response selection process and the execution of the database query (Kaplan, 1978). In structured database query languages, these two processes may conflate, but with a natural language interface, they must be distinguished. This is because users expect more cooperative behaviour from a natural language speaking database. Cooperative behaviour includes for example:

- Signal erroneous *presumptions* (presuppositions), and give a corrective indirect response. For example, a query contains a subquery that always yields an empty set. This corresponds to the inappropriate use of a definite term ("the king of France") in everyday language.
- Avoid negative and trivial answers. If the result of the database query is empty, then answer by providing the reason for that, rather than simply saying "no" or "zero";
- Recognize the *focus* of a query in order to anticipate follow-up questions.† For example, the focus of the query "how many more trains leave for N.Y. this evening?", is the question term "how many more trains". If the database result is "zero", a cooperative answer could be: "None, but there are 3 busses".

An extensive discussion of the problems encountered in human-computer interfaces and the existing solutions and tools is beyond the scope of this chapter. The idea of dialogue independence is relevant for the specification of knowledge bases. It occurs to me that the *conceptual level* should be specified in the knowledge base whereas the *communication level* is better kept separate. In principle, it is possible to generate a communication module automatically once the conceptual level is fully specified. In practice, some adaptations to the user's taste and working habits will be necessary. A natural language interface is a communication module consisting of a parser and a generator. The lexicon is in the knowledge base; if necessary, parts of it can be imported in the communication module.

Separating the communication level from the knowledge base may have consequences for implementation design. In a distributed system environment, the communication module may be loaded at the user's workstation, as an application, whereas the knowledge base management system takes a special server.

Both the conceptual level of the interface and the communication level should incorporate general linguistic principles such as

(1) *feedback* Humans constantly expect feedback at different levels: is the other one still listening, does he understand me, does he agree.

(2) *cooperation* (see above) The underlying goal of human communication is to maximize the mutual knowledge (relevancy) and agreement.

(3) *context-dependence*. In human communication, the highest level of communication is not the sentence (although it is the largest *syntactic* unit). In particular, speech act patterns and topic choices have a scope that goes beyond the single sentence. Linguistic agents expect that the partner reckons with contextual features such as the current discourse topic and the current discourse goal.

If these principles are truly universal, they should not be programmed each time

† The focus is defined by Kaplan as "that aspect of the question that is most likely to shift in a follow-up question", which is more about the effect of focus than about its essence. Grosz (1978;1985) uses the term "focus space" (of a discourse segment): those entities that are salient. In (Dik et al, 1981), Focus is defined as "the (relatively) most salient information of the sentence" (with respect to the pragmatic information of the Speaker and the Addressee), and several kinds of Focus are distinguished, such as Question Focus and Contrastive Focus.

anew for each application, but must be incorporated in the communication component. As far as I know, there is no system in which this is the case yet.

7.1.7. Summary

By way of conclusion, I recall the arguments that I consider to be the most relevant:

(1) A knowledge base is typically part of an information system; the propositions are typically embedded in messages;

(2) A knowledge base that takes data independence serious, not only at the internal level, but also at the external level, provides not only a model of the Universe of Discourse, but also one of the Environment of Discourse;

(3) In modelling the Environment of Discourse, a significant increase in analytical accuracy can be gained by using linguistic knowledge, in particular the theory of speech acts;

(4) Dialogue independence means that the semantic structure of the dialogue is described independently from the syntactic and keystroke level. This can be achieved by having the semantic structure be described explicitly in the knowledge base and putting the keystroke and syntactic level in a separate communication module.

7.2. DEFINITION

The highest level of the predication is called the message. I distinguish six types of messages:

(a)	ASSERT	the Speaker presents a proposition with his own support
(b)	ASK	the Speaker presents a proposition without his support
(c)	DIRECT	the Speaker presents an action with his own support
(d)	PROPOSE	the Speaker presents an action without his own support
(e)	EXPRESS	he Speaker presents a feeling with his own support
(f)	INVITE	the Speaker presents a feeling without his own support

Several secondary distinctions can be made; for example, the message type DIRECT can be a command or a promise, depending on who is the responsible agent of the action.

In each case, the expected and desired response of the Addressee is cooperative support: †

AGREE take over the proposition

† See (Pomerantz, 1984; Houtkoop,1987). Apparent exceptions to this rule are utterances of self-deprecation and compliment, in which case the preferred response is disagreement. This is probably because such expressions endanger the supposed symmetry in the relationship of Speaker and Adressee as partners in the transcendental language game. I have put together the expected response of EXPRESS and INVITE actions under the heading RELATE. There is much more to say about these kinds of speech acts, and they are far from marginal in the whole of communication, but at the same time they are perhaps the most difficult to model and to support by means of information systems. Therefore I largely ignore them here.

ANSWER	lend support to (one of) the unsupported propositions
COMPLY	take up a commitment
COMMIT	confirm the commitment of the Speaker
RELATE	express support with the feeling

The FG underlying clause is not a speech event, but a speech event type (not an utterance, but a sentence). The general format is as follows:

$\pi_4\ ILL(\pi_3\ p)$

where π_3 is an *epistemological* proposition operator, *ILL* is the *illocutionary frame* and π_4 is an *illocutionary* operator. *ILL* is of one the following three forms:

DECL	declarative
INT	interrogative
IMP	imperative

The value of *ILL* is called the sentence type; it must be distinguished from the message type, as we will see shortly. In the next section, I give the f-structure format of the illocutionary frame. A special section is devoted to the epistemological operators.

7.2.1. Illocutionary frame

In f-structure format, the message is represented as:

```
OP(pred => OP(p);
   cat => ILL;
   type => ilforce
   prag => (g-top => ...; n-top => ...);
   res => ...
   sit => ...
   sat => (theme => ...;
           tail => ...))
```

Example:

```
(pred => PRES(pred => (pred => (pred => IN;
                        cat => q;
                                    sem => (ref => Amsterdam));
                          cat => p;
                          syn => (subj => X:(pred => john)));
                   prag => (topic => -));
 cat => int;
 type => [ask];
 prag => (g-top  => X))
```

Is John in Amsterdam?

Remarks:

- The address `pred` points to the embedded proposition, whose structure has been defined in the preceding chapters. In the example, we don't have epistemological operators, only the tense operator. I will return on these operators shortly.

- The value of the `cat` address is `decl`, `int` or `imp`.

- The `type` specifies the illocutionary force of the clause, that is, `assert`, `ask`, `direct`, `propose`, `express`, `invite`. Perhaps some subtypes can be defined too, such as "promise" and "warn" (subtypes of "direct"), "apologize" (a subtype of "express"), "greet" (subtype of "invite"). Note that the illocutionary force is given independent from the sentence type (cat). This means that an utterance can be of the sentence type INT (interrogative) whereas the type (illocutionary force) is [direct]. Examples are polite requests, such as: "Would you please come in?"

The `type` information is missing in the traditional FG representation. In my opinion, this is not correct, because the type (illocutionary force) can influence the formal expression, in particular, the prosodic contour. Think, for example, about the prosody of warnings. Therefore, the underlying clause is not complete when the type is not specified. Moreover, the `type` determines the (pre and post) conditions of the speech act, which can function in the same way as the secondary semantic functions in predicate frames (4.4.4).

- Just as predicate frames have semantic functions, and predications have syntactic functions, so messages have pragmatic functions. In the example, the pragmatic function `g-top` (given topic) co-refers with the subject function. Following (Dik,1989) and many others, a topic can be Given, New or Resumed.

- Restrictors on the message are adverbs like "briefly". Adverbs like these do not qualify the proposition or SoA, but the message as a whole.

- Satellites on the message level are Theme and Tail. They fall outside the scope of the clause. The *Theme* presents a "domain or universe of discourse with respect to which it is relevant to pronounce the following predication" (Dik, 1978:130). A constituent with *Tail* function presents, as an 'afterthought' to the predication, information meant to clarify or modify some constituent in the predication. *Theme* and *Tail* are optional slots of the message frame, and therefore we represent them as satellites.
It is not unlikely that more message satellites have to be distinguished. A candidate is "Address", the title used by the Speaker to address the Addressee ("Dear John, ...").

- Illocutionary operators are not given in the example. The most important ones are *mitigation* and *aggravation* which determine the degree of politeness or indirectness of the message (Labov & Fanshell, 1977; Levinson, 1983).

The structure presented here defines a message *type*. If we want to represent a particular message instance (an utterance), for example, when we deal with a particular knowledge base session, the message frame must be extended with a `frame` slot specifying the context, including the Speaker, the Addressee, the speech time, and discourse location.

7.2.2. Epistemological modality

Epistemological modality is defined as "all those linguistic means through which the Speaker can show his attitude towards the proposition" (Hengeveld, 1988). Two subgroups can be distinguished. First, we have "those modal distinctions which evaluate the actuality of an event with respect to a source", such as:

(1) inferential mode - in which the predication is characterized as inferred from evidence ("evidently");

(2) quotative mode - in which the predication is reported from another source ("allegedly");

(3) experiential mode - in which the predication is characterized as experienced by the source ("apparently");

(the English expressions are to be taken as paraphrases). The second group is where the predication is marked explicitly as constructed by the Speaker himself:

(4) subjective mode - in which the predication is presented as a statement for which the Speaker takes responsibility, within a certain degree of commitment. A decreasing degree of commitment is reflected in the following series of modal adverbs: certainly - probably - possibly.

Some examples (EXP stands for experiential, CERT for subjective certainty):

(1) `EXP p (PROG e repair(subj ag d[s] x: John)(go d[s] y car: french)`
"Apparently, John is repairing the French car"

(2) `CERT p (POS e: have(subj d[s] x John)(co e repair(ag x)(go d[s] y car: french))]`
"Certainly, John may have to repair the French car"

Note that we consider the subjective mode as an epistemological operator too. "The very essence [of subjective modality] is to express the speaker's reservations about giving an unqualified "I-say-so" to the factuality of the proposition" (Lyons, 1977:799). The Speaker suggests rather than states a proposition. He can express more or less support to the proposition. This is indicated by an operator `[c]` which could be either a numerical value of belief support (certainty factor) or some support type (like `CERT` for certain). A somewhat complex example (we ignore irrelevant SoA markers):

(a) `([0.7] p4 (e streptococcus(subj d[s] x organism))`
"Probably (CF=0.7) the organism is streptococcus"

(b)
```
([0.7] p4 (e streptococcus(subj x))
        (cond p3 ([t] gram-positive(subj i[s] x organism))))
```
"If an organism is gram-positive, then probably (CF=0.7) it is streptococcus"

Note the correspondence between the belief support operator and the quantitative operators we defined for terms and predications. It seems that a quantitative operator is universal for all parts of the underlying clause.

The mathematical basis for computations on certainty factors or belief functions is a can of worms that we will not open here. Shortliffe and Buchanan (1984) discuss several models. For the interested reader, we only remark that within the functional-linguistic framework I am working in, a Subjective Theory of probability (Ramsay, 1931; Finetti, 1972;cited in Shortliffe and Buchanan) seems to be more promising than a statistical one. As Finetti writes:

> We hold it to be chimerical for anyone to arrive at beliefs, opinions, or determinations without the intervention of his personal judgment.

which is in line with Aristotle's conception of knowledge as involving judgment.

7.3. COMMUNICATION MODEL

The formal semantics of messages and the Environment of Discourse model are less worked out than the logical semantics of propositions and the description of the Universe of Discourse. This is an area in which more research is barely needed. In this section, I introduce a communication model based on ideas in modular programming. In the next section, I will argue that the EoD model can be specified essentially in the same way as the UoD model, namely, by means of lexical definitions and deontic constraints. The only difference is that the actions and entities are speech acts and linguistic entities (messages and propositions). The "ontology" of the EoD is to be discovered in the communication model.

The communication model makes use of the SPE model developed in (Kersten, 1985). The SPE model is designed to model access control in a programming environment, in which *agents*, *objects*, *regions*, and *import/export* actions are central. An agent differs from an object in the ability to initiate a state change under a procedural interpretation of the model. The *regions* are artificial objects, introduced to represent domains to which agents and objects are bound. They are also called *mediating regions*. Consider the following diagram:

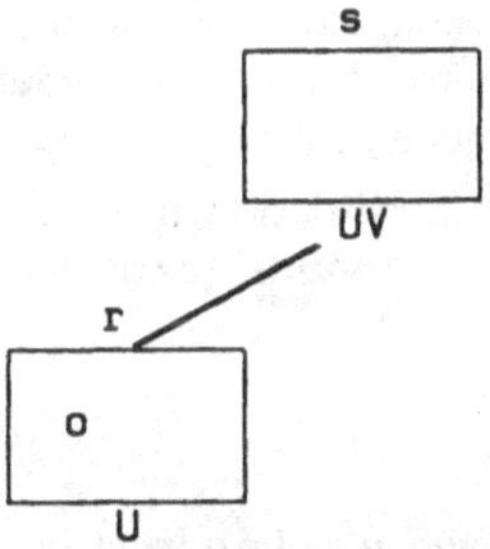

Fig. 7.2 basic model

This diagram models two regions *r* and *s*, and two agents *u* and *v*, and one object *o*. Object *o* is bound to region *r*. The agent *u* is bound to *r*, and also to *s* (together with *v*). Moreover, there is a relationship between the regions represented by an arrow. Formally, we can define the model as follows:

Definition 7.1 A communication model *COM* is defined as a tuple

$<A,R,O,OWN,DEF,MED>$

where

A = the set of agents
R = the set of regions
O = the set of objects

and

OWN $\subsetneq$ A $\times$ R = a relation between agents and regions
DEF $\subsetneq$ O $\times$ R = a relation between objects and regions
MED $\subsetneq$ A $\times$ A = a partial ordering between regions

end 7.1

When a MED relation is defined between region r and s, as in Fig. 7.2, we say that r is *mediated* by s. Agent u is the *owner* of r

Now suppose we extend the previous diagram in the following way:

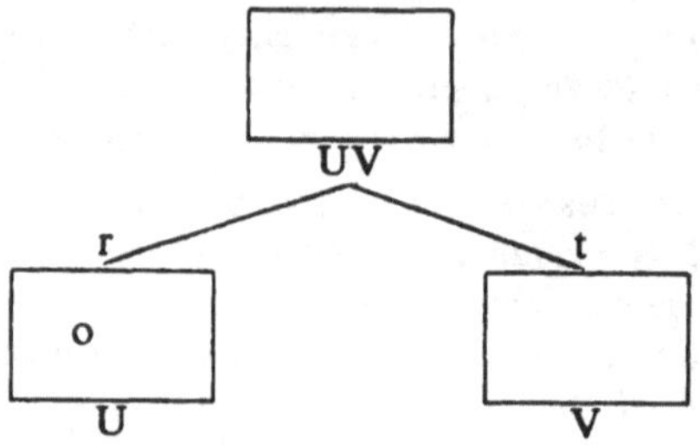

Fig. 7.3 Example communication setting

Object o is bound to region r. Suppose agent u wants to make it accessible to agent v in region t. To make this possible we define two dynamic relations: *import* and *export*. These relations can move objects, or rather, they change the accessibility.

Definition 7.2 IMPORT (EXPORT) is a relation over A×O×R×R, where a tuple (a,o,r_1,r_2) is to be read as: agent a imports (exports) object o from region r_1 into region r_2.

An object is *accessible* in region s iff

(1) it is defined in region s, or

(2) it is accessible in some region t and it is imported or exported from t to s.

An agent a can *export* an object o from region r to region s iff

(1) object o is accessible in region r, and

(2) a is owner of r and s, and

(3) r is mediated by s.

An agent a can *import* an object o from region s to region r iff

(1) object o is accessible in region s,

(2) a is owner of r, and

(3) r is mediated by s.

end 7.2

The action "to import" is to be read as the insertion of a tuple in the relation IMPORT. Similarly for "to export". Later we will also consider an action "to retract" for deleting a tuple from IMPORT or EXPORT.

In the example above, u can *export* o to region s. After that, he cannot do anything more to it, but agent v can now *import* it in his own region t, if he wishes. The new situation after import is shown in the following diagram:

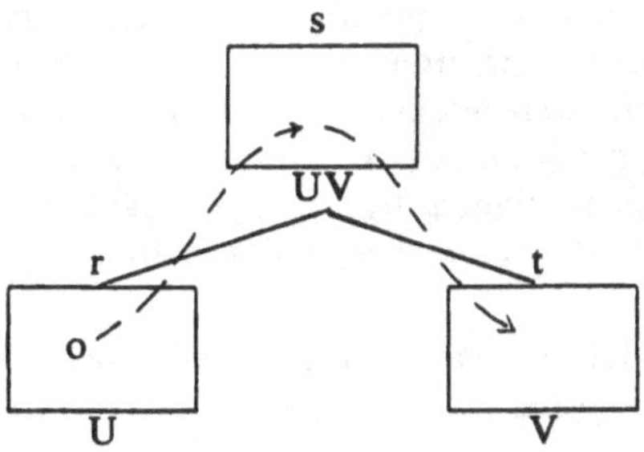

Fig. 7.4 situation after export and import

Now object o is accessible in all three regions, according to the definition. For the security of information systems, it is also interesting to know whether an object can be *made* accessible, with or without the help of others. It is also useful to define accessibility to *agents*, rather than regions. For this purpose, we also define the notion of *visibility*:

Definition 7.3 Let OWN(a) be the set of regions owned by agent a. The *environment* (ENV) of a region r is the set of regions $\{ s \mid (r,s) \in \text{MED}\}$.
The environment of an agent a is the set of regions $\bigcup_{r \in OWN(a)} ENV(r)$.
An object o is called *visible* to agent a iff $o \in r$, for some region $r \in$ ENV(a).
end 7.3

Note the asymmetry in the definitions of import and export. An agent can *export* to some region s only if he is owner of that region, whereas an agent can *import* from s even if he is not an owner of s. For example, suppose that in Fig. 7.4 U is the sole owner of the mediating region. Then the described export and import could still take place, but an inverse transportation would be impossible. So if the mediating region is owned by just one of the agents, we have an asymmetric communication situation. If the mediating region is owned by both, we have duplex symmetric communication. If the mediating is owned by none of the agents, there is no communication. In that case, there is only data sharing, since both agents can still import whatever they want. The three configurations correspond to the classical distinction made by Thompson (1967) between *reciprocal*, *sequential* and *pooled* interdependence (see Fig. 7.5).

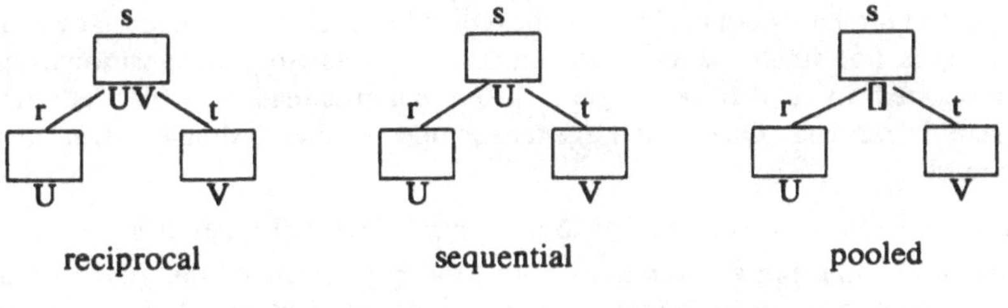

Fig. 7.5 Reciprocal, sequential and pooled interdependence

In the case of reciprocal interdependence, both agents can export objects to the mediating region. In the case of sequential interdependence, only one of them can do that. In the case of pooled interdependence, no agent is allowed to export into the mediating region. Interdependence is defined between two agents, it is not a property of the mediating region per se. Suppose that *u* and *v* have a region *s* in their common environment owned by *z*. They cannot export to the mediating region, so they stand in pooled interdependence to each other, but in sequential interdependence to *z*.

The communication model we want to set up takes over the SPE framework, but differs in its further elaboration.

7.3.1. A simple model of dialogue

In the following, we will assume that each agent u owns one region that is mediated by all the other regions he owns. This region is called the *private region*, written as [u]. [u] is so to say the lower bound of the region structures owned by u.

In our dialectical model of communication the passive objects of the SPE model are replaced by FG objects. We will consider several kinds of these, starting with the most fundamental one, the proposition. The elementary 'moves' of the communication game are the export and the import. Later on we will see that several sequences of basic moves allow for more complex communication moves. The moves do not only restrict the way communication flows from one agent to another, but at the same time they determine patterns of interaction, because each move constrains and alters the set of possible subsequent moves.

Consider again a communication situation such as in Fig. 7.3. Agent *u* owns a proposition *p*. Recall that propositions may be positive or negative, depending on the polarity operator (6.4.5). The only action possible for agent *u* is to export it to region s. In principle, three reactions of *v* are possible:

(a) Agent *v* imports *p* into his own region. This is the situation in which *v accepts* p;

(b) Agent *v* exports *p* from his own region. That is, *v* had *p* already, and *agrees* with *u*;

(c) Agent *v* exports $\neg$p. Now region *t* contains both *p* and $\neg$p. We say that *v* *disagrees* with *u*.

In (a) and (b), the proposition *p* is *mutually* supported. Since communication is aimed at mutual knowledge, (b) can be considered a stable state. However, the state in (c) is not stable, since there are two contradictory propositions, each of them supported by a different agent. More communication is needed before a stable state is reached. One of the agents, or both of them, should retract or adapt his proposal.

(d) Agent *v* exports *?p* (equivalent to p $\vee$ $\neg p$) That is, he *questions p*.

In trying to explain human communication, the hypothesis of the goal of maximal mutual knowledge is, in my view, a good way to account for all kinds of particularities. However, it is virtually impossible to formalize it. Perhaps this is because the goal of maximal mutual knowledge is a part of what Karl-Otto Apel calls the *transcendental language game* (Apel, 1987). The line of explanation, in linguistics, is from syntax to semantics and from semantics to pragmatics, as Dik put it (Dik, 1978). However, the pragmatics, as a formal theory, cannot be self-contained. It must be grounded itself in a transcendental pragmatics which can be explored but never grasped in full.

The following definitions formalizes the support relationship.

Definition 7.4 An agent u *supports* a proposition p in region r iff (i) p is accessible in r, and (ii) u has either imported or exported p to or from his private region. If P is a set of literals (conjunction), then u supports P iff u supports p for all $p \in P$ (support is distributive)

end 7.4

It has been suggested already that propositions are not the only objects that are supported by the linguistic agents. Other objects are:

- topics
- commitments
- messages

The communication model is general enough to be of value for these objects as well. Discourse topics can be proposed, accepted, supported, rejected, questioned, just like propositions. The same holds for commitments and for feelings. Commitments are to be understood as controlled SoAs, usually actions. It seems that IMP messages do not take a proposition, but a predication as their content. Evidence for this is that tense and modality cannot be specified for imperative sentences. If this is true, we cannot speak about the propositional content of an imperative sentence. A better term would be "action content".

The appearance of messages as objects of communication may be surprising. However, as Austin has remarked, it is possible to understand a message without taking it up (Wunderlich makes a similar distinction between Verstehen and Akzeptieren). Uptake means supporting the proposition. Understanding means that the agent has received (imported) the message. The "yes" response is ambiguous between these two. On the one hand, it can mean: "Yes, I have got the message", and on the other hand it can mean: "Yes, I agree". In the first case, he shows that he has imported the message, but does not commit himself yet to the proposition. In the second case, he has not only imported the message, but also the propositional content. Because of this distinction, it is necessary to treat messages as communication objects independent from the propositions.

7.3.2. Epistemological modality

The model of Fig. 7.3 contains one non-private region only. This is not very realistic. We may assume that at any moment the linguistic actors are involved in a large number of discourses, i.e., mediating regions. We can make a distinction between "open" and "closed" regions. A discourse is open as long as the participants contribute to it. After it is closed, it remains accessible as such to both of them. Closed regions are therefore still relevant to the communication in the open regions. A typical example is a refusal to answer. It might look as if this violates the cooperative principle that participants want to increase their mutual knowledge. However, the linguistic agent may be confronted with conflicting beliefs in different regions. In such a case, pretending ignorance is not optimal with respect to the mutual knowledge in the region in question, but it may be an optimal strategy with respect to the totality of mutual knowledge over all regions.

When two linguistic agents communicate by some mediating region, they carry with them their own set of "closed" regions. These two sets may overlap; in that case we speak of "*common background*". The situation is depicted in Fig. 7.6:

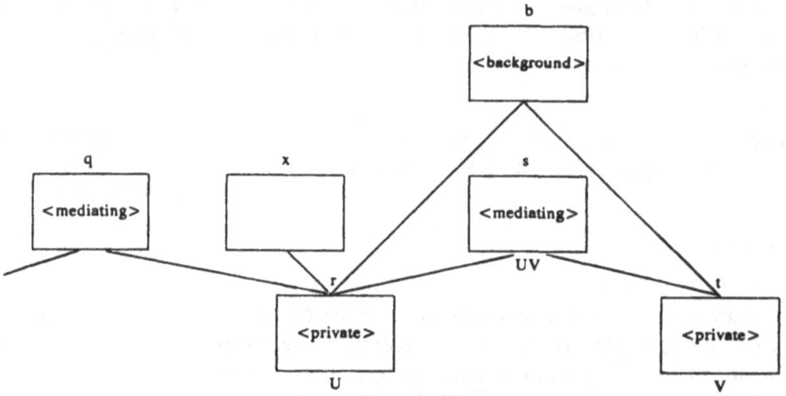

Fig. 7.6 extended communicative setting

Here *b* is a common background of *u* and *v*. This common background may consist of previous discourse, common experience, shared cultural values, general world knowledge, etc.

Furthermore, *x* is a region that is accessible to *u* only, whereas *q* is a (closed) mediating region of *u* with some other agent. A typical example of an x-type region is some visual experience of *u*. The regions *b*, *x* and *q* can be taken as representatives for all possible configurations.

In the extended setting, the simple moves of import and export can be combined in several ways, each combination being a meaningful communicative alternative. Let us take the perspective of one of the linguistic agents as reference point, say, *u*. Then *u* can make the following moves:

(1) if *p* is an object in *q*, then *u* can *import* p and *export* it through to *s*: **quotative modality**;

(2) the same if *p* is an object in *x*: **experiential modality**;

(3) if *p* is an object in *r* (imported or created), then *u* can *export* it to *s*: **subjective modality**;

(4) if *p* is an object in *b*, then *u* can *import p* and *export* it through to *s*: **inferential modality**;

In an information system, the modalities distinguished here can be equated with the following types:

(1) quotative - the source of the information is some third agent or database

(2) experiential - the source of the information is some sensory device or internal monitor

(3) subjective - the information is a suggestion from the user or created by the knowledge base itself by means of inductive reasoning

(4) inferential - the information is retrieved or deduced from what the is common knowledge

These four distinctions represent *types*. Each type can be further specified, for instance, for the name of the third agent in the case of quotative. Epistemological modality qualifies the proposition as a whole. A direct way to represent it in the knowledge base, is to store the export trace in the following format:

EXPORT(proposition, source)

where the source may be either the identifier of a specific region (e.g., "john") or a type (e.g. QUOTE). If we treat messages as communication objects, as I argued in the last section, then this trace is already accounted for by the bookkeeping of the messages import and export, if "source" is a satellite in the extended proposition.

For subjective modality, further subdistinctions are to be made indicating the level of commitment of the speaker. This is not worked out here.

7.4. EoD SPECIFICATION

The model introduced in the previous section is intended to model discourses at a general level. In everyday life, the mediating regions are dialogues. I now give a sketch of the way in which the model may reappear in an actual knowledge base.

I assume that the knowledge base consists of several regions, representing different users and different shared knowledge bases. It is neither necessary nor desirable that each user has access to all the knowledge stored in the system. The modularization of the knowledge base is *functional*, that is, it depends on the communication functions established between the participating users of the system. The *import* and *export* are familiar constructs in modular languages.

Using this framework, there are still two possible views on the role of the KBMS. One is that the KBMS is just a mediating region between two users. That is, one user exports a certain proposition to the KBMS, and another user imports the proposition. The KBMS consists of all objects that are supported by the users in the mediating region, including propositions and topics. In this view, the KBMS is just an interface between human users. In the other view, the KBMS takes a more active role. It becomes an agent itself, that can import and export objects between regions. It communicates with users by means of passive mediating regions. Under this view, human tasks can be delegated to the KBMS. For example, a question can be answered by the KBMS in behalf of the human user who built up the database. In the first view, the KBMS would just record the question and the answer that must be given by the other user. Of course, the KBMS would be *visible* to its users (it would be possible to brows through it, for example), but it is not possible to start a dialogue with it.

At a certain level of abstraction, the KBMS is just an interface between users. But at a more detailed level, it is profitable to view it as an agent with delegated tasks. These tasks include taking up propositions, answering questions, reasoning, but also sending notifications or other messages to users and perhaps other knowledge bases. The behavior of the KBMS can be controlled by means of constraints given in deontic logic. We call these constraints EoD constraints, since they refer to the Environment of Discourse. The following examples make use of FG frames, but the conditions of the rules are written as IF parts of IF-THEN rules rather than as satellites. This is to increase the readability.

```
IF
   ask(ag [s] m manufacturer)(go e permit(ag 1P)(rec m)(go operate) &
   PROG operate(ag [<3] x manufacturer)
THEN
   OBL permit(ag KB)(rec m)(go operate)
```

If a manufacturer asks for permission to operate and less than three manufacturers are operating, then the KB must permit him to operate.

```
IF p
  fuel consumption(m manufacturer)(tmp y year) >
        maximum fuel consumption(y)
THEN
 OBL warn(ag KB)(rec m)(reason p) &
 OBL inform(ag KB)(rec d[s] y government)(go p)
```

If the fuel consumption of a manufacturer in some year is more than the maximum fuel consumption of that year, the KB must warn the manufacturer and the government.

In these examples, we use speech act types such as `permit` and `warn`. The pre- and postconditions for such speech acts must be described in the lexicon, and they are subject to other deontic constraints as well. For example, it can be specified that if the KB warns a manufacturer, then the manager of the registration authority should be informed of this. Then, as soon as the system knows that some manufacturer has a fuel consumption that is too high, then it must warn the manufacturer. As soon as it does this, it must inform the manager. In this way, the behaviour of the KBMS can become quite complex.

In giving meaning conditions for the various speech acts, we may use the basic moves *accept, reject* etc defined in the previous section as primitives. This is not to say that their meaning can be exhaustively described in this way; but they can be used to give necessary meaning conditions.

Advantages of the specification format proposed in this section in comparison with traditional methods are:

(1) the behaviour specification is "declarative": it consists of separate constraints that can be inserted and retracted independently (by sending messages to the KB);

(2) the EoD constraints can be given a logical interpretation. There is no formal difference between the EoD constraints and the UoD constraints treated in chapter 6. The only difference is that we have not only entities and SoAs, but also propositions and messages as possible objects.

(3) the EoD constraints not only prescribe the behaviour of the KBMS, but may also specify the behaviour of other agents in the EoD. They do not only make

the application work, but also provide a general model of the EoD. This model can be analyzed, queried, etc.

At this point, it is worthwhile to look back and see what kinds of integrity constraints we have distinguished. Firstly, we have the lexicon with the meaning conditions (necessary analytic) and meaning definitions (characterizing). In some sense, all structures in the lexicon are constraining, including the subtype definitions, the arity of predications and selection restrictions. Secondly, we have deontic propositions in the knowledge base that describe what is obliged, forbidden and permitted in the UoD. Universal and necessary propositions can be used to express empirical constraints (third form). Fourthly, deontic propositions in the knowledge base describe the rules for the EoD (including the KB itself). These rules capture, among others, what are called *authorization constraints* in traditional databases. Finally, we may think of constraints for the interface module, with respect to allowable sentences and keystrokes, but these fall out of the scope of the KB and of this thesis. In my opinion, the diversity of integrity constraints must be evaluated positively, because it makes us understand better the specific meaning of each one of them.

7.5. REASONING AS A LANGUAGE-GAME

In this thesis, I have given an algebraic model-theoretic semantics for FG propositions. I have not given a proof-theory. Such a theory consists of certain axioms and derivation rules. For example, in classical propositional logic, we have axioms such as $p \vee \neg p$, and the derivation rule is Modus Ponens:

$$\frac{p,\ p \supset q}{q}$$

In a proof-theory for FG propositions, we will have a similar rule. An important role will also be played by subsumption rules; for *positive* propositions, we have that

$$\frac{p,\ p \leq q}{q}$$

where $\leq$ is the subsumption ordering on frames. From a functional point of view, the question is not only whether such a proof-theory can be found, but also how it can be explained. This means that we are interested in a linguistic-constructive logic, in the line of Lorenzen (Lorenzen & Lorenz, 1978; Barth & Krabbe, 1982; Felscher, 1986). In the time that the Dutch logician Beth developed the tableaux method for theorem proving, the German philosopher Lorenzen was investigating the possibilities of using dialogues as a foundation for intuitionistic logic. Barth reports this as follows (Barth, 1980; cited in van Eemeren, Grootendorst, Kruiger, 1987):

> In about 1960, Paul Lorenzen wrote ... Beth a letter, which I once read. In my view this letter deserves to be regarded as a historic document; unfortunately it cannot now be found. In this letter Lorenzen wrote to Beth: I set myself the task of taking the connectives and other logically important non-referring words and *defining* them by describing the ways in which they are used in a *dispute*: that is to say, in a discussion between people who are disagreed about something. ... So Lorenzen took

> the interaction between a speaker a *critical* listener — not just a passive or amenable listener prepared to allow himself to be swept along by a *rhetor*, but one who not only adopts a critical attitude but also puts it into words. On the rules for use which emerged in this way Lorenzen wrote to Beth ...: "*und dann entstehen eben Ihre Tableaus*" [and that is just when your tableaux are created].

The work of Lorenzen leads into another view on logic and knowledge representation. In the traditional view, logic is a solitary enterprise, in which more and more facts ("truths") are proved from some set of "evidential" postulates. However, it is also possible to see knowledge about a topic as a snapshot in the process of human interaction, consisting of sets of propositions and proof procedures that are agreed upon at a particular moment by the people working on that topic. In Lorenzen's dialogue tablaeux theory, a logical proof is pictured as a discussion between two parties. The formula to be proved, called initial thesis (T), is defended by one party, which thereby takes up the role of the so called proponent (P), against the criticism of the other party accordingly taking up the role of opponent (O). A discussion about T represents a logical proof of T, provided that P is able to defend T against all possible criticism, i.e. that P has a winning strategy for T. There are several kinds of games, depending on how we formulate the dialogue rules and winning rules. In the so-called formal game (Kamlah & Lorenzen), the proponent wins if he has to defend a formula already put forward by the opponent (the *ipse dixisti!* remark, "you said it yourself").

Felscher (1986) describes a D-dialogue (with D-strategy) for which the following equivalence theorem holds:

Theoreom 7.5 There exists a recursive algorithm which, for every formula ϕ, transforms a proof of the sequent $\Rightarrow \phi$ in Gentzen's calculus LJ (for intuitionistic logic) into a D-strategy - and vice versa.

end 7.5

The D-dialogue is roughly as follows. The argumentation forms specify how a proposition can be attacked and how the attack should be answered. The argumentation forms for the connectives in propositional logic are:

$\wedge$ assertion: P$w_1 \wedge w_2$
attack: O i (i=1 or i=2)
answer: P w_i

$\vee$ assertion: P$w_1 \vee w_2$
attack: O $\vee$
answer: Pw_i (i=1 or i=2)

$\rightarrow$ assertion: P$w_1 \rightarrow w_2$
attack: Ow_1
answer: Pw_2

$\neg$ assertion: P$\neg w$
attack: Ow
answer: *no answer possible*

In the first case, the Opponent chooses one of the conjuncts and the Proponent has to defend this conjunct. In the case of disjunction, O can only attack the disjunction as such; P can choose himself which disjunct to defend. The argumentation form for the implication is such that the Proponent is obliged to affirm the consequent when the Opponent supports the condition (of course, he can also attack O's w_1, if this is allowed by other rules). A negated formula can be attacked by stating the positive part; the proposer cannot answer this attack but he can hope that O contradicts himself. If no answer is possible, this does not mean that O has won already.

A D-dialogue must also satisfy the following properties:

D1 P may assert an atomic formula only after it has been asserted by Q before;

D2 If, at some position, there are several open attacks suitable to be answered, then only the *latest* of them may be answered;

D3 An attack may be answered at most once;

D4 A P-formula may be attacked at most once

A dialogue is said to be won by P if it ends in finite time, all attacks have been answered, and O cannot continue with another attack or answer.

The first rule is to ensure the relevance of the dialogue. The Proponent may not assert additional material. The only exception is that he may recall what O has said before (as "ipse dixisti"). The other rules are also necessary for the proper continuing of the dialogue; see Felscher (1986) for motivations.

The Dialogue Tableaux Theory shows that it is possible to ground intuitionistic logic in a theory of dialogues. The dialogue rules are rather strict and should not be taken as descriptive of actual dialogues. They are an abstraction. Nonetheless, they are interesting because the abstraction can be linguistically motivated. And, given the abstraction, it is possible to see how the semantics of propositions is grounded in the pragmatics. This is in line with one of the paradigms of Functional Grammar, that says that the direction of explanation in linguistics must be from syntax to semantics and from semantics to pragmatics. That is, the formal proof calculus must be grounded in the semantics (a model-theory), and the semantics must be grounded in pragmatics (a dialogue Theory). We can also put it as follows. A certain theory is consistent iff it is satisfiable (has a model — semantic definition of consistency). A theory is satisfiable iff it is defendable (in a D-dialogue — pragmatic definition of satisfiability).

The Dialogue Tableaux Theory is also interesting for other reasons. Hoepelman and van Hoof (1987) have extended the D-theory with a "fail operator" F. The F operator does not replace negation, but it functions in the same way as negation by failure in Prolog. It can be used for certain kinds of non-monotonic reasoning. The same authors have also implemented a theorem prover based on DTT in C-Prolog. In other words, the Dialogue Tableaux Theory has not only theoretical interest, but it can be used in the KBMS for the inference engine.

The Dialogue Tableaux Theory can be embedded in our SPE dialogue model. In 7.3.1, we hypothesized the principle of maximal mutual knowledge as a transcendental goal of language. Faithfulness may be another rule. In order to participate in the language game, the agent's yes must be yes and no must be no. This principle can be embedded in SPE by restricting the actions of the agents to the argumentation forms given by the D-theory. This is obviously a topic for future research. A careful choice must be made from the various possible dialogue rules.

7.6. SUMMARY

In the first half of the chapter, we have reviewed some research on information system modelling and interface design. A KBMS should not only contain an explicit model of the Universe of Discourse, but also one of the Environment of Discourse. A key concept is the principle of *dialogue independence*. This principle urges us to specify the Environment of Discourse description independently from the syntax of the interface (communication module). The communication module supports the syntactic and keystroke level. For the semantics of this language, we need the EoD and UoD models contained in the KBMS.

In FG, propositions are embedded in illocutionary frames. The underlying clause is not just a proposition, but a message containing a proposition. In this chapter, we have defined the syntactic form of messages and the interpretation of basic messages in a communication model. We have also argued that a model of the Environment of Discourse can be specified in a declarative (logical) form, using speech acts and deontic operators. Such a model specification is a necessary part of the KBMS.

The message level has often been neglected in knowledge base research. In this chapter, I have tried to develop a "knowledge-based" approach. Obviously, much more research is needed before practical results can be expected. But so much is clear that many problems are linguistic in nature. Progress in this area can be expected only when linguistic theory is taken seriously.

Appendix A

F-STRUCTURES

F-structures (feature structures) were introduced in 2.8. In this appendix, I only give the formal definitions and some results.

Formally, an f-structure consists of a list of addresses, where an address is a string of labels (for example, `id`, `id.last`), and a symbol function ψ that attaches to each address a certain symbol. The symbols may be predicates, like `person`, or values, like `philadelphia`. The symbols are taken from a family of domains Σ_i. It may happen that $i = 1$ in which case we have only one symbol domain. Each domain is partially ordered. By default, the ordering is represented by "<".

Definition A1 Let L be a finite set whose elements are called labels. An *address* is a finite string of labels. L^* is the set of all addresses over L. We use the notation $u.v$ for the concatenation of addresses u and v. If $w = u.v$, then u is a prefix of w.
end A1

We put some requirements on the set of addresses A.

Definition A2 Let A be a set of addresses. A is called *prefix-closed* iff

if $u,v \in L^*$, and $u.v \in A$, then $u \in A$

A is *finitely branching* iff

if $u \in A$ then the set $\{u.a \in A \mid a \in L\}$ is finite.

If A is prefix-closed and finitely branching, we call it an *address tree* (on L).

end A2

An f-structure can be *tagged* with variable symbols. This is the way to enforce structure-sharing. A tagging is a function from addresses to variable symbols.

We now define the f-structure. I will use the term "frame" as a synomym.

Definition A3 Let Σ_i be a family of symbol domains, each with a partial ordering $<$ and including a top element Δ. Let L be a set of labels, and T be a set of tag symbols.

An *f-structure* is a triple (A,ψ,τ), where A is an address tree on L, ψ is a symbol function from L^* to Σ such that $\psi(L^* - A) = \{\Delta\}$ and τ is a tag function from A to T.

end A3

The symbol function ψ is defined in such a way that it maps all addresses not occurring in A to the top element Δ.

The tag function τ is defined as a function from addresses to T. In the examples above, we used some "syntactic sugar": we omit writing explicitly tags for addresses that do not share. Hence not every address has an explicit tag symbol.

Addresses in a tree which are not the prefix of any other address in the tree are called *leaves*. The empty string ϵ is called the *root* address.

An f-structure (A,ψ,τ) is finite iff A is finite. In what follows, I will consider only finite f-structures.

A *subtree* of A at address w is the tree $A\backslash w = \{w' \mid w.w' \in A\}$. Given a frame $f = (A,\psi,\tau)$, and an address w in A, the *subframe* of f at address w is the frame $f\backslash w = (A\backslash w,\psi\backslash w,\tau\backslash w)$ where $\psi\backslash w$ and $\tau\backslash w$ are defined by:

$$\psi\backslash w(w') = \psi(w.w') \quad \forall w' \in L^*$$
$$\tau\backslash w(w') = \tau(w.w') \quad \forall w' \in A\backslash w$$

For example, in the following frame of `sheep`:

```
sheep = (pred => (stem => "sheep"; cat => n;
                  forms => (plur => "sheep"));
         cat => t;
         type => [animate])
```

the addresses are:

$A = \{\epsilon,$ `pred, pred.stem, pred.cat, pred.forms, pred.forms.plur, cat, type`$\}$

The *leaves* in A are

`{pred.stem, pred.cat,pred.forms.plur,cat,type}`

A subtree of A at address `pred` is the tree with addresses:

$\{\epsilon,$`stem, cat, forms, forms.plur`$\}$

STRUCTURE SHARING

The following two definitions give content to the co-reference idea.

Definition A4 In an f-structure, any two addresses bearing the same tag are said to *co-refer*. Thus the *co-reference* relation $\varkappa$ of a frame $f = (A,\psi,\tau)$ is a relation defined on A as the *kernel* of the tag function τ, i.e. $\varkappa = \mathbf{Ker}(\tau) = \tau \circ \tau^{-1}$.
end A4

Note that $\varkappa$ is an equivalence relation since it is the kernel of a function. A $\varkappa$-class is called a coreference class.

We say that a frame f is *referentially consistent* if the same subframe occurs at all addresses in a co-reference class. That is, if C is a set of co-referring addresses, then $f\backslash w$ is identical for all addresses w in C. If a frame is referentially consistent, then $\varkappa$ is a *right-invariant* equivalence on A, that is:

$$\forall w_1, w_2 \in A\ (\varkappa(w_1,w_2) \Rightarrow \forall u \in L^*: w_1.u \in A \Rightarrow \varkappa(w_1.u,w_2.u)\ )$$

A frame is *well-formed* if is referentially consistent. The set of well-formed frames is denoted as *WFF*.

Under *expanding* a frame f we understand the process of extending the address tree of f so as to become referentially consistent. This is a finite process iff the frame is referentially acyclic. We can explain this notion as follows.

F-structures can be mapped to (finite) labeled directed graphs provided that the domain A/x is finite:

> Let the frame be (A,ψ,τ). The construction of the graph G(V,E) is as follows: the set of vertices V = A/x. This is a finite set. As for the edges, (U,V) $\in$ E iff $v=u.l$, for some $l \in L$, $u \in U$ and $v \in V$, and this edge is labeled with l. The labels of the vertices are given by the function ψ.

For an example, see Fig. A.1.

```
term(pred => (pred => Y:(stem => "man";
                          cat => n);
              num => X:plur);
     head => Y)
     num => X)
```

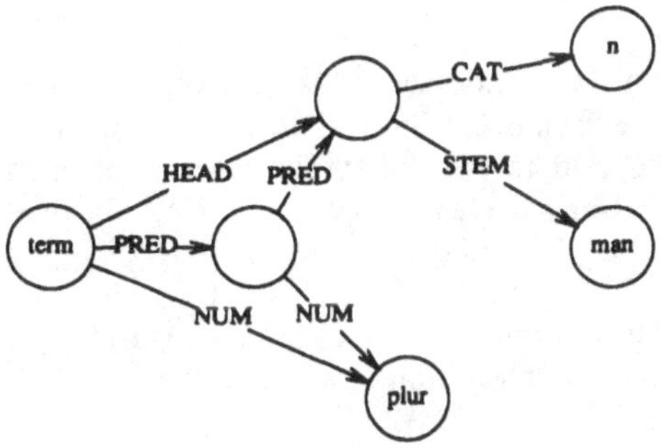

Fig. A.1 Graph representation of a well-formed frame

Let us now consider frames with a cyclic tagging. This means that an address is in the same co-reference class as one of its genuine prefixes. An example is the following frame f:

```
person(id => name(last => X:string);
       father => Y:person(id => name(last =>X);
                          son => person(father => Y)))
```

because the addresses `father` and `father.son.father` co-refer. If we expand this structure, we get:

```
person(id => name(last => X:string);
   father => Y:person(id => name(last => X);
               son => person(father => Y:person(id => name(last => X));
                                              son => person(father => Y)))
```

etcetera. A frame is called *referentially acyclic* if there is no cyclic tagging occurring in it.

Proposition A6 Let f be a well-formed frame. The labeled directed graph of f is acyclic iff the frame is referentially acyclic.

Proof. If the frame is referentially acyclic, there is no $v \in A$ such that $\varkappa(v,v.w)$, for some $w \neq \epsilon$. Hence there is no vertex v such that $v \rightarrow \ldots \rightarrow v$ is a non-empty path in the graph. The same holds for the reverse.□

end A6

In this thesis, I only consider frames that are well-formed and referentially acyclic. These can be mapped to DAGs. Cyclic frames are not without interest; they can be given a fixed-point semantics (Aït-Kaci, 1986ab) and can be used for logic programming.

The tag symbols have no semantic value aside from the coreference classes they define. Therefore, if one frame is identical to another frame up to a renaming of the tags, the two can be said to be alphabetic variants of each other. We also put all frames that contain a bottom element ($\psi(w) = [\nabla]$), in one class "bottom" (∇). These frames are said to be *inconsistent*.

Definition A7. Two f-structures $f_1 = (A_1, \psi_1, \tau_1)$ and $f_2 = (A_2, \psi_2, \tau_2)$ are *alphabetic variants* of one another (noted $\simeq$) iff either:

1. $A_1 = A_2$;
2. $\mathbf{Ker}(\tau_1) = \mathbf{Ker}(\tau_2)$;
3. $\psi_1 = \psi_2$

or both are inconsistent.

end A7

The alphabetic variant relation is an equivalence relation. Therefore we can define the set $\Psi = WFT/\simeq$. The elements of this set are called *ψ-types*. If f is an f-structure, then $[f]$ denotes the ψ-type of which f is an element.

In this thesis, we represent ψ-types by one of their representatives. So in each case what is meant is an f-structure modulo tag renaming and "smashing" to bottom.

SUBSUMPTION

The partial ordering on the symbols of Σ_i induce a *subsumption ordering* on f-structures, and hence on Ψ.

Definition A8 A frame $f_1 = (A_1, \psi_1, \tau_1)$ *is subsumed by* a frame $f_2 = (A_2, \psi_2, \tau_2)$, noted $f_1 \leq f_2$, if either $f_1 \simeq \nabla$ or

1. $A_2 \subseteq A_1$
2. $\mathbf{Ker}(\tau_2) \subseteq \mathbf{Ker}(\tau_1)$
3. $\psi_1(w) < \psi_2(w), \forall w \in L^*$

end A8

Proposition A9. The relationship $\leq$ between ψ-types, defined by $[f_1] \leq [f_2]$ iff $f_1 \leq f_2$ is well-defined and it is an ordering

Proof. Straightforward.

end A9

The ordering on the f-structures is induced by the ordering on Σ. If Σ is an information system domain, then the intersection of two elements of Σ is an element of Σ (see 3.2.1). The intersection corresponds with the *generalization* operation. For example, the generalization of [john] and [mary] may be [human,english]. The generalization operation is also called "join" and indicated by $\bigvee$. The dual operator is *unification* (meet, written as $\bigwedge$). This corresponds with taking the *sup* of two elements of Σ, written as $x \underline{\cup} y$, that is the deductive closure of the union of x and y, if this exists. In the system containing ∇, the union always exist, but may include ∇ as a member (for example, the meet of [john] and [mary] will include bottom since [male,female] $\vdash \nabla$). Above, we defined an f-structure to be inconsistent (identical to ∇) if it contained ∇.

So we can assume that in the information system, both the LUB and the GLB are defined, what makes it a complete lattice. This property carries over to ψ-types (Ait-Kaci,1986a).

Theorem A10 If the domain Σ is a lattice, then so is Ψ.

Proof See Ait-Kaci(1986b:315). □

end

We have the following properties of unification and generalization:

(idempotency)	$A \bigwedge A = A$
(commutativity)	$A \bigwedge B = B \bigwedge A$
(associativity)	$(A \bigwedge B) \bigwedge C = A \bigwedge (B \bigwedge C)$
(top)	$\Delta \bigwedge A = A$
(bottom)	$\nabla \bigwedge A = \nabla$
(interdefinability of $\leq$ and $\bigwedge$)	$A \leq B$ iff $A \bigwedge B = A$

We also observe that the $\bigwedge$ and $\bigvee$ are in general not distributive (Ait-Kaci, 1986; see also Plotkin, 1977). However, it is possible to augment the f-structures (ψ-types) so that Ψ becomes a distributive lattice. To this end, we must allow disjunctive information. This may have useful applications, but the manipulation of disjunctive f-structures is more difficult. Rounds and Kasper (1986) proved that the problem of unifying disjunctive structures is NP-complete. For a concise review of research in this area, see Knight(1989).

EXTENSIONS

• *nil addresses*. Sometimes we want to say that a certain address is *nil*, that is, no subframes can be inserted there. For example, most T-frames have no semantic functions. We indicate this by a hyphen at the address in question:

```
(pred => sheep;
 cat => t;
 sem => -)
```

Formally, we can represent this by extending the f-structure so as to include a set $Z \subseteq L^*$ of *dead-ends* such that $A \cap \{w \mid \exists \delta \in Z: w = \delta.u\} = \emptyset$. If this intersection is not empty, the ψ-type is ∇.

• *symbol sets*. If Σ_i is the domain of an f-structure, then we sometimes want to represent *sets* of elements of Σ rather than single elements. For example, a frame may contain a set of meaning conditions or a set of primitive types. The subsumption on these sets must be defined in such a way that, if $f_1 \leq f_2$, then every condition in f_2 is also in f_1.

If Σ_s is a particular domain, then we can form the powerset $\mathcal{P}(\Sigma_s)$. The ordering on this domain is as follows.

Definition A11 Let Σ be a (partially ordered) domain and $\mathcal{P}(\Sigma)$ be its set domain, with elements V_i. Then the ordering on the set domain is derived from the ordering on Σ. $V_1 < V_2$ iff

$$\forall x \in V_2\ \exists v \in V_1: v < x.$$

end A11

Example. Suppose `mammal` $\leq$ `animate`. Then

```
(type => {female, mammal, herbivorous}) ≤
                  (type => {female,animate})
```

• *address sets*. Sometimes, we want the frame to contain *sets* of subframes. Examples include the representations of restrictors and conditions.

```
(pred => table;
 res => {(pred => green; cat => q);
         (pred => small; cat =>q);
         (pred => expensive; cat => q) })
```

Note the difference with symbol sets. Here, we have several subframes at the address `res`, which is different from ψ(`res`) being a set. There are two ways to extend the framework with address sets. The first way is to define equivalence classes of frames, and the second way is to merge the symbol domain and the frame domain.

The use of equivalence classes goes as follows. Let us first translate the notation above to a genuine f-structure.

```
(pred => table;
 res => cons(head => (pred => green; cat => q);
             tail => cons(head => (pred => small; cat =>q);
                          tail => (pred => expensive; cat => q) )))
```

Here we have simulated the set notation by means of a list structure. This list structure is ordered. To ensure that the order does not matter, we have to state that two f-structures are equivalent if they are *permutational variants*.

Definition A12.

(i) Two frames are permutational variants when they are the same up to permutational variants of their subframes.

(ii) The frame `cons(head => A; tail B)` is a permutational variant of `cons(head => B; tail => A)`.

A ψ*-type is an equivalence class under alphabetic and permutational variants.

end A12

In this thesis, when I use address sets, the f-structure is to be read as a representative of its ψ*-type.

The second solution to the problem of address sets consists in merging the symbol domain and the frame domain. In the example above, we could say that the address `res` is a leaf, and that ψ(`res`) is some symbol. However, this symbol is itself an f-structure, or to be more precise, a set of f-structures. If we allow the domain of qualifiers to be a symbol domain, we can use the symbol set construct defined in A11 to have sets of f-structures. In this solution, the qualifiers are not subframes in the strict sense of the word. This is not unproblematic. In particular, we cannot use tag symbols anymore, or we should adapt the definition of the tag function. Although this seems to be a promising direction of research, I consider it to be beyond the scope of this thesis.

BIBLIOGRAPHY

F-structures were first introduced by Kay(1979). The formalization is based on Ait-Kaci (Ait-Kaci,1986ab). For more information on f-structures and ψ-types, see also (Shieber, 1986), (Pollard & Sag,1987), (Rounds & Kasper, 1986), and (Klein & Van Benthem, 1987). (Knight,1989) presents a survey on unification and contains many references to relevant sources.

Appendix B

ISO CAR EXAMPLE

At various places in this thesis, reference was made to the ISO car example described in (van Griethuysen, 1982; cf. Weigand, 1986). In this appendix, we give the text of the example and recapture the pieces of our conceptual model for it.

The case is described in English as follows.

> "The universe of discourse to be described has to do with the registration of cars and is limited to the scope of interest of the registration authority. The registration authority exists for the purpose of:
>
> 1. Knowing who is or was the registered owner of a car at any time from construction to destruction of the car.
> 2. To monitor certain laws, for example regarding fuel consumption of cars and their transfer of ownership".
>
> **Manufacturers of cars** There are a number of manufacturers, each with one unique name. Manufacturers may start operation, with the permission of the registration authority (which permission cannot be withdrawn). No more than five manufacturers may be in operation at any time. A manufacturer may ceas to operate provided he owns no cars, in which case permission to operate lapses.
>
> **Cars** A car is of a particular model and is given a serial number by its manufacturer that is unique among the cars made by that manufacturer. The manufacturer is registered as the owner of the car as soon as practicable. At this time it is given one registration number, unique for all cars and for all time. The year of production is also recorded. During the month of January only, a car may be declared to have been produced in the previous year. Eventually a car is destroyed and the date of destruction is registered. The history of a car must be kept until the end of the second calendar year following its destruction.
>
> **Car models** A model of a car has one universally unique name. Cars of each model are made by only one manufacturer. New models may be introduced without limit. All cars of one model are recorded as having the same fuel consumption.
>
> **Fuel consumption** Fuel consumption is a number of litres of hydrocarbon fuel per 100 kilometers which will be between 4 and 25 litres. The fuel consumption averaged over all registered cars produced by a particular manufacturer in a particular year is required not to exceed a certain maximum value, which is the same for each manufacturer and may change from year to year. At the end of each January an appropriate message is sent by the registration authority to each manufacturer which has failed to meet this requirement.
>
> **Garages** There are a number of garages, each with one unique name. New garages may start trading. Garages may own cars, but at any time the cars

they own must have originated from no more than three manufacturers (which three is unimportant, and may vary with time). A garage cannot cease to trade as long as it owns cars.

Persons There are a number of persons who can own one or more cars. Each person has one unique name. Only those persons are of interest who own, or have at some time owned, a car still known to the registration authority.

Car ownership At any time a car may be owned by either its manufacturer, or a trading garage, or a person or group of persons. If a car is owned by a group of persons, each is regarded as an owner.

Transfer of ownership Ownership of a car is transferred by registration of the actual transfer, including the date. A manufacturer can transfer only to garages, and cannot be a transferee. After destruction of the car it cannot be transfered anymore. Earlier transfer though still can be recorded.

The case includes also some things and happenings in the Universe of Discourse, as actual data, but there are no more specifications except as above.

Environment of Discourse

As we saw in chapter 7, we can describe both the Universe of Discourse and the Environment of Discourse. In the example, it is specified explicitly that the UoD is described from the perspective of the registration authority. So the registration authority is part of the EoD. The other agents with which this agent has to deal (communicates) are the *manufacturers* and the *government*. With the other agents (garages and persons), there appears to be no communication, only observation and registration.

The communication between manufacturers and registration authority consists of several speech acts, such as:

- asking permission to operate
- reporting the introduction of a model
- reporting the production of a car

The registration authority's responses are, among others,

- granting permission to operate
- confirming the acceptability of a model
- expressing a warning about excessive fuel consumption
- declaring a car to be registered

The government is not explicitly present in the model description, but plays an important role too. It is the source of various laws that the registration authority is held to monitor. The communication with the government includes:

- the government declares a law
- each year, the government declares what is the maximum fuel consumption
- the registration authority informs the government about violations of the law

Note that the communicative acts are interrelated in several ways. In the first place, there is the connection between statement and answer. For example, the manufacturer asks permission to operate and the registration authority grants permission. In the second place, one message can contain instructions for dealing with other messages. For example, the government sends a message to the registration authority specifying the conditions under which a new manufacturer can be registered.

According to the example, the registration authority is also bound to certain rules on what should be recorded. For example, the year of production of a car must be recorded. The history of a car must be kept until the end of the second calendar year following its destruction. These are EoD rules, not about the UoD objects themselves but about recorded facts about these objects.

Various speech acts can be recognized in the case. Examples:

assertive:	car XY10103 has been produced in September, 1988.
commissive:	the fuel consumption of our cars will be reduced.
directive:	please registrate us as car manufacturer under the name ..
declarative:	the maximum fuel consumption is 120.
expressive:	we express you our concerns about the fuel consumption of your company which already exceeds the maximum value.

The EoD specification contains not only the agents involved in the EoD and the message types occurring there, but also constraints that specify how messages must be processed. For readability, we write these rules if an IF-THEN format rather than by means of a condition satellite. In chapter 7, the following rules were given:

```
IF
   ask(ag [s] m manufacturer)(go e permit(ag 1P)(rec m)(go operate) &
   PROG operate(ag [<3] x manufacturer)
THEN
   OBL permit(ag KB)(rec m)(go operate)
```

If a manufacturer asks for permission to operate and less than three manufacturers are operating, then the KB must permit him to operate.

```
IF p
  fuel consumption(m manufacturer)(tmp y year) >
          maximum fuel consumption(y)
THEN
 OBL warn(ag KB)(rec m)(reason p) &
 OBL inform(ag KB)(rec d[s] y government)(go p)
```

If the fuel consumption of a manufacturer in some year is more than the maximum fuel consumption of that year, the KB must warn the manufacturer and the government.

In these examples, we use speech act types such as `permit` and `warn`. The pre- and postconditions for such speech acts must be described in the lexicon, and they are subject to other deontic constraints as well. For example, it can be specified that if the KB warns a manufacturer, then the manager of the registration authority should be informed of this. Then, as soon as the system knows that some manufacturer has a fuel consumption that is too high, it must warn the manufacturer. This triggers again the obligation to inform the manager.

Lexicon

The UoD is specified at two levels. First, we circumscribe the sublanguage involved (the lexicon), and secondly, integrity constraints are specified. The lexicon is as follows (the ≺ denotes a taxonomic ordering):

Taxonomy of T-frames:

```
car < vehicle
company < [human,collective]
fuel < liquid
fuel consumption(car) < [quality]
fuel consumption(manufacturer) < [quality]
garage < company
manufacturer  < company
maximum fuel consumption(year) < [quality]
model(car) < [quality]
person < [human]
registration authority  < company
registration number(car)  < number
serial number(car)  < number
number(thing) < [quality]
```

T-frames and conditions:

```
fuel consumption(X car)
     :-- fuel : consume(fo X car)(go .)([per] [100] Z kilometer).
fuel consumption(M manufacturer)(tmp Y year)
     :-- AVG(fuel consumption(X car : produce(ag M)(go .)(tmp Y year))).
maximum fuel consumption(Y year)
     :-- fuel.
maximum fuel consumption(Y year)
     ->> MAX(fuel consumption(M manufacturer)(tmp Y year)) < Z.
registration number(Y car)
     :-- number : assign(ag X registration authority)(go .)(rec Y car).
serial number(C car)
     :-- number : assign(ag X manufacturer : produce(ag .)(go C car))
                   (go N)(rec Y car).

model(car) <=> Citroen, Ford, VW, Daf, Honda, ....
```

Taxonomy of P-frames:

```
assign < [action]
consume < use < [action]
destroy < [action]
establish < [action]
operate < [position]
own < have < [position]
produce < make < [action]
register < [action]
sell < transfer < [action,material]
converse(sell,buy)
```

P-schemata and conditions:

```
assign(ag X [human])(go Z number)(rec Y car).
consume(fo X car)(go Y fuel).
destroy(ag X [human])(go Y car)
     <-- exist(Y).
establish(ag X registration authority)(go Z [soa])
     --> Z.
operate(po X manufacturer).
own(po X [human])(go Y car).
produce(ag X manufacturer)(go Y car)
     --> exist(Y), own(po X)(go Y).
register(ag X registration authority)(go Y car)([id] Z number)
     :- assign(ag X)(go Z number)(rec Y car).
sell(ag X [human])(go Y car)(rec Z [human])
     <-- own(po X)(go Y).
sell(ag X [human])(go Y car)(rec Z [human])
     --> own(po Z)(go Y).
```

Remarks:

1. Most schemata are subtypes of lexical predicate frames. "Fuel consumption" is a composite frame derived by noun phrase formation and composition, just as registration number. For example, "company" is defined in the general dictionary as being of type `[human,collective]`. The action `sell` has a selection restriction of the agent argument in the form of the primitive type [human]. So it follows immediately that person, garages and manufacturers can sell cars. Furthermore, no special words are needed to express that a group of persons may be the seller or owner of cars as well, since FG terms may be singular or plural, or conjunctions, and the selection restriction only specifies the type which is the same for singular and plural terms.

2. The definition of maximum fuel consumption is a bit complicated. It is defined in the first place as an amount of fuel. For example "50 dollar" is not a good value. The maximum fuel consumption is further defined by its purpose: all fuel consumptions of manufacturers must remain below it (note that the "maximum fuel consumption" is not simply the maximal value of all fuel consumptions). Maximum fuel consumptions are established by the registration authority. *To establish*

is a predicate frame which takes a SoA as goal argument with the intended meaning that the SoA holds afterwards. In this case, the registration authority can only establish that the maximum fuel consumption is such and such, but this restriction must be specified by deontic rules.

3. We have used MAX and AVG as abstract functions on terms (comparable to place functions), with the intended meaning of "maximum" and "average".

4. The meaning definitions of the predicate frames can be worked out in more detail (or imported from a general dictionary). But the specification given here already gives the system the opportunity to answer questions on the conceptual level:

U: *What is the fuel consumption of a manufacturer?*
A: *The fuel consumption of the cars produced by the manufacturer.*

U: What is the fuel consumption of a car?
A: *The fuel consumed by the car per 100 kilometers.*

Integrity constraints

In chapter 6, we have made a distinction between necessary/analytical, empirical, and deontic integrity constraints. The analytical integrity constraints are already dealt with in the lexicon. An example is that the agent of *to sell* is human. These constraints do not need further specification.

An empirical constraint is something which in true in every state of the UoD but not because of analytical necessity or deontic obligation. An example in the ISO case is the statement that the fuel consumption of cars will be between 4 and 25 litres. This just happens to be true (as long as no counterevidence is found). In our model, such a constraint can be represented in two ways, in the lexicon or in the rule base. It can be specified in the lexicon by creating a *prototypical* predicate schema for car. In this schema, characteristics of car are given: that they have four wheels, a certain size, maximum speed, typical costs, as well as a typical fuel consumption. If we specify here that the fuel consumption is between 4 and 25, this implies that the system is not inconsistent when a car with fuel consumption 2 is inserted (although the car will be marked as being atypical). Instead of one prototype schema, we can also have several prototype schemata for different kinds of cars.

The empirical constraint can also be specified as a categorical assertion: the fuel-consumption of each car is always (in all possible worlds) between 4 and 25. Then, if we would enter the data about the car with fuel consumption 2, the knowledge base would become inconsistent. Either the proposition is refused or the constraint must be adapted.

Deontic constraints are obligations, permissions and prohibitions that can be violated without causing an inconsistency in the knowledge base. Examples are:

[1] a manufacturer may start operation with the permission of the registration authority;

```
P INGR operate(pos i[s] X manufacturer) (cond PERF permit(ag d[s] Y
registration authority)(go e operate(pos X))
```

[2] a manufacturer may cease to operate provided he owns no cars;

```
P EGR operate(pos i[s] X manufacturer) (cond NEG own(pos X)(go i[p]
C car)
```

[3] the manufacturer [of the car] is registered as the owner of the car as soon as practicable;

```
OBL register(go i[s] X manufacturer < owner([go] Y car)) (tmp t
PERF: produce(ag X)(go i[s] Y car)(tmp t)
```

[4] the fuel consumption [of a manufacturer] is not to exceed a maximum value;

[5] the cars that garages own must have originated from no more than three manufacturers

[6] a garage can transfer only to people;

```
P transfer(ag X[s] garage)(res_focus rec Y people) =
F transfer(ag X[s] garage)(rec Y [human] : NEG people)
```

[7] a manufacturer can transfer only to garages;

```
P transfer(ag X[s] manufacturer)(res_focus rec Y garage) =
F transfer(ag X[s] manufacturer)(rec Y [human] : NEG garage)
```

In our deontic logic, only *dynamic* deontic predications can be interpreted. That is the reason why we do not give the predication form of rules [4] and [5], although it is no problem to write it down syntactically. Rule [5] can be paraphrased dynamically as follows: garages cannot buy a car of a certain manufacturer if he already has cars from three other manufacturers. In this way, a the deontic operator works on an action, *buy*, and can be interpreted in our logic. For rule [4], such a paraphrase is more difficult. A possible solution is by use of a purely formal "newyear" action, an action that automatically occurs at the first of January. Then we can say that "newyear" is forbidden if the fuel consumption of the manufacturer exceeds the maximum value. If this nonetheless happens, a violation is recorded that can be the trigger for appropriate action.

Terms

In the example, cars can be bought by groups of persons. For example, we have the fact that John and Mary buy a certain Rolls. In this predication, *John and Mary* is a collective term: they buy it together. We can not infer from this that John has bought a Rolls. On the other hand, if we have that fact that John and Mary are owners of a certain Rolls, then then the predication is static and the nominal predicate *owner of Rolls x* applies to John and Mary, but also to John individually. This follows from our treatment of collective conjuncts (5.4.3).

Uniqueness

At several places, the case description alludes to uniqueness: a manufacturer has a unique name, registration numbers for cars are unique for all cars and for all times, garages and persons have a unique name, etc. Probably, these sentences originate from the authors' preoccupation with an implementation of the model in a relational database. In an object-oriented implementation, uniqueness is not so strong a requirement. In our modeling approach, we do not have special constructs for marking uniqueness. For example, `name([thing]) < string` is defined in the general lexicon, but no uniqueness is implied. The uniqueness may be required deontically — then it may happen that two persons have the same name —, empirically or analytically. In the latter case, we introduce specialized predicate schemas, for example, for *assign* that check the uniqueness:

```
assign(ag X [human])(go Z number)(rec Y car)
  <- NEG registration number(i[s] car)(subj Z)).
```

In this way, an inconsistency occurs when we want to assign a number that is already in use.

Conclusion

We have presentend both the EoD and the UoD specification of the car case in a linguistic framework. A big part of the specification is got for free because it is already part of the (presumed) general dictionary. Several constraints must be rewritten first before they can be interpreted. However, in most cases this rewriting can be done in natural language. This makes the resulting model directly translatable to natural language.

REFERENCES

Aarts, J.M.G., 1976. *Adjective-Noun Combinations: A Model for their Semantic Interpretation*. Doctoral Dissertation, University of Nijmegen.

Abbott, R.J., 1987. Knowledge Abstraction. *CACM* **30**,8.

Abrial, J.R., 1974. Data semantics. In: Klimbie & Koffeman (eds), *Data Base Management*. North-Holland, pp.1-60.

Aït-Kaci, H., 1986a. Type Subsumption as a Model of Computation. In: Kerschberg (ed), 1986, pp.115-140.

Aït-Kaci, H., 1986b. An algebraic semantics approach to the effective resolution of type equations. *Theoretical Computer Science* **45**, pp.293-351.

Akama, S. & M. Kawamori, 1988. Data semantics in logic programming framework. In: Dahl & Saint-Dizier (eds), *Natural Language Understanding and Logic Programming*. Elsevier North-Holland.

Almeida, M. J., 1987. *Reasoning about the temporal structure of narratives*. Ph.D. Thesis, SUNY, Buffalo NY.

Anderson, A.R., 1967. Some Nasty Problems in the Formalization of Ethics. *Nous* **1**, pp.345-360

Anderson, T.L., 1981. *The database semantics of time*. Ph. D. Thesis, Univ of Washington.

ANSI, 1975. ANSI/SPARC Study Group on Data Base Management Systems. *ACM SIGMOD Newsletter* **7**, 2.

Apel, K-O., 1987 (75). The Problem of Philosophical Foundations in Light of a Transcendental Pragmatics of Language. In: Baynes et al (ed), pp.245-290.

Aristotle, 1954. *Metaphysics*. Translated under the editorship of W.D. Ross. Oxford Univ Press, London

Aristotle, 1968. *Topics*. Translated under the editorship of W.D. Ross. Oxford Univ Press, London

Auramäki, E., E. Lehtinen, K. Lyytinen, 1988. A Speech-Act based office modelling approach. *TOIS* **6**,2.

Austin, J.L., 1962. *How to do things with words*. Clarendon Press, London.

Auwera, J. van der, 1987. Complementizers as P2 Fillers. In: Nuyts & de Schutter (eds), 1987.

Auwera, J. van der & L. Goossens, 1987. *Ins and Outs of the Predication*. Foris, Dordrecht.

Bancilhon, F. & S.N. Khoshafian, 1986. Objects Calculus. *Proc. PODS*, 1986.

Barth, E.M. & E.C.W. Krabbe, 1982. *From axiom to dialogue*. Walter de Gruyter, Berlin.

Bartlett, F.C., 1932. *Remembering*. Cambridge Univ Press, Cambridge.

Barwise, J. & R. Cooper, 1981. Generalized quantifiers in natural language. *Linguistics and Philosophy* **4**, pp.159-219.

Barwise, J. & J. Perry, 1983. *Situations and Attitudes*. MIT Press, Cambridge MA.

Baynes, K., J. Bohman, Thomas McCarthy, 1987. *After Philosophy: End or Transformation?* MIT Press, Cambridge MA.

Benthem, J.F.A.K. Van, 1983. *The logic of time*. Reidel, Dordrecht.

Bolinger, D., 1961. Syntactic blends and other matters. *Language* **37**, 3, pp.366-381.

Bolinger, D., 1976. Meaning and memory. *Forum Linguisticum* **1**, 1, pp.1-14.

Bolkestein, A.M., C. de Groot, J.L. Machenzie (eds), 1985a. *Syntax and Pragmatics in Functional Grammar*. Foris, Dordrecht.

Bolkestein et al, (eds) 1985b. *Predicates and Terms in Functional Grammar*. Foris, Dordrecht.

Borgida, A., J. Mylopoulos, H.K.T. Wong, 1984. Generalization/Specialization as a basis for software specification. In: Brodie et al (eds), 1984.

Bracchi, G., P. Paolini, G. Pelagatti, 1976. Binary Logical Associations in Data Modelling. In: Nijssen (ed), *Modelling in database management systems*. North-Holland, pp.125-148.

Brachman, R.J., 1983. What IS-A Is and Isn't: An Analysis of Taxonomic Links in Semantic Networks. *IEEE Computer* **16**,10, pp.30-36.

Brachman, R.J. & R.E. Fikes & H.J. Levesque, 1983. *KRYPTON: A Functional Approach to Knowledge Representation*. FLAIR Technical Report 16, Palo Alto CA.

Brachman, R.J. & J. Schmolze, 1985. An overview of the KL-ONE Knowledge Representation System. *Cognitive Science* **10**.

Brachman, R.J. & H.J. Levesque, 1986. What makes a knowledge base knowledgeable? In: Kerschberg (ed), 1986, pp.69-78.

Brodie, M.L., 1978. *Specification and Verification of Database Semantic Integrity*. Ph.D. Thesis, Univ of Toronto.

Brodie, M. T., J. Mylopoulos, J. W. Schmidt (eds), 1984. *On conceptual modelling*. Springer-Verlag, Berlin.

Brown, G. & G. Yule, 1983. *Discourse Analysis*. Cambridge Univ Press, Cambridge.

Brown, D.R., 1985. Term Operators. In: Bolkestein et al (ed), 1985b.

Burgess, J.P., 1984 . Basic tense logic. In: Gabbay & Guenthner (eds), *Handbook of Philosophical Logic*, Vol II. Reidel, Dordrecht.

Cammarata, S.J. & M.A. Melkanoff, 1986. An interactive data dictionary facility for CAD/CAM databases. In: Kerschberg (ed), 1986, pp.423-442.

Caruso, M. & E. Sciore, 1988. Meta-functions and Contexts in an Object-oriented Database Language. *Proc SIGMOD*, 1988, pp.56-65.

Chen, P.P.S., 1976. The Entity-Relationship Model: Toward a Unified View of Data. *TODS* **1**, 1.

Chen, Q. & G. Gardarin, 1988. An implementation model for reasoning with complex objects. *Proc SIGMOD*, 1988, pp.164-172.

Chisholm, R.M., 1966. Comments on Davidson's "The logical form of action". In: Rescher (ed), 1966.

Clifford, J. & D. Warren, 1983. Formal semantics for time in databases.*TODS* **8**,2, pp.214-264.

Codd, E.F., 1970 . A relational model of data for large shared data banks. *CACM* **13**,6.

Codd, E.F., 1979. Extending the relational model to capture more meaning. *TODS* **5**.

Cyert, R. & J. March, 1963. *A Behavioral Theory of the Firm*. Prentice-Hall, Englewood Cliffs, NJ.

Date, C.J., 1977. *An introduction to database systems*. Addison-Wesley, Reading.

Date, C.J., 1986. *Relational Databases. Selected writings*. Addison-Wesley, Reading.

Davidson, D., 1966. The logical form of action. In: Rescher (ed), 1966.

Davidson, D., 1987 (77). The Method of Truth in Metaphysics. In: Baynes et al (ed).

De Antonellis, V. & A. Di Leva, 1984. *DATAID: A Database Design Methodology*. IEEE Tutorial Notes 3.

DeJong, G., 1978. Prediction and substantiation: a new approach to natural language processing. *Cognitive Science* **3**, pp.251-273.

DeMarco, T., 1978. *Structured Analysis and Systems Specification*. Yourdon Press, New York, 1978.

Derrida, J., 1976. *Of Grammatology*. John Hopkins Univ Press, Baltimore.

Dignum, F.P.M., T. Kemme, W. Kreuzen, H. Weigand, R.P. van de Riet, 1987. Constraint modelling using a conceptual prototyping language. *Data & Knowledge Engeneering* **2**, 2, pp.213-254.

Dignum, F.P.M., 1989. *A Language for Modelling Knowledge Bases based on Linguistics and Founded in Logic*. Ph.D. Thesis, Vrije Universiteit, Amsterdam.

Dik, S.C., 1978. *Functional Grammar*. North-Holland, Amsterdam.

Dik, S.C., 1985. Formal and semantic adjustment of derived constructions. In: Bolkestein et al (eds), 1985b, pp.1-28.

Dik, S.C., 1987a. Linguistically motivated knowledge representation. In: Nagoa (ed), 1987.

Dik, S.C., 1987b. A typology of entities. In: van der Auwera & Goossens (eds), 1987.

Dik, S.C., 1989fc. *A Theory of Functional Grammar*. Foris, Dordrecht.

Dik, S.C. & J. Connolly (eds), 1989. *FG and the Computer*. Foris, Dordrecht.

Dik, S.C. et al, 1981. On the typology of focus phenomena. In: Hoekstra et al (eds), 1981, pp.41-74.

Dik, S.C. et al, 1989. A Computational Model of the Natural Language User. In: Dik & Connolly, (eds), 1989.

Dummet, M., 1987 (75). Can Analytic Philosophy Be Systematic?. In: Baynes et al (ed).

Eemeren, F.J. van, R. Grootendorst, Tj. Kruiger, 1987. *Handbook of Argumentation Theory*. Foris, Dordrecht.

Ehrich, R.W. & H.R. Hartson, 1981. DMS — An environment for dialogue management. *Proc COMPCON81*, IEEE, New York.

Felscher, W., 1986. Dialogues as a Foundation for Intuitionistic Logic. In: Gabbay & Guenthner (eds), *Handbook of Philosophical Logic*, Vol III. Reidel, Dordrecht.

Fillmore, Ch.L., 1968. The case for case. In: Bach & Harms (eds), *Universals in linguistics*. Holt, Rinehart and Winston, New York, pp.1-88.

Fillmore, Ch.L., 1977. The case for case reopened. In: Cole & Sadock (eds), *Syntax and Semantics* **8**, Seminar Press.

Flores, F., M. Graves, B. Hartfield, T. Winograd, 1988. Computer Systems and the Design of Organizational Interaction. *TOIS* **6**,2, pp.153-172.

Fodor, J.A., 1975. *The language of thought*. Thomas Y. Crowell, New York.

Fodor, J.A., 1983. *The Modularity of the Mind. An Essay on Faculty Psychology*. Bradford Books.

Foley, W.A. & R.D. van Valin, 1984. *Functional Syntax and universal grammar*. Cambridge Univ Press, Cambridge.

Gabbay, D.M. & M.J. Sergot, 1986. Negation as Inconsistency I. *Journal of Logic Programming* **3**, 1, pp.1-35.

Gadamer, H-G., 1976. *Philosophical Hermeneutics*. Univ of California Press, Berkeley.

Gadia, S.K., 1988 . A homogeneous relational model and query language for temporal databases. *TODS* **13**,4, pp.418-48.

Gallaire, H., & J. Minker (eds), 1978. *Logic and Databases*. Plenum Press, New York.

Gane, Ch. & T. Sarson, 1977. *Structured Systems Analysis: Tools & Techniques*. Improved System Technologies Inc.

Gardner, A. von der Lieth, 1987. *An artificial intellligence approach to legal reasoning*. MIT Press, Cambridge, MA.

Gierz, G. et al, 1980. *A Compendium of Continuous Lattices*. Springer-Verlag, Berlin.

Grandy, R.E., 1987. In Defense of Semantic Fields. In: LePore (ed), *New Directions in Semantics*. Academic Press, London.

Griethuysen, J.J. van (ed), 1982. *Concepts and terminology for the conceptual schema and the information base*. Report ISO/TC97/SC5-N695, ISO.

Groenendijk, J. & M. Stokhof, 1988. Context and Information in Dynamic Semantics. In: Elsendoorn. & Bouma, *Working Models of Human Perception*. Academic Press, New York, pp.457-488.

Grosz, B., 1978. Discourse Analysis. In: Walker (ed), *Understanding Spoken Language*. Elsevier North-Holland, New York, pp.235-268.

Grosz, B. & C.L. Sidner, 1985. *The structures of discourse structure*. CSLI-85-39, Stanford University.

Halliday, M.A.K., 1985. *An introduction to Functional Grammar*. Edward Arnold, London.

Hannay, M., 1985. Inferability, discourse-boundedness, and sub-topics. In: Bolkestein et al (eds), 1985a.

Harel, D., 1984. Dynamic Logic. In: Gabbay & Guenthner (eds), *Handbook of Philosophical Logic*, Vol II. Reidel, Dordrecht.

Harnad, S., 1987. Category induction and representation. In: Harnad (ed), *Categorical perception*, Cambridge Univ Press, pp.535-565.

Harré, R., 1987. Enlarging the paradigm. *New Ideas in Psychology* **5**,1, pp.3-12.

Hart, H.L.A., 1961. *The concept of law*. Clarendon Press, Oxford.

Hartson, H.R. & D. Hix, 1989. Human-Computer Interface Development. *ACM Computing Surveys* **21**,1, 1989, pp.5-92.

Heim, I., 1982. *The Semantics of Definite and Indefinite Noun Phrases*. Dissertation, Univ of Massachusetts.

Hendriks, H., 1987. *Type Change in Semantics: the Scope of Quantification and Cordination*. In: Klein & van Benthem (eds), 1987, pp.95-120.

Hengeveld, K., 1988. Layers and Operators. *WPFG* **27**.

Heyer, G., 1985. Generic descriptions, default reasoning and typicality. *Theoretical Linguistics* **12**, 1985, pp.33-72.

Higginbotham, J., 1989. Elucidations of meaning. *Linguistics and Philosophy* **12**,4.

Hinrichs, E., 1989. Review of Lo Cascio & Vet, 1988. *Linguistics and Philosophy* **12**, 2, pp.243-267.

Hintikka, J., 1962. Cogito, Ergo Sum: Inference or Performance? *Philosophical Review* **71**, pp.3-32.

Hirschheim, R., 1986. Understanding the Office: A Social-Analytic Perspective. *TOIS* **4**,4.

Hoekstra, T., H. van der Hulst, M. Moortgat (eds), 1981. *Perspectives on functional grammar*. Foris, Dordrecht.

Hoepelman, J.Ph. & A.J.M. van Hoof, 1987. *The Success of Failure*. Paper presented at the 6th Amsterdam Colloquium, ITLI, Amsterdam.

Houtkoop, H., 1987. *Establishing Agreement*. Foris, Dordrecht.

Jackendoff, R., 1983. *Semantics and cognition*. MIT Press, Cambridge, MA.

Jakobson, R., 1956. The metaphoric and metonymic poles. *Fundamentals of Language*, 's Gravenhage, pp.76-82.

Janssen, Th., 1981. Montague Grammar and Functional Grammar. In: Hoekstra et al (eds), 1981.

Johnson-Laird, P., 1983. *Mental models*. Cambridge Univ Press, Cambridge.

Jones, S., P. Mason, R. Stamper, 1979. Legol 2.0: A relational specification language for complex rules. *Information Systems* **4**, pp. 28-48.

Kamp, H., 1981. A theory of truth and semantic representation. In: Groenendijk, Janssen, Stokhof, *Formal methods in the study of language*. Mathematical Center, Amsterdam.

Kaplan, S.J., 1978. On the difference between natural language and high level query languages. *Proc 1978 Annual Conference of the ACM*, pp.27-38.

Karttunen, L,, 1972. Possible and Must. In: Kimball (ed), *Syntax and Semantics* **1**. Seminar Press, New York.

Kawamura, M., 1986. *Hoe identificeren wij de goal?* (How to identify the goal?). Draft.

Kay, M., 1979. Functional Grammar. *Proc. 5th Ann. Meeting of the Berkeley Linguistic Society*, Berkeley CA, 1979.

Kay, M, 1984. Functional Unification Grammar: A Formalism for Machine Translation. *Proc. COLING* 1984, pp.75-78.

Kerschberg, L. (ed), 1986. *Expert Database Systems*, Benjamin/Cummings, Menlo Park CA.

Kersten, M.L., 1985. *A model for a secure programming environment*. Ph.D. Thesis, Vrije Universiteit, Amsterdam.

Khoshafian, S. & G. Copeland, 1986. Object identity. *Proc 1st Conf on OOPSLA*, Portland, 1986.

Khosla, S., S.E. Maibaum, M. Sadler, 1986. Database Specification. In: Steel & Meersman (eds), 1986.

King, M., 1987. On the proper place of semantics in machine translation. In: Nagoa (ed), 1987.

Kittredge, R. & J. Lehrberger, 1982. *Sublanguage*. De Gruyter, Berlin.

Klein, E. & J. Van Benthem, 1987. *Categories, Polymorphism and Unification*. Centre for Cognitive Science, Edinburgh / ITLI, Amsterdam.

Knight, K., 1989. Unification: a multidisciplinary survey. *ACM Computing Surveys* **21**,1, March 1989.

Krifka, M., 1987. Nominal Reference and Temporal Constitution: Towards a Semantics of Quantity. *Proc 6th Amsterdam Colloquium*, Univ of Amsterdam, 1987.

Kung Chen ho., 1984. *A temporal framework for information systems specification and verification*. Ph.D. Thesis, Univ of Trondheim.

Labov, W. & D. Fanshel, 1977. *Therapeutic Discourse: psychotherapy as conversation*. Academic Press, New York.

Lacroix, M. & A. Pirotte, 1977. Domain-oriented relational languages. *Proc VLDB* 3, Tokyo.

Lai Kum-Yew, Th.W. Malone, Ken-Chiang Yu, 1988. Object Lens: A Spreadsheet for Cooperative Work. *TOIS* **6**, 4.

Landman, F., 1987. Groups, Plurals, Individuals and Intentionality. *Proc 6th Amsterdam Colloquium*, Univ of Amsterdam, 1987.

Laymon, R., 1987. Using Scott domains to explicate the notions of approximate and idealized data. *Philosophy of Science* **54**, 1987, pp.194-221.

Lee, R., 1988. Bureaucracies as Deontic Systems. *TOIS* **6**, 2, pp. 87-108.

Lehnert, W. G., 1978. *The Process of Question Answering*. Lawrence Erlbaum, Hillsdale, NJ.

Lehtinen, E. & K. Lyytinen, 1986. Action based model of information system. *Information Systems* **11**, 4, 1986, pp.299-317.

Lesniewski, S., 1929. Grundzüge eines neuen Systems der Grundlagen der Mathematik. *Fundamenta Mathematicae* **14**, pp.1-81.

Levesque, H.J., 1988. Logic and the complexity of reasoning. *Journal of Philosophical Logic* **17**, pp.355-389.

Levinson, S.C., 1983. *Pragmatics*. Cambridge Univ Press, Cambridge.

Lindberg, D.A.B & B.L. Humphreys, 1987. Toward a unified medical language. *Proc. MIE*, Rome, Sept 1987.

Lingat, J.Y., P. Nobecourt, C. Rolland, 1987. Behaviour Management in database applications. *Proc VLDB* 13, pp.185-196.

Link, G., 1983. The logical analysis of plurals and mass terms. A lattice-theoretic approach. In: Bauerle, Schwarze, von Stechow (eds), *Meaning, Use and the Interpretation of Language*. De Gruyter, Berlin.

Lipeck, U.W. & G. Saake, 1988. Monitoring Dynamic Integrity Constraints Based on Temporal Logic. *Information Systems* **12**,3, pp.225-269.

Lo Cascio V. & C. Vet (eds), 1988. *Temporal Structure in Sentence and Discourse*. Foris Publications, Dordrecht.

Lorenzen, P. & K. Lorenz, 1978. *Dialogische Logik*. Wissenschafliche Buchgesellschaft, Darmstadt.

Lundeberg, M., G. Goldkuhl, A. Nilsson, 1979. A Systematic Approach to Information Systems Development. *Information Systems* **4**, 1979.

Lyons, J., 1977. *Semantics*. Cambridge Univ Press, Cambridge.

Mackenzie, J.L., 1986. Aspects of nominalization in English and Dutch. *WPFG* **15**.

Mackenzie, J.L., 1987. The representation of nominal predicates in the fund. *WPFG* **25**.

Maier, D., J.D. Ullman, M.Y. Vardi, 1984. On the foundations of the universal relation model. *TODS* **9**,2.

Malone, Th.W., et al, 1987. Intelligent Information-Sharing Systems. *CACM* **30**, 5, 1987, pp.390-402.

Mays, E., 1986. A temporal logic for reasoning about changing databases in the context of natural language questions-answering. In: Kerschberg (ed), 1986, pp.559-578.

McArthur, R.P., 1981. Anderson's Deontic Logic and Relevant Implication. *Notre Dame Journal of Symbolic Logic* **22**, 1981, pp.145-154.

McCarty, L.Th, N.S. Sridharan, 1981. The representation of an evolving system of legal concepts II: Prototypes and Deformations. *Proc IJCAI* 7, Vancouver, 1981, pp.246-253.

McCarty, L.Th., 1977. Reflections on TAXMAN: An experiment in AI and Legal Reasoning. *Harvard Law Review* **90**, pp.839-893.

McDermott, D., 1982. A temporal logic for reasoning about processes and plans. *Cognitive Science* **6**, pp. 101-155.

Meijer, J.-J.Ch., 1987. A Simple Solution to the "Deepest" Paradox in Deontic Logic. *Logique et Analyse* **30**, pp.81-90.

Minksy, M., 1975. A framework for representing knowledge. In: Winston (ed), *The Psychology of Computer Vision*. McGraw-Hill, New York, pp.211-280.

Mittwoch, A., 1988. Aspects of English Aspect. *Linguistics and Philosophy***11** ,2.

Moran, T.P., 1981. The command language grammar: a representation for the user interface of interactive computer systems. *Int. J. Man-Machine Studies* **15**, 1981, pp.3-51.

Moto-Oka, T., 1982. *Fifth Generation Computer Systems*. North-Holland.

Nagoa, M. (ed), 1987. *Language and Artifical Intelligence*. North-Holland.

Nicolas, J.M. & H. Gallaire, 1978. Database: Theory vs. Interpretation. In: Gallaire & Minker (eds), 1978, pp.33-54.

Nicolas, J.M. & K. Yazdanian, 1978. Integrity Checking in Deductive Databases. In: Gallaire & Minker (eds), 1978,pp.325-44.

Nida, E.A, 1975. *Componential analysis of meaning*. Mouton, The Hague.

Nijssen, G.M., 1980. A framework for advanced mass storage applications. *MEDINFO 80*. North-Holland.

Nuyts, J. & G. de Schutter (eds), 1987. *Getting One's Words into Line*. Foris Publications, Dordrecht.

Nuyts, J., 1989. Functional Procedural Grammar: an overview. *WPFG* **31**.

Ogden, C.K. & I.A. Richards, 1930. *B.A.S.I.C. English*, London.

Okada, N., 1987. Towards a Unified Understanding of Natural Language and Picture Patterns. In: Nagoa (ed), 1987.

Ouchi, W.G., 1979. A Conceptual Framework for the Design and Organizational Control Mechanisms. *Management Science* **25**, 9, 1979, pp.833-848.

Palmer, F.R., 1986. *Mood and Modality*. Cambridge Univ Press, Cambridge.

Peirce, C.S., 1933-58. *Collected papers of Charles Sanders Peirce*. Edited by Charles Hartshorne, Paul Weiss and Arthur Burks. Harvard Univ Press, Cambridge, MA.

Pirotte, A., 1977. Database models for natural language users. In: Mey M. de (ed), *Int. Workshop on the cognitive viewpoint*, Gent. pp.165-172.

Plotkin, G.D., 1977. *Lattice theoretic properties of subsumption*. MIP-R-77, Dept. Machine Intelligence and Perception, Univ of Edinburgh.

Polanyi, M., 1969. *Personal Knowledge*. Routledge & Kegan Paul, London.

Pollard, C. & I. Sag, 1987. *Information-based syntax and semantics I*. CSLI Lecture Notes, Stanford CA.

Pomerantz, A., 1984. Agreeing and disagreeing with assessments: some features of preferred/dispreferred turn shapes. In: Atkinson & Heritage (eds), *Structures of social action: Studies in conversation analysis*. Cambridge Univ Press, Cambridge, pp.57-101.

Prior, A., 1967. *Past, Present, Future*. Oxford Univ Press.

Prat, I., 1987. Constraints, Meaning and Information. *Linguistics & Philosophy* **10**, 3, pp.289-324.

Quine, W.V., 1960. *Word and Object*. MIT Press, Cambridge MA.

Quine, W.V., 1961. *From a Logical Point of View*. Harper and Row, New York.

Reichenbach, H., 1947. *Elements of symbolic logic*.Macmillan Co.

Reichman-Adar, R., 1984. Extended Person-Machine Interface. *Artificial Intelligence* **22**, 1984, pp.157-218.

Reiter, R., 1978. On closed world databases. In: Gallaire & Minker (eds), 1978, pp.55-76.

Reiter, R., 1984. Towards a logical reconstruction of relational database theory. In: Brodie et al (ed), 1984, pp.191-233.

Rescher, N. (ed),, 1966. *The Logic of Decision and Action*. Univ of Pittsburg Press, Pittsburg.

Rieber, R.W. (ed), 1983. *Dialogues on the psychology of language and thought*. Plenum Press, New York.

Rijkhoff, J., 1986. Word order universals revisited: the Principle of Head Proximity. *WPFG* 14.

Rijkhoff, J., 1988. A typology of operators. *WPFG* **29**.

Roberts, C., 1987. Distributivity. In: *Proc 6th Amsterdam Colloquium*, Univ of Amsterdam, 1987.

Rounds, W.C. & R. Kasper, 1986. A complete logical calculus for record structures representing linguistic information. *Proc. 1st Ann. Symp. on Logic in Computer Science*. IEEE, Cambridge MA.

Rumelhart, D.E. & J.L. McClelland, 1986. *Parallel distributed processing*. MIT Press.

Russel, B., 1956. *Logic and Knowledge: Essays 1901-1950*. Edited by R.C. Marsh. Allan and Unwin, London.

Sacks, H., E.A. Schegloff, G. Jefferson, 1974. A simplest systematics for the organization of turn-taking for conversation. *Language* **50**, 1974.

Scha, R., 1981. Distributive, Collective and Cumulative Quantification. In: Groenendijk, Janssen, Stokhof (eds), *Formal methods in the study of language*. Mathematical Center, Amsterdam.

Schachter, P., 1976. The Subject in Philippine languages: topic, actor, actor-topic, or none of the above. In: Li (ed), *Subject and Topic*. Academic Press, New York, pp.491-518.

Schank, R.C. (ed), 1975. *Conceptual Information Processing*. North-Holland, Amsterdam.

Schank, R.C. & R.P. Abelson, 1977. *Scripts, Plans, Goals and Understanding*. Lawrence Erlbaum, New York.

Schmidt, L. (Hg), 1973. *Wortfeldforschung*. Wissenschaftliche Buchgesellschaft, Darmstadt.

Scott, D., 1982. Domains for denotational semantics. *Proc 9th Int Conf on Automata Languages and Programming*, LNCS **140**, Berlin, pp.577-613.

Scott, D., 1986. Capturing concepts with data structures. *Proc IFIP TC2/WG 2.6 Conference on "Knowledge and Data"*, Algarve, Portugal.

Searle, J.R., 1969. *Speech Acts - An Essay in the Philosophy of Language*. Cambridge Univ Press, London.

Searle, J.R., 1983. *Intentionality - an essay in the philosophy of mind*. Cambridge Univ

Press, London.

Searle, J.R. & D. Vanderveken, 1985. *Foundations of Illocutionary Logic*. Cambridge Univ Press, London.

Sellars, W., 1967. *Science, Perception and Reality*. Routledge and Kegan Paul, London.

Sernadas, A., 1980. *Logic Procedure Definition for Information System Specification*. Ph.D. Thesis, London School of Economics, Univ of London.

Shapiro, S.C. & W.J. Rapaport, 1987. SNePS considered as a fully intensional propositional semantic network. In: Cercone& McCalla (eds), *The Knowledge Frontier*, Springer-Verlag.

Shieber, S., 1986. *An Introduction to Unification-based Approaches to Grammar*. CSLI Lecture Notes, Stanford CA.

Shneiderman, B., 1982. Multi-party grammars and related features for designing interactive systems. *IEEE Trans. Syst. Man Cybern* **12**,2, 1982, pp.148-154.

Shoham, Y., 1988. *Reasoning about change*. MIT Press,Cambridge, MA.

Shortliffe, E.H. & B.G. Buchanan, 1984. A Model of Inexact Reasoning in Medicine. In: Buchanan & Shortliffe (eds), *Rule-based Expert Systems*. Addison-Wesley.

Small, D.W., L. Weldon, 1983. An experimental comparison of natural and structured query languages. In:*Human Factors* **25**,3 pp. 253-263.

Smith, B.C., 1982. *Reflection and Semantics in a procedural language*. Ph.D. Thesis, MIT.

Smith, J.M. & D.C.P. Smith, 1977. Database abstractions: aggregation and generalization. *TODS* **2**,2, pp.105-133.

Snodgrass, R., 1987. The temporal query language TQUEL. *TODS* **12**,2, pp.247-298.

Sowa, J., 1984. *Conceptual Structures*. Addison-Wesley.

Stamper, R., 1985. Management Epistemology: Garbage In, Garbage Out. In: Methlie & Sprague (eds), *Knowledge Representation for Decision Support Systems*, North-Holland, 1985.

Stamper, R., 1987. The processing of business semantics: necessity and tools. *Proc IFIP TC2/WG2.6 Conference on "Knowledge and Data"*, Algarve, Portugal.

Steel, T.B. & Meersman, R. (eds), 1986. *Database Semantics (DS-1)*, North-Holland, Amsterdam.

Stefik, M., 1986. The next knowledge medium. *The AI Magazine*, Spring 1986, pp.34-36.

Tannen, D., 1982. Analyzing discourse: text and talk. Georgetown Univ Round Table on Languages and Linguistics, Georgetown Univ Press.

Tannen, D., 1987. The interactional development of all texts: repetition in talk as spontaneous idiomaticity. *Proc 14th Int. Congress of Linguists*, Berlin, 1987.

Taylor, Ch., 1987 (75). Overcoming Epistemology. In: Baynes et al (ed), pp.459-488.

Thompson, R., 1967. *Organization in action*. McGraw-Hill, New York.

Uzkoreit, H., 1987. *Word Order and Constituent Structure in German*. CSLI Lecture Notes 8, Stanford CA.

Veltman, F., 1985. *Logics for conditionals*. Ph.D. Thesis, University of Amsterdam.

Voogt, H., 1987. Constructing an FG lexicon on the basis of LDOCE. *WPFG* **24**.

Wasserman, A.I & D.T. Shewmake, 1985. The role of prototypes in the user software engeneering methodology. In: Hartson (ed), *Advances in Human-Computer Interaction*. Ablex, Norwood NJ, pp.191-210.

Weigand, H., 1986. Conceptual Models in Prolog. In: Steel & Meersman (eds), 1986.

Weigand, H., 1989. A dialectical model of modality. In: Dik & Connolly (eds), 1989.

Weigand, H., in prep. Expression rules for f-structures.

Wieringa, R., J.-J.Ch. Meijer, H. Weigand, 1989. Specifying Dynamic and Deontic Integrity Constraints. *Data & Knowledge Engeneering* **4**, pp.157-190

Wierzbicka, A., 1980. *Lingua Mentalis*. Academic Press, London.

Wierzbicka, A., 1985. *Lexicography and conceptual analysis*. Karomo Publ, Ann Arbor.

Wierzbicka, A., 1989. *The alphabet of human thought*. Proc. L.A.U.D. Symposium, Duisburg.

Wilensky, R., 1983. *Planning and understanding*. Addison-Wesley, Reading MA.

Wilks, Y., 1977. *Good and bad arguments about semantic primitives*. Research Report 42, Dept of Artificial Intellligence, Univ of Edinburgh.

Winograd, T., 1983. *Language as a cognitive process. Volume I: Syntax*. Addison-Wesley, Reading MA.

Winograd, T. & F. Flores, 1986. *Understanding language and cognition*. Ablex, Norwood NJ.

Wittgenstein, L., 1953. *Philosophical Investigations*. Macmillan, New York.

Woods, W.A., 1975. What's in a link: foundations for semantic networks. In: Bobrow & Collins, (eds), *Representation and Understanding: Studies in Cognitive Science*, pp.35-82.

Yamanashi, M-A, 1987. Metonymic Interpretation and Associative Processes in Natural Language. In: Nagoa (ed), 1987.

Yourdon, E. & L.L. Constantine, 1979. *Structured Design*. Prentice-Hall, Englewood Cliffs NJ.

Yule, G., 1981. *Aspects of the information structure of spoken discourse*. Unpublished Ph.D. Thesis, Univ of Edinburgh.

Zaniolo, C., 1985. The representation and deductive retrieval of complex objects. *Proc. VLDB* 10, Stockholm, 1985.

Zeevat, H., 1989. A Compositional Approach to Discourse Representation Theory. *Linguistics and Philosophy* **12**, 1.

ABBREVIATIONS

CACM	Communications of the ACM
TODS	ACM Transactions on Database Systems
TOIS	ACM Transactions on Information Systems
VLDB	International Conference on Very Large Data Bases
WPFG	Working Papers in Functional Grammar

ERRATA

p11, below: Fig. 1.2 should be Fig. 1.1.

p14, below: section 3.10 should be section 4.5.3

p50, 3.7(i): definition 3.4 should be definition 3.5

p51, below: definition 3.5 should be definition 3.8

p100, Fig. 4.8: node labelled "dead" should be "material"

p141, 5.4(ii): x **in** y should be x_i **in** x_j

p172, below: theorem 3.11 should be theorem 3.23. Definition 3.15 should be definition 3.27, and proposition 3.1 should be proposition 3.2.

Throughout the work, the reference to Dik and Connolly, 1989 should be Connolly and Dik, 1989. The reference: "Bunt, H.C., 1981. *The formal semantics of mass terms*. Ph.D. Thesis, University of Amsterdam" should be added to the list.

Kolibri 360 GmbH
Ferdinand-Jühlke-Straße 7
99095 Erfurt, Deutschland
produktsicherheit@kolibri360.de